The Secret History
of the Blitz

The Secret History of the Blitz

How we behaved during our darkest
days and created modern Britain

JOSHUA LEVINE

**SIMON &
SCHUSTER**

London · New York · Sydney · Toronto · New Delhi

A CBS COMPANY

First published in Great Britain by Simon & Schuster UK Ltd, 2015
A CBS COMPANY

1 3 5 7 9 10 8 6 4 2

Simon & Schuster UK Ltd
1st Floor
222 Gray's Inn Road
London WC1X 8HB

www.simonandschuster.co.uk

Simon & Schuster Australia, Sydney
Simon & Schuster India, New Delhi

A CIP catalogue record for this book
is available from the British Library

Hardback ISBN: 978-1-4711-3101-1
Ebook ISBN: 978-1-4711-3103-5

Typeset in the UK by M Rules
Printed and bound by CPI Group (UK) Ltd, Croydon, CR0 4YY

MIX
Paper from
responsible sources
FSC® C020471

Simon & Schuster UK Ltd are committed to sourcing paper
that is made from wood grown in sustainable forests and supports the Forest
Stewardship Council, the leading international forest certification organisation.
Our books displaying the FSC logo are printed on FSC certified paper.

To Frances Drysdale
1970–2015

Contents

Do not try to persuade us to come to an agreement with the barbarian. We shall not be persuaded. And now carry back to Mardonius this message from the Athenians: *So long as the sun traverses the same course he traverses now we shall never make terms with Xerxes. We shall go forth to defend ourselves against him trusting to find at our side the gods and heroes whose dwellings and images he has impiously burnt.*

Herodotus, *The Persian Wars* (c. 440 BC)

We must all stick together, all stick together
And the clouds will soon roll by
We must all stick together, all stick together
Never mind the old school tie

'We Must All Stick Together', Billy Cotton Band (1939)

'A short time ago, we were just an undisciplined mob. Now we can deal with tanks. We can kill with our pikes. We can make them all sneeze with our pepper. And, after all, even the Hun is a very poor fighter with his head buried in a handkerchief. But remember, men, we have one invaluable weapon on our side. We have an unbreakable spirit to win. A bulldog tenacity that will help us to hang on while there's breath left in our bodies. You don't get that with Gestapos and jackboots. You get that by being British! So come on, Adolf! We're ready for you!'

Captain Mainwaring, *Dad's Army* (Episode One, 1968)

CHAPTER ONE

A Time of Extremes

No single artistic endeavour of the Blitz period – no film, no song, no radio programme – reveals more of the prevailing mood than a stage play called *Thunder Rock*. Phyllis Warner, a young middle-class Londoner, went to see it in the West End in March 1941, and described it in her diary as going 'straight to the heart of the times'. It left her feeling 'equipped for the ordeal that awaits'. She was not alone: 'This play ought not to be missed,' wrote George Orwell, reviewing it for *Time and Tide* magazine. And it became a huge hit – to the surprise of many who could remember the entertainment on offer during the First World War. A walk around the West End in search of a diverting evening in 1916 would have revealed musical revues such as *Chu Chin Chow* and melodramas like Edward Sheldon's *Romance*, but not much in the way of serious theatre. These, though, were different times.

Thunder Rock is a claustrophobic tale of ghosts and politics set on a remote lighthouse on Lake Michigan – not an obvious recipe to inspire the British public. Its central character, disillusioned political journalist David Charleston, has renounced his former life, and retreated to the Thunder Rock lighthouse, where he is able to avoid human company for months on end. When visited by a former col-league, he explains that the problems thrown up by the modern world, with its currency of greed, expansion and destruction, are so insoluble that the only rational response is to run away. 'I took this job,' says Charleston, 'to put myself out of circulation.'

But Charleston is not quite alone: he has created an imaginary world peopled by men and women who drowned during a storm on the lake ninety years earlier. These 'ghosts' are Charleston's com-panions, his comfort, and the reason he eventually decides to re-enter the real world. They explain how, as they headed west across America in 1849, they were running away from the problems of their time – ignorance, social injustice, misogyny and disease. These problems might have seemed part of the order of nature in 1849 but, Charleston tells them, they would, in time, be tackled and overcome. Why, he asks, did they not stand up and fight when they had the chance? The 'ghosts' turn his own argument back on himself: why is *he* disengaging? Why is *he* failing to stand up and fight when *he* has the chance? Emboldened, he resolves to leave the lighthouse and rejoin the 1940 struggle. In a rousing finale, delivered to a former col-league, Streeter, he declares:

> We've reason to believe that wars will cease one day, but only if we stop them ourselves. Get into it to get out, Street. We've got to create a new order out of the chaos of the old, and already its shape is becoming clear. A new order that will eradicate oppression, unemployment, starvation and wars as the old order eradicated plague and pestilences. And that is what we've to fight and work for, Street; not fighting for fighting's sake, but to make a new world of the old. That's our job, Street, and we can do it.

This is what a besieged Blitz audience wanted to hear. The fight against Hitler, the fight against oppression and chaos, the fight for a better future – these were really one fight, and it was winnable. Hitler was a symptom rather than a cause, and his passing would herald the dawn of the entire world. 'Quite possibly our present evils, even including war, will disappear like leprosy and bubonic plague,' wrote Orwell in his review. And it is interesting that this message of shining hope was brought to Britain by an American playwright, Robert Ardrey, just as the United States ambassador Joseph Kennedy – that 'foul specimen of double-crosser and defeatist' in the memorable words of Lord Vansittart – had done all he could to keep his country out of the war.

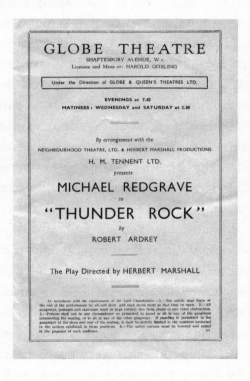

Thunder Rock had flopped in New York, closing after just a week. Ardrey wrote of his own play, 'If the audience is cynical or satisfied or subjected to no sense of pressing danger, then the play does not exist. It is strictly a play for desperate people.' It might not have existed for isolationist New Yorkers but it certainly did for blitzed Londoners. As well as for the British government – which paid for *Thunder Rock's* transfer from a fringe theatre in Kensington to the West End. Michael Redgrave, the actor playing Charleston, met Treasury officials who told him that the government had bankrolled the play, but that its involvement must be kept secret. Such cloak-and-dagger state involvement might seem anti-democratic but the war years are usually excused: the ultimate survival of democracy allows for its brief suspension. And the fact is that the play did not, in truth, influence the people's mood; it reflected it.

But it reflected only *one element* of the mood. As Tom Harrisson – anthropologist and co-founder of Mass-Observation, the extraordinary and controversial wartime barometer of public opinion – has written: 'At no time in the Second World War generally, and in the Blitz particularly were British civilians united on anything, though they might be ready to appear so in public on certain issues.'

This book is a biography of the period, and as such it will try to look beyond the public faces to the real experiences behind events. It can certainly be difficult nowadays to express a contrary view on controversial events. It sometimes seems that we prefer ideas – as well as people – to be simplified into good or bad, right or wrong, black or white. A person, a dispute, a country, all are too often reduced to tabloid-friendly shorthand. Perhaps we are scared of thinking for ourselves. Perhaps we mistake nuance for weakness. And if this is how we contemplate the present, how much harder to make meaningful sense of the past, that foreign country where things are done differently? Here we often find ourselves guided by consensus; by received wisdoms that have been worn down by the years until they achieve the status of truth. So is it safe to pay heed to received wisdoms about the Blitz? A version of the consensus narrative, the sort one is used to hearing, might run something like this:

The Blitz began on 7 September 1940 with a huge raid on London, as the Luftwaffe changed its focus from trying to destroy the Royal Air Force's fighter defences, to trying to crush civilian morale with a sustained aerial onslaught on the capital. From that day, London was attacked on fifty-seven consecutive nights. The East End was hit hardest – and responded to the danger and hardship with typical resolute humour – although other areas of London were also badly affected. Buckingham Palace, for example, suffered nine direct hits – allowing the King and Queen to 'look the East End squarely in the face'. Thanks to grass-roots pressure on the authorities, London Underground stations were opened as deep shelters; inhabitants enjoyed the sense of community, and many were loath to leave at the end of the war. In November, Hitler ordered the Blitz to be widened to target the major ports and industrial cities, in an attempt to shatter the nation's economy. This phase began with a horrifying attack on Coventry on 14 November. Attacks followed on Southampton, Birmingham, Liverpool, Manchester and Sheffield.

All the while, Winston Churchill's carefully crafted words rallied the country, while some unprecedented social effects took hold. For the first time, British people of different classes and localities started talking to each other. Bombing ensured that people not only shared the same danger, but also sheltered together, fire-watched together, and served in the Air Raid Precautions (ARP) and Home Guard together. Evacuation meant that understanding replaced mistrust. Rationing and austerity measures meant that people wore the same clothes, ate the same food, bought the same furniture – and occasionally dabbled in the black market together. Women took jobs which had long been the preserve of men. Legislation was passed ensuring factory workers a guaranteed wage, a newly gained importance from which there would be no going back after the war. A surreptitious social revolution was taking place, paving the way for the Beveridge Report and the post-war welfare state.

On 10 May 1941 London suffered its worst raid. The Luftwaffe took advantage of a full moon and a low tide to start almost 2,500 fires. The House of Commons burnt to the ground, and nearly 1,500 people were killed. And this night, although nobody in Britain knew it at the time, marked the last night of the Blitz. Six weeks later, Hitler launched Operation Barbarossa, his attack on the Soviet Union. He expected a quick victory, which would allow him to return his attention, once again, to Britain. That quick victory, of course, never came. Britain, standing alone with its colonies and dominions, had resisted Adolf Hitler. Before the entry into the war of the United States or the Soviet Union, the citizens of this country had kept the light of liberty shining. They had saved the world for democracy and freedom.

The conclusion of that narrative was invoked by Labour Party leader, Michael Foot, in April 1982, the day after the Argentinian invasion of the Falkland Islands. In supporting military action, Foot proudly reminded the House of Commons of 'the claim of our country to be a defender of people's freedom throughout the world, particularly those who look to us for special protection'. Not only did Foot live through the events of 1940 and 1941, he was one of the authors of 'Guilty Men', a criticism, published in July 1940, of Britain's unpreparedness for war. So we should be very careful before dismissing his words simply because they are familiar. They may contain substantial truth.

The consensus is often known today – perhaps harshly – as 'the myth of the Blitz', which was the title of a 1991 book by Angus Calder. Calder was keen to stress that his use of the word 'myth' did not imply that it was founded on lies, but rather that it presented a purified story, stripped of complexity and conflict, which invoked some truths and ignored others in its effort to appear historically destined. Far from striking the reader as gratuitous revisionism, Calder's work is notable for his belief that the 'myth' is not a crude propagandist distortion. He accepts significant parts of it, and commends it, in his final chapter for promoting 'a juster and friendlier society'. But it is difficult to disagree that, ultimately, the 'myth' does not – *cannot* – tell the whole story.

But care must be taken when digging deeper into such an emotive, politically charged period of history. The 'myth' has guardians fiercer than any dragon slain by Hercules. When it is suggested that people sometimes behaved badly during the Blitz, the guardians are liable to react with fury. An individual born long after 1940 will assert that nothing like that ever happened, while another will scoff that far worse things happen today – as though that has any bearing on the discussion. And, conversely, the suggestion that a 'Blitz Spirit' existed also has the power to infuriate. When writer Matt Wingett was putting together a theatre piece set in 1940, an artist friend asked him whether this would be another 'bloody thing where we all pull together'. The friend, it seemed, had once met an old woman who told him of her miserable experiences during the Blitz. For the friend, there was now only one reality.

So how *did* the people of Britain behave during the Blitz? Did they sing 'Roll out the Barrel' in communal shelters, shaking their fists at 'bloody Adolf', before cheerfully dodging the debris next morning on their way to work? Or did they loot from bombed-out houses, fiddle their rations and curse foreigners, while hoping for a negotiated peace that would save their wretched lives?

Faces of 'Blitz Spirit'. London firemen photographed in May 1941.

The answer, of course, is that they did both, and they did neither. Life was dangerous, hard, and lived in the shadow of invasion and death. It was also exciting and shot through with optimism. People pulled together and helped strangers; they broke rules and exploited neighbours. They bonded with, and stole from one another, they grew to understand, and to dislike each other. They tolerated without complaint and they complained without tolerance. They were scared and fearless, they coped and they cracked. They lost all hope, and they looked to the future. They behaved, in short, like a lot of human beings. Everything they did both confirms and refutes the 'myth' of the Blitz.

Over the course of this book, we will meet a widely ranging cast of characters. From the woman who experienced the Blitz as a time of 'triumph and happiness' to the man who described it as a time when he learned that 'the world was a dark place', to the opportunist who 'used to pray for a fucking [air raid] warning, 'cos a lot of these shopkeepers used to run out and leave their shops . . .'

But while there was no single reaction nor a reliable formula to predict behaviour, it must always be borne in mind that large numbers of British people were faced with a period of brutal and intense terror that is almost unimaginable today. Even at the time, nobody could predict what months of intensive air raids would do to the morale of a nation. Our parents, grandparents and great-grandparents were guinea pigs – and extraordinary things happened to them.

Albert Dance was a lance corporal in the Rifle Brigade who had been one of the last soldiers brought home from Dunkirk. A two-man yacht had spotted him lying asleep on a jetty near La Panne on 4 June. Seven months later, he married his sweetheart, Maisie, a factory worker, at the garrison church in Woolwich. And just a fortnight after that, he was called out of his army billet by an officer who poured him a whisky. 'I'm sorry,' said the officer, 'but your wife has been very badly injured in a bombing raid.'

Maisie Dance was working at the Varley Magnet Company in

Woolwich, making radio components. On the night of 28 January 1941 an air raid siren sounded, aeroplanes were spotted overhead, and the foreman sent workers into the shelter. Maisie was one of the last to enter, and as she did, a bomb exploded. She caught the blast. Albert was sent directly to Woolwich where he was escorted by Maisie's father to St Nicholas' Hospital. He remembers his initial reaction on seeing his wife: 'She was a beautiful girl with lovely hair. Her hair was all matted with oil, her face was bashed, stones were embedded in her cheeks. She was crying with pain because her back was shattered and her arm was shattered. It was awful.'

Albert Dance – photographed later in the war as a staff sergeant in the Glider Pilot Regiment.

Albert spent the subsequent days at the hospital, and the nights at his mother's house. He remembers the smell coming from underneath Maisie's plaster casts; to distract her from it he started bringing in bunches of lavender. After a while, to his relief, her spirits seemed to lift. But throughout this time, the doctors were able to tell him very little. 'They didn't know what she'd be like when she came out,' he says.

After a few weeks, Maisie was moved to a hospital in Darenth, and Albert returned to his unit. He had been gone just three days when a telegram arrived. Maisie had developed tetanus. Albert hurried back – to find his wife unable to recognise him. Her body was rigid and her face was locked. He fell to his knees and prayed to God to end her suffering. 'I walked out to get a nurse and a doctor,' he says, 'and as I walked back in, she died.'

Albert Dance was interviewed by the Imperial War Museum in 1999, specifically about his experiences at Dunkirk and, later, in the Glider Pilot Regiment. This story of his wife's death was not the main focus of the interview. It was incidental and nearly lost to the years, as have been countless other stories. And just as there were all sorts of different kinds of behaviour during the Blitz, so there were different reactions to the grief it caused. Joan Batt was living in Coventry in November 1940 when the city centre was all but destroyed. Years later, she said, 'I still feel hatred for the Germans, they took everything off me.' Ethel Clarke's son was killed in an air raid, but she felt empathy with the Germans: 'They didn't ask for war. They lost their sons, we lost our sons.' However understandable it is that a particular reaction be viewed as the only possible or rational one, however neatly it slots into the received wisdom, we must remain alert across a much wider spectrum.

And if it is human nature to fail to acknowledge the attitudes of others, it is equally human nature to become set in unquestioned ways of behaviour. All of us do it all of the time – and it can take a startling event to wake us up to other possibilities. The Blitz was such an event: it shocked people out of their rhythms. It encouraged unaccustomed 'good' behaviour and unaccustomed 'bad' behaviour – sometimes from the same individual. The Blitz was, above all, a time of extremes. Extremes of experience, extremes of behaviour, extremes of reaction. In all directions.

A very small thing happens in Patrick Hamilton's beautiful wartime novel, *The Slaves of Solitude*. Miss Roach, a sensible young middle-class woman, is staying in a boarding house in a suburban town, beyond the reach of the bombs. While living this unfamiliar life, she enters a pub and has a drink. She is alone. There is no one else with her. And then she shares a drink with, and gets drunk with, a male stranger. As a poster girl for rebellion Miss Roach hardly stands with Emily Davison or Rosa Parks – but she is a rebel, all the same. She would not have contemplated such behaviour before the war. The Blitz was a time of intensity; people took risks, and they did new things – to greater and lesser degrees. They related to each other in wholly new ways. And their social, economic and political expectations grew as the world became a less permanent and more mobile place.

The year 2015 marks the seventy-fifth anniversary of Dunkirk, the Battle of Britain, and the start of the Blitz – and this is a significant time-lapse. It marks the point where living memory starts to turn into history, when the muddy soup of perceptions, memories, and interpretations – or 'real life' – begins to thicken into historical fact, ready to be used to shore up old prejudices. But before it solidifies, we have a chance to look closer. To speak to survivors, to search out old interviews, to study newly released documents.

And let's not focus on the familiar stories, but on a wider picture of Britain around the time of the Blitz. Not in order to prove a point, or to confirm a thesis, but to gain a sense of a complicated, nuanced, uncertain time. Don't allow the myth-defenders to convince you that people behaved in a certain way. And don't let the myth-deniers tell you that they didn't. For a little while, at least, let us look beyond the theories that pretend to account for the entire throbbing mass of free-willed Britons.

We could start by probing a fact or two. It is well known, for example, that the Blitz began on 7 September 1940. Certainly, that was the day that Hermann Goering took personal command of the air offensive against Britain, and the day when that offensive was directed on London. In Goering's mind, a concerted attack on London made sense. It was an attack on the Port of London through which food and supplies arrived, on the political and administrative centre of Britain from which the war was run, and on densely populated urban areas whose morale could be affected. But from the German perspective, this attack on London heralded no change in strategy. It was simply the continuation of Adolf Hitler's effort to bring Britain to heel, whether by invasion, negotiation, or popular uprising. For the British, the Battle of Britain and the Blitz were fought over different territory with entirely different forces. But for the Germans, it amounted to a single aerial assault, carried out by the same forces from the same airfields with the same basic objectives.

And 7 September was not even the first attack on London. That took place a fortnight earlier. For a period of about four-and-a-half hours, from 11 p.m. on 24 August, bombs were dropped across the capital from West Ham, Stepney and Bethnal Green in the east to Esher and Staines in the west. Two weeks before 'Black Saturday', the London sky had glowed red.

And the serious bombing of British civilians had already taken place sometime before that. On the night of 18 June 1940, a bright 'bomber's moon' had shone over southern and eastern England as seventy-one German aircraft set out across the Channel. Some were attempting to destroy the oil storage tanks at Thameshaven, others were targeting the airfields at Mildenhall and Honington. Heinkel 111s of Kampfgeschwader 4, meanwhile, were on their way to attack railway installations. It represented the first major raid on Great Britain.

That night, Michael Bowyer, a schoolboy living near the river in Cambridge, was at home with his parents. Michael knew a lot about aeroplanes; he could distinguish the unsynchronised revving of a Heinkel 111 from the rattling of a Dornier 17 and the smooth tone of a Junkers 88. And so he was excited, just before midnight, to hear a

Heinkel passing low over the house. This was followed by a piercing whistle – the sound of bombs falling, and then by two huge explosions. The windows rattled, the pressure in the room changed suddenly, and a pig's carcass, hanging from the ceiling, swung to and fro. 'Oh hell!' Michael exclaimed. 'Don't swear in front of your mother!' said his father. A few seconds later, a British Merlin engine roared overhead, and then came the sound of human activity outside. An excited air raid warden blew his whistle and swung his rattle, before hammering at the front door, and shouting for the Bowyers to follow him into the shelter opposite. They did as they were told. Michael's father brought with him an attaché case that he had ready. It contained his will, savings certificates, cheque book, some cash, and the deeds to the house. He looked, says Michael, as though he was going on holiday. Inside the shelter, Mr Clover, the chief warden, made a solemn announcement: 'Bombs have fallen. There have been casualties. I am not permitted to tell you any more.' At that moment, a man rushed in, shouting, 'They've got Vicarage Terrace.'

Vicarage Terrace was a few minutes' walk away. It consisted of modest two-storey houses, with front doors leading directly into front rooms, and toilets in sheds at the bottom of gardens. The terrace had no electricity, only gas lighting downstairs and candles upstairs. For its residents, and for the country as a whole, the last month had brought a flow of depressing news. German Panzer divisions had thundered through the supposedly impenetrable – and barely defended – Ardennes area, forcing the British army to withdraw haphazardly to the Channel coast. A desperate operation had managed to bring its remnants – men such as Albert Dance – back to England. Holland and Belgium had quickly surrendered, and just four days earlier, the first German troops had entered Paris. France was falling, and church bells in Britain had been silenced to be rung only in the event of a German invasion – as now seemed likely.

The air raid siren had sounded in Vicarage Terrace just before 11.30 p.m. that night. There was nothing unusual in this. Sirens had been sounding across the country for eight and a half months. When they had first sounded on the morning of 3 September 1939 – minutes after Neville Chamberlain's radio announcement that Britain was at war with Germany – people had genuinely expected the skies to blacken with Nazi bombers sent to deliver the 'knock-out blow'. Private and public shelters had quickly filled with the stoic, the nervous, and the downright hysterical, all carrying their gas masks. The evacuation of hundreds of thousands of children from vulnerable cities to safer areas (such as Cambridge) had already begun, and hospitals had been discharging their non-essential patients to make room for the tens of thousands of air raid casualties expected imminently. But they did not arrive. The knock-out blow was not delivered. Weeks of waiting turned into months, and people, unsurprisingly, became less vigilant. A handful of civilians, it is true, *were* killed. One on Orkney, by a misdirected bomb, and two in Clacton-on-Sea when a Heinkel crash-landed into a house. But these were rare and isolated events. And so, when the siren sounded in Cambridge on 18 June, the residents of Vicarage Terrace felt they had little to fear.

A few of the residents responded to the alarm by walking to the public shelter. Most did not. Olive Unwin, in number seven, was going over the details of her wedding, due to take place that weekend. On hearing the siren, she made her way downstairs to the front room, where she sat beneath the stairs. She was joined by the other four members of the family. This spot, they felt, was the safest part of the house. Further down the terrace, the Deere family – father, mother, and five-month-old baby – also moved downstairs, but after fifteen minutes returned to bed, believing this to be yet another false alarm. Others in the terrace took no precautions at all. Edna Clark was in bed with her younger sister, Gladys. As the Heinkel approached the terrace, she got up to ask her father whether everything was all right. 'Yes, my duck, get back to bed,' he soothed. Seconds later, at some point around midnight, the Heinkel 111, which had just passed over Michael Bowyer's house, dropped two 50kg bombs on Vicarage

Terrace. Numbers one to six were demolished; numbers seven to ten were badly damaged.

The Unwins in number seven were fortunate. The roof collapsed, but the family was sheltered underneath the stairs. Olive's brother was able to push aside timber and masonry to clear a path, allowing all five members to escape. The Deeres, asleep upstairs in the bedroom, fell through the collapsed floor, and were buried by the remains of the roof. They were eventually dug out by rescue workers; the parents survived but baby Heather did not. Edna Clarke was knocked to the ground, but her sister Gladys – in the bed to which Edna was returning – was killed by a falling beam. All three members of the Beresford family, in number six, were killed, including a two-year-old boy. Three hours after the explosion, faint cries were heard in the wreckage. A tunnel was dug, and forty-seven-year-old Lily Langley was dragged to safety. But her husband William and eighteen-year-old son Sam were both dead. In all, nine people were killed and eight injured by the bombs. One of the injured was Lily Itzcovitch, an eleven-year-old Londoner who had been evacuated to quiet Cambridge.

At nine o'clock the next morning, Michael Bowyer cycled past Vicarage Terrace on his way to school. Seventy-four years later, I accompanied him as he retraced his steps. The terrace today consists of modern two-storey buildings with a gap at one end, and as Michael looked around, he was struck by how ordinary everything seemed. 'You just wouldn't know that anything terrible had happened here,' he says. 'It's amazing, isn't it?' His strongest memories of the morning after were of the powerful smell of dust, and the desperate feeling of invaded privacy: 'I thought that was awful, your house and the miserable conditions in which you lived were exposed for the whole world to see.' As we walked to the end of the terrace, Michael pointed out where a barricade had been placed, behind which officials were studying the state of the gas and water mains. And he recalled two particularly poignant sights: a piano standing in the middle of the shattered street, and a child's doll, lying in the gutter, missing its head.

For a while after the bombing, Michael says, local people started taking shelter whenever the sirens sounded. Only for a while, however. 'Pretty soon,' he says, 'the attitude was, "Damn it, I can't be bothered!"' And he is convinced that the Heinkel was intending to drop its bombs on the huge railway goods yard nearby. Having heard the sound of the engine change over his house, he believes that it was simply too low when it dropped its bombs. 'If he'd been a little bit higher, he might have got nearer to the yard. There were something like fifty tracks there, so it was a prime target. But the bombs were dropped too soon.'

Michael can remember that, late on the night of the bombing, the head warden returned to his shelter with an exciting announcement: 'They've shot the blighter down, killed them all!' 'Where?' asked Michael. 'Ah, son, that's a military secret!' replied the warden who kept the secret for a few seconds before proclaiming, 'Fulbourn!' He then announced that a Spitfire had shot the Heinkel down, which Michael doubted. How could a Spitfire have downed a German bomber *at night*? When another warden added that the Heinkel pilot had been a Cambridge undergraduate, the tale's peculiarity increased.

Yet these Chinese whispers were not quite as fanciful as they seemed. Heinkel *5J+AM* of Kampfgeschwader 4, piloted by Oberleutnant Joachim von Arnim, did indeed crash at Fulbourn in the early morning of 19 June 1940. Von Arnim, writing many years later to aviation historian Andy Saunders, related his surprise at being attacked by British fighters that night. He and his crew had been anticipating only anti-aircraft fire. It seems that his Heinkel was caught in a searchlight, and attacked by a Spitfire of 19 Squadron, flown by Flying Officer Petra, and a Blenheim of 23 Squadron, captained by Squadron Leader O'Brien. The Spitfire was about to open fire when the Blenheim arrived, so it banked away and started pouring tracer into the Heinkel from one side as the Blenheim fired several long bursts. Smoke started to gush from one of the Heinkel's

engines, but its upper gunner was now firing back at the Spitfire
which was itself illuminated by a searchlight. Explosive bullets struck
the Spitfire's fuel tank, setting it on fire. Petra baled out with severe
burns to his face and hands. The Blenheim also came under fire from
the Heinkel's guns, and went into an uncontrollable spin. O'Brien
managed to bale out safely, but his navigator, Pilot Officer King-
Clark, was killed by a propeller as he tried to jump clear, and his air
gunner, Corporal Little, was killed as it hit the ground. The Heinkel,
meanwhile, was sent out of control by the combined fire of the two
fighters. 'We had to bale out in a hurry,' Von Arnim writes. He and
two of his crew members parachuted down safely, while the fourth
was killed. The survivors landed in a potato field, and two hours later,
they were taken prisoner by Local Defence Volunteers – the fore-
runners of the Home Guard – and escorted to barracks in Bury St
Edmunds.

   The first LDV to respond was Ron Barnes, a farm labourer. He had

Oberleutnant Joachim von Arnim and Feldwebel Wilhelm Maier
in the cockpit of Heinkel He. 111H *5J+AM.*

The wreckage of Heinkel He. 111H *5J+AM* at Fulbourn.

been woken by a commotion outside, and somebody shouting, 'Paratroops have landed!' As we shall discover, airmen parachuting from doomed aeroplanes were often mistaken for parachute troops: at a time of invasion fears, people saw what they wanted to see. Ron grabbed his rifle and set off across fields. After a while, he noticed movement, and shouted a challenge. A man – who was probably Joachim von Arnim – threw up his hands and replied in German. Ron escorted him to a searchlight post, and handed him over. Ron was later interviewed by the London *Evening Standard*, in which he was celebrated as the first LDV to capture a member of the German armed forces.

So what can we make of the rumours heard by young Michael Bowyer in his shelter? To begin with, a Heinkel 111 *had* crashed at Fulbourn. And it *had* been shot down (or shared, at least) by a Spitfire. There is little, however, to back up the warden's claim that a member of its crew had spent time at Cambridge University. And this Heinkel, we can be sure, was not the aircraft that bombed Vicarage

Terrace. Joachim Von Armin's Heinkel crashed at Fulbourn over an hour after the bombs landed; Fulbourn is only five miles from Cambridge.

All the same, this was clearly the night when the Blitz came to Cambridge. Even though, as any fule kno, it hadn't started yet.

CHAPTER TWO

Homeless and Helpless

Olive Unwin, the young woman due to get married on the Saturday following the Vicarage Road bombing, defied the circumstances and went ahead with the ceremony. On 22 June 1940 she married Private George Brown at St Matthews Church, only yards from her bombed house. Her wedding dress had not survived the raid, so she had little choice but to wear something borrowed.

As she walked down the aisle, a nineteen-year-old undergraduate at University College, Oxford, was awaiting trial at Stafford Assizes for a much darker act of defiance. His was the sort of crime that has, in recent years, become common in countries where firearms are freely available. In 1940 an unstable British teenager had little difficulty in finding a gun. In Hackney, in east London, meanwhile, an old woman was living in rented rooms with her blind husband. The couple had enjoyed a long and happy marriage, but the old man was becoming increasingly senile and dependent on his wife. Life was about to become even harder for them. The young Oxford student and the elderly London couple had little in common – but their extraordinary responses to national events reveal a great deal about Britain in summer and autumn 1940.

On the afternoon of 17 May, John Fulljames walked into a college friend's room, picked up the Lee Enfield rifle propped up in a corner, and wandered back to his own room. He loaded a cartridge, steadied himself at the window, and opened fire on fellow students crossing the quad. Charles Moffat was shot in the abdomen. As he fell, groaning, another shot struck him in the neck, killing him. The second bullet also injured Dennis Melrose in the chest. A third shot missed, but a fourth struck Pierre de Kock in the calf. John Fulljames was not firing indiscriminately; his targets were all members of a particular college 'set'. After the shooting, Fulljames walked up to the dean of the college. The dean asked him whether he knew from which room the shots had come. 'I'm afraid they came from mine,' said Fulljames. 'Do you know who had the gun?' 'I'm afraid I did. What do you want me to do, sir?'

A police photograph of the quad at University College, Oxford.
Taken shortly after the shooting, a bloodstain is clearly visible.

Fulljames had been approaching the end of his first year at Oxford. He was a quiet young man with an excellent school record, who had recently turned moody and apathetic. Nowadays he would probably be described as 'disaffected'. Certainly, his behaviour had been erratic. While declaring himself to be a pacifist, he tried – and failed – to enlist in the Territorial Army. He told a college friend that he might 'get a kick out of killing', but when he went to see the Bette Davis film *Dark Victory*, he had to leave the cinema owing to his 'horror of bloodshed'. He developed a dislike for a boisterous 'set' of college people – including Moffat, Melrose and de Kock – even though he had barely spoken to them. And he was described by his closest friend as being 'very worried about the war'.

At 9 a.m. on the morning of the shooting, Fulljames was seen searching a room for rifle ammunition. Later that morning, he wrote a casual note to a young man at another college:

> Thank you very much for your invitation and I'm sorry if you have ordered my dinner for nothing but I'm afraid I won't be able to come to Oriel tonight. Probably unforeseen and pressing engagements will detain me in durance vile. Still, iron bars, etc . . . or is it 'stone walls'?

In durance vile is an archaic expression for a long prison term, while the final sentence refers to a line from Richard Lovelace's 1642 poem 'To Althea, From Prison': 'Stone walls do not a prison make, Nor iron bars a cage'. In the hours before the shooting, Fulljames wrote to another friend:

> Michael, I want you to know, though I feel that you do, that during the second and the age that I have known you, life has opened out for me.

Hidden in the adolescent love pangs are clues as to his state of mind:

I want you to believe that what I do today, because I know what is
going to happen, cannot separate us – I know that physically we
shall be apart, but I shall always feel that somewhere, though you
may not understand any more than I do, why I am going to do I
have felt this coming all term [sic], and most of last. But I never
really believed even when I saw ten cartridges at home, even until
last night, and not until I woke this morning that I should ever do
anything quite so utterly foolish.

So while the act (or at least, *some* act) had been brewing for a while,
it seems Fulljames only finally decided on it that morning. After the
shooting, Fulljames sat in the porter's lodge with the Master of the
college, Sir William Beveridge, the economist whose 1942 report
would inspire the creation of the welfare state. Beveridge asked
Fulljames whether he had been ill. 'No,' he said.

While on remand in Brixton Prison, Fulljames was examined by
the senior medical officer who found him to be suffering from para-
noid schizophrenia. 'His antipathy,' wrote the doctor, 'seems to have
generated in his own mind without any stimulating factors of any
kind.' But he went on to state that his schizophrenia was at an early
stage of development. He was fit to stand trial for murder.

The trial was held in early July. Counsel for Fulljames had to
prove insanity. He submitted that when his client fired the four
shots, he did not know that what he was doing was wrong. He presented the concept of schizophrenia to the jury by referring them to
'the famous horror story' involving Dr Jekyll and Mr Hyde. 'The
mind,' he said, 'disintegrated and the whole personality was with-
drawn from reality into a world of fantasy.' He called an eminent
psychologist, Dr Henry Yellowlees, to give evidence that Fulljames
was insane in law. In rebuttal, the prosecution called the senior
medical officer from Brixton Prison, who restated his opinion that
the schizophrenia was not advanced, and that Fulljames *had*
known, when he fired, that what he was doing was wrong. The jury

was presented with a straight choice. The young man's life rested on its decision.

The jury retired for just twenty-five minutes. It returned a verdict of guilty, but insane. Fulljames had escaped the hangman and was committed to Broadmoor. He smiled as he left the dock. In one respect, his story seems startlingly modern; we think of campus shooting sprees as a contemporary American phenomenon. But this spree was very much of its time. Britain was in crisis, its army on the run in France, its identity no longer certain. John Fulljames, a pacifist, horrified by the sight of blood, tried to join up – and failed. Even in its darkest hour, his country rejected him, and he went to an extreme to demonstrate his own existence. His defiance was the dark reflection of the optimism of *Thunder Rock*. And his survival was every bit as fortunate as the survival of his countrymen rescued from Dunkirk. A letter in his prison file, opened in 2014, reveals that, despite the jury's verdict and the evidence of Dr Yellowlees, the medical authorities at Broadmoor did not believe him ever to have been insane, and were content to advise the Home Secretary to agree to his release in 1945, after just five years of detention. Fulljames, it seems, might very easily have been hanged for the murder of Charles Moffat.

The case of Ida Rodway, meanwhile, exposes the truth about the early weeks of the London Blitz. On 14 November 1940 she was arraigned at the Old Bailey for the murder of her blind husband Joseph. She had attacked him with a chopper and a carving knife, almost severing his head from his body. It is perhaps difficult to conceive how a domestic incident, however tragic, could cast much light on the period – but a closer look reveals that both Ida and Joseph Rodway were just as much victims of the Blitz as anybody killed by an aerial mine.

Ida and Joseph were married in April 1901. They had lived together for almost forty years. In that time, Joseph's brother, Albert, had never known them to share a cross word. 'They were always happy,' he told the police. Joseph had worked as a carman, a horse-drawn delivery driver, but this was a dying trade, and he had been out of work for ten years. Ida had been working as a boot machinist, but when Joseph's sight began to deteriorate, she started caring for him. When he lost his sight entirely, and his mind began to fail, he became entirely dependent on her. As a result, Ida's attendance at work fell away, and she lost her job. They had now to survive, each week, on 10 shillings from Joseph's pension and 26 shillings from the labour exchange, with the knowledge that the latter would soon be stopped.

On 21 September 1940 the east London house, in which they rented rooms, was bombed. Ida and Joseph, in their garden shelter, were physically unhurt, but Joseph was admitted to Hackney Hospital in a state of distress, and Ida went to stay with friends. After three days, the hospital discharged Joseph, leaving the couple with nowhere to go, until Ida's sister agreed to take them in. For the next week, they slept on the floor of her back room. Throughout this time, Joseph never understood where he was. Ida had trouble looking after him in a strange house, and he was becoming more confused. She had other anxieties, too: she would soon lose her labour money, leaving them with just ten shillings a week (about £20 today), and no idea what to do about the bombed house which still contained their furniture and possessions. She told her sister that she wished the bomb had killed them, and she started think about suicide – but decided that it would not be fair on her helpless husband. 'I thought to myself,' she later told police, '"Oh, what shall I do?"'

Her answer to that question came on the morning of 1 October. Instead of bringing her husband a cup of tea in bed, as she had begun to do, she picked up a chopper and a carving knife. She went into the back room, and found Joseph sitting up in bed. She hit him first with the chopper – but it broke. 'What are you doing this for?' asked Joseph, startled. And then she cut his throat.

A little later, Ida's upstairs neighbour, Lily Beauchamp, met her walking down the street. Ida appeared dazed, and said, 'Lil, I've murdered my husband. I want to find a policeman. Will you get one of the wardens?' The astonished Mrs Beauchamp fetched a warden who accompanied them to the house. When the police arrived, Ida said, 'He was my husband. I was worried about him. He was blind. We were bombed out of our home and I had nowhere to go and nobody to help me. I was worried to death. I don't know what made me do it.'

Ida was placed on remand in the hospital wing of Holloway Prison, where she spent her days sitting quietly, showing no emotion. She told the medical officer that she had done the right thing, as her husband was now out of his misery. On the morning of her Old Bailey trial, 13 November, the medical officer spoke to her once more. Ida told him that she intended to plead guilty to murder, as that would get everything settled. She said again that she had done the right thing, and seemed to the doctor to be entirely unconcerned about the result of the trial. On the basis of this interview, the doctor gave evidence to the court that Ida was insane and unfit to plead. The jury returned a formal verdict to that effect, and Ida Rodway, like John Fulljames before her, was committed to Broadmoor. Unlike Fulljames, she would never be released. She died in the asylum on 25 April 1946.

When speaking to the court, the medical officer made much of the fact that Ida believed that she had done nothing wrong. This, to his thinking, was strong evidence of her insanity. But 'nothing wrong' to Ida Rodway meant that she had done *the right thing in the circumstances*. And given her husband's mental and physical condition, given the huge difficulty Ida was having looking after him, and given their desperate future prospects, who could say with certainty that she had not? The insanity finding, of course, saved her from the hangman, but it is striking that in the surviving case papers, the only recognition of the practical difficulties faced by the Rodways can be found on Ida's application for legal aid, made eight days after she had been charged with murder. The form reads: 'The attack appears to have been the result of worry and agitation through war conditions.' And 'war conditions' in east London, at the start of the Blitz, could be deeply distressing. As air

'Homeless' by Clifford Hall. For many thousands of people – and
certainly for Ida Rodway – being left homeless and helpless
led to unthinkable misery.

raid warden Barbara Nixon noted, for many of the poor, the loss of a
home was 'a disaster comparable with the loss of life.'

One of the surprising features of the Blitz, when it arrived, was the
relatively small loss of life compared with the unexpectedly large
amount of damage to buildings. Over 13,000 people were killed in
September and October, and however much suffering this represented, it was a much smaller figure than had been feared. The
number of Londoners made homeless by the middle of October, on
the other hand, was around 250,000 – far greater than expected. The
homeless might be left with nowhere to sleep, nowhere to eat,
nowhere to wash, no money, no ration book, no clothes except those

they were wearing, goods and furniture that needed salvaging, a damaged house that needed repairs, and no idea of what to do about any of these things. For the first few weeks of the Blitz, the authorities were taken by surprise. They could not control the situation. The result was described by social scientist Richard Titmuss, in his official history of wartime social policy, as a 'crisis in London'. It was the central factor in Ida Rodway's sense of helplessness and hopelessness. And she was not alone in her despair.

When a family or an individual was bombed out, the first port of call was usually a rest centre. Often situated in an evacuated school, offering tea, bread, shelter, and sanitation, rest centres were intended merely as casualty clearing stations, to be emptied each day to make room for the next wave of homeless. But a daily turnover relied on housing being found each day, and though the bombs kept falling, the replacement housing did not arrive. In the first six weeks of the Blitz, only around 7,000 Londoners were rehoused, compared with the quarter of a million who were made homeless. The discrepancy is startling. Some people were staying with friends and family, some were living half-lives between shelters and bombed-out houses, some were living rough. By 26 September, there were 25,000 people in London rest centres, and the congestion was growing.

Gioya Steinke worked in a rest centre. Once the 'all clear' had sounded, she became used to receiving wardens and firemen who arrived with people caked in thick bomb dust and debris. 'It was very distressing,' she says, 'there was a lot of grief and crying.' At first, Gioya spent much of the time in tears, but was told to learn to control herself. 'You didn't know who was a street market person and who was a person from the posh flats,' she says, 'they were all reduced down, and this, I think, had a lot to do with the wonderful camaraderie of the war.' One wonders, though, how much camaraderie was felt at the time.

When Lily Merriman's house was destroyed, she and her mother and father were put on a bus and sent to a rest centre in a nearby school where they remained for a month. 'We felt like refugees,' she says. The centre had separate rooms for men and women, as well as a family room where Lily's family slept on mattresses on the floor alongside strangers. As a result she refused to undress. And there were washing facilities, but no baths. 'I used to feel dirty,' she says. When the family was eventually rehoused, it was to a new area: 'We didn't see any of our old neighbours any more. We was shifted, and that was it.'

But people were being shifted very slowly. Part of the problem was that the homeless did not know where to go for help. Often it was not clear where they *should* be going. There were too many assistance bodies, with badly defined responsibilities, and little co-ordination between them. The London County Council and a metropolitan borough, for example, might both try to billet different families in the same house. Richard Titmuss records how a damaged house resulted in visits to separate offices for cash advances, clothing, ration books, repairs, the salvage of furniture, the reconnection of utilities, and information about evacuation. And there was no guarantee of help in any of them. A sixteen-year-old girl, bombed out in November, needed to get hold of a few pounds for clothes. She spent an entire day visiting offices across Norbury and Croydon – and came away with nothing.

To make matters worse, people desperate for relief were being received in the spirit of the poor law: hurdles were placed in their path as though they were paupers begging money for gin rather than victims of a national emergency. The most unsympathetic agency was proving to be the Assistance Board, the body responsible for dispensing financial aid, which usually erred, according to Richard Titmuss, 'on the side of parsimony'.

But perhaps we should not be surprised that this mentality persisted into the 1940s. This was a time, after all, when workhouses, those totems of Dickensian London, were still in existence. Doreen Kluczynska spent the Blitz working in the nursery section of

Knaresborough Workhouse in Yorkshire. Some of her charges were abandoned children, while others were the illegitimate offspring of 'shamed' young women who had been forced into the workhouse. 'The children didn't have any sweet ration,' says Doreen, 'no toys, no books, and clothes that didn't fit them.' The clothing was not even their own; each morning they were dressed in clothes another child had worn the day before.

One possible solution to the crisis in London was to move 'useless mouths' (as those not contributing to the war effort were known) out of the city.

The result – Evacuation Plan VII – was introduced on 22 September. Under this scheme, the government would pay for homeless mothers and children to be evacuated away, but only from a handful of east London boroughs; the plan was limited lest hordes of Cockney refugees were to apply and overwhelm the system. The government needn't have worried: only about 2,600 mothers and children took up the offer in the last week of September. The scheme was then extended to cover the whole of London, and in October about 89,000 mothers and children were evacuated. But this figure was still lower than hoped, and the government responded with a propaganda campaign. One mother recalls the stern tones of 'The Radio Doctor', Charles Hill, as he 'kept on about the selfish mothers who would not consider the offer of safety for their children'. The woman gave in to his bullying, and she and her daughter were evacuated to Devon.

There were, in truth, plenty of reasons why homeless people did not leave London in the expected numbers. Many simply preferred familiar surroundings – however dismal the circumstances. Some were tied to jobs locally, others had been evacuated in 1939 and were not keen to repeat the experience. And there were those, like Maggie Edwards' mother, who wanted to stay near their damaged houses. When Maggie's house was bombed in November, the family went to stay with her grandmother nearby, but they visited their own house regularly 'to light the fire and make sure everything was secure'. On one visit, Maggie's mother noticed that the front door was slightly ajar. She went in, and found that the gas and electricity meters had been cracked open, and the money taken. On the floor nearby was a lead truncheon. 'Obviously the burglar had intended using it if we'd caught him in the act,' says Maggie, 'and we had to reimburse the Gas and Electricity Boards ourselves.'

Some people did leave London – before coming quickly back. Eileen Brome went to Bournemouth with her sister, stepdaughter, sister's daughter, and friend's daughter. All five of them shared a single room, which was testing enough, but then 'we were called bomb-dodgers by the people of Bournemouth. They didn't want us down there, they told us to go home again.' Eventually, life became so unpleasant that Eileen and her group caught the train back to London. 'We really thought bombs were better than people,' she says. But things were to get even worse. A fortnight later, Eileen opened her jewellery box – to find that there were lots of pieces missing. 'So I went to the police and they made enquiries, and it turned out the people we'd been staying with were known very well to the police. He was the biggest thief in Bournemouth!'

In the end, the real solution to the crisis did not lie in relocation, but in reorganisation. On 26 September, Henry Willink, MP for Croydon, was appointed Special Commissioner for the Homeless. Three days later, he gave a press conference at which he acknowledged the extent of the problems. He promised that the 'pillar to post' chasing after different officials 'which too often has been demanded of the homeless' would end at once. In future there would, he said, be one place for the homeless to go for all the primary necessities. He intended to clear the rest centres, as they were meant for only for emergency use. And he intended to sweep away the poor law mentality. From now on, he promised, 'London Region will do its utmost for those who have suffered in the front line.' Willink had been a battery commander on the Somme; he understood the concept of a front line.

Henry Willink: the Conservative Member of Parliament
who kick-started the welfare state.

In a matter of days, Willink set out clear and practical principles. He
placed his greatest emphasis on providing new homes. This would be
the responsibility of the local authorities, working seven days a week
with extra staff. They would continually re-survey all of the available
housing stock, personally escort people to their new billets, and
resolve any disputes. They would take responsibility for requisition-
ing houses, and for supplying and salvaging furniture. Meanwhile the
London County Council would be responsible for providing the
immediate necessities of life. The LCC and the local authorities would
liaise closely with each other, and members of Willink's staff would
monitor the whole of London to ensure that his improvements were
properly carried through. And in a forward-thinking move, a permanent staff of social workers – known as 'welfare inspectors' –
would be employed to deal with individual cases of distress.

Willink also dealt with the lack of information reaching the public, and the widely dispersed government agencies. He established Information Centres across the capital, and placed housing and welfare advisers in every rest centre. Assistance Board officials were sent into rest centres to make payments on the spot, while mobile units equipped as fully functioning offices went on the road, dispensing money in recently bombed areas. And most important of all, Administrative Centres were established in which the relevant agencies were finally gathered together under a single roof.

This was all too late to help Ida Rodway, but the 'crisis in London' was tackled effectively. Measures were also taken to improve the rate and quality of housing repairs. In December the military call-up of workers engaged on repairs was suspended, and a repair service was created of men specially released from the army. This was particularly important: people wanted to return to their own homes, and unlikely as it often seemed in the aftermath of a raid, most houses *were* repairable. Indeed by January 1941, eighty per cent of the houses damaged in London had already been repaired.

If Henry Willink was the man with the administrative skill to resolve the crisis, his example came from the Citizens Advice Bureaux (CAB). Described by the *Manchester Guardian* as a 'clearinghouse for information', the CAB was formed in 1938, but it came into its own during the Blitz, as its staff of keen volunteers helped to fill the governmental void before Willink's improvements could take hold. The CAB motto, tellingly, was 'We're all in it together'.

As the organisation grew in size and standing, bureaux started opening in shelters, rest centres, and in private homes and offices across the country. Advisers were trained in post-raid welfare, so that they could inform the public where to apply for housing, clothes, emergency money, repair work – the information that the government should have been providing. In 1940 and 1941, this was the information that most people wanted, but surviving records reveal a wide range of applicants with a huge variety of problems.

Advisers were surprised by the numbers of people who needed

help filling in forms. Illiteracy was a serious problem in Britain. A soldier came in to a bureau asking for help for his mother. Neither of them could fill in her evacuation form, or her compensation form for furniture lost in a raid. The woman's husband and daughter had been killed in the raid, and she had nowhere to go. She was referred to a rest centre in Southwark, but the soldier was asked to bring his mother to the office so that she could be dealt with personally. In cases like this, pastoral care was as important as advice.

Elizabeth Atkin, the daughter of a House of Lords judge and one of the first CAB workers, understood the importance of listening. One evening, she was locking up the bureau in the Charing Cross Road. She wanted to get home before the bombing started. At that moment a man knocked on the door, and said, 'I won't keep you a moment. I just want your advice.' Elizabeth let him in. He told her that he'd been offered a job in the north of England but that his wife didn't want to leave London. 'I think it's a better job, but, of course, I don't want to upset her.' The man embarked on an hour-long monologue, while Elizabeth offered only the occasional yes or no. Eventually he left. The next morning, a letter came through the door. It read, 'Thank you very much for your advice. I've taken it.'

Advisers had to become familiar with a wide range of charities offering different forms of assistance. One woman, having lost 'everything' in a raid, including £12 in cash and her spectacles, was referred to the Lord Mayor's Fund for new spectacles, to the Personal Service League for clothes, to the Soldiers', Sailors' and Airmen's Family Association for billeting expenses, and to the Women's Holiday Fund. She was also offered an escort to her billet: assistance sometimes took more active forms.

Some queries required a detailed knowledge of law. An ARP man had been admitted to hospital after a raid, just as his army call-up papers were arriving. The ARP authorities could not pay his wages as he was technically now a soldier. And he had been refused compensation for his injuries despite their being caused by enemy action. The

CAB took these matters up on his behalf. Other queries were of a personal nature. A woman whose husband was in the army abroad showed up in a panic; her husband had written her a letter saying that he had 'heard things about her'. It is not clear (and not recorded) how the CAB could help. Another bureau was located near a camp of Dutch soldiers who had been evacuated from Dunkirk. A surprisingly short time later, one of the Dutch sergeants was being held responsible for a dozen local babies. According to an adviser, the Dutch authorities were very good about maintenance. 'But it took a bit of sorting out . . .'

Elizabeth Atkin's work extended well beyond office duties. Illustrating the debt owed by the government to the organisation, Elizabeth was to visit bombed houses to decide whether repairs should be carried out at the government's expense or at the householder's. The answer depended on who was living there. She remembers visiting a nice young man in a house in south London with shattered windows. 'Is there a child or old person in the house?' she asked. The answer was no. 'I'm terribly sorry. I can't help you. You'll have to do it yourself.'

The CAB was only one of many voluntary organisations – and individuals – to come to the fore during the period. Bernard Nicholls was a social worker (and a conscientious objector) who tried to ease the plight of London's down-and-outs. He helped to transform the crypt of St Martin-in-the-Fields into a dedicated shelter, removing the centuries-old coffins – one of which was Nell Gwyn's – and reinterring them in the country. He and his colleagues replaced them with the long-term homeless.

'At the time,' Bernard says, 'many shelters were experiencing problems with homeless people who usually slept in the parks.' Many of these were verminous, many were alcoholics, and they were finding it difficult to find shelter. 'We took people from the "submerged" thousands of Westminster's population who had lived mostly out of sight of the generality of the population.'

One of these people was a drinker of neat methylated spirits whom Bernard succeeded in rehabilitating. A short while later, having been reunited with his family, the young man showed up again at the crypt, reeling and barely able to stand. Bernard was furious. 'I took one look at him and said, "It's perfectly obvious that I haven't communicated with you. Let's see if this will," and I slapped him hard in the jaw. He went straight down. Then I realised the awfulness of what I'd just done.'

Bernard and his colleagues helped far more vulnerable people than they slapped, however, including one man so infested with lice, after months living in St James's Park, that the skin on his back was a 'wet pus-y mass'. After the war, a Social Care Unit was formed at St Martin's to provide support for the homeless, and that work continues today, very much a legacy of the Blitz.

The Women's Voluntary Service was a jill-of-all-trades which took on a staggering variety of functions during the Blitz. It was founded in 1938 by Stella Isaacs, Marchioness of Reading, described by friend Isobel Catto as 'a remarkable person, who cut through any type of red tape, and got things done'. The organisation's non-rank structure allowed members to share out roles according to individual strengths. This made it adaptable enough to staff rest centres, care for the homeless, set up mobile canteens, drive ambulances, man observation posts, carry out ARP duties, assist with evacuations, remove iron railings from buildings, collect a mass of rosehips (a source of Vitamin C), and far more besides.

Isobel Catto, a young woman from a well-to-do family, was given an administrative job at WVS Headquarters in Tothill Street, near Westminster. 'We were the powerhouse sending out news and instructions to the local centres,' she says. Women applied to join at these local centres, and word of mouth quickly increased the size of the organisation. 'We really wanted to get as much time as people had to give.'

When the Blitz started, Isobel became involved in one of the

WVS's most important roles. 'We were getting clothes for people who were bombed.' Some of these clothes were donated, but Isobel's job was to negotiate with clothing companies to buy coats, skirts and jerseys at wholesale prices. She would then distribute them to the local centres according to need. In December 1940 Isobel placed a large order with the Houndsditch Warehouse, a well-known East End department store. 'I had not arranged to get it collected. It was Christmas, and I thought that it could wait.'

The night of 29 December 1940 saw the largest attack on London yet. Ten Heinkel 111s laid a carpet of 10,000 incendiary bombs, followed by more than a hundred other aircraft dropping high-explosive bombs and parachute mines. In the resulting conflagration 9,000 firemen battled to prevent the entire City of London from burning to the ground. Had it not been for fog on the Channel coast preventing follow-up raids, it might well have done so. Isobel Catto could see the flames from her home in Surrey, and her thoughts were focused on her clothes in the Houndsditch Warehouse. What would become of them?

> The next morning I went off to London. It was all guarded with the police. You weren't supposed to go through, but I was in uniform, and I said I had these things in the Warehouse, and I didn't know if any could be saved. I'd managed to get hold of three lorries, and we were in these, and they let us through. When we got to the Warehouse, it hadn't received a direct hit, but half the side of the building was down. But the clothes were still hanging on their rails, some of them soaked with water, but they would dry out. So we got a lot of people to help, and we shoved them off the rails and threw them into the lorries, and we saved most of them. I realised that once you've received the order, you must get them out and get them distributed! Don't leave them all in one place! We were fortunate!

Having learned her lesson, Isobel moved on to the organisation of troop canteens, a role in which she found herself pitched against

A mobile canteen paid for by the people of the Bahamas.

formidable local women – 'Lady Bountifuls' in her phrase – who had set up their own canteens and were fiercely resisting interference from the WVS.

It is clear that the country benefited from a tidal wave of volunteerism; large numbers of people gave up time and energy in a common effort to boost the country's ability to defend and organise itself. Which is not to say that everyone's experience was positive; having already failed in her efforts to join the CAB, Vera Reid, a well-educated young woman from London, received a note from the Minister of Labour and National Service, in May 1940, telling her that her services were not wanted. 'Strange that in times like these,' she wrote in her diary, 'the individual is so often thrown back on his own resources.' Nevertheless, the growth of volunteer spirit undoubtedly brought people together. It could hardly have any other effect.

It is worth noting that the work of Henry Willink – in making agencies more accessible, in promoting social workers, in protecting the vulnerable from exploitation and neglect – represents the early stirrings of the welfare state. Yet it is testament to these extreme times that far from being a socialist agitator or leftist thinker, Henry Willink was a Conservative Member of Parliament. In this age of transition from Victorian to modern, in which workhouses overlapped with social workers, and where problem-solving was more important than ideology or allegiance, a truly imaginative and progressive voice could come from almost any direction.

And what of John Fulljames, the young man who carried out a modern-style campus shooting spree? In 1945, only five years after the shooting, a prison reformer named Alexander Peterson, with connections to University College, attempted to find Fulljames a job. He approached Archibald Balfour, the head of a large trading company in South America, asking whether a position could be found for him as an English teacher in Peru. He described Fulljames to Balfour as 'a young fellow of 24, of excellent physique, good appearance, manners and a very useful brain'. Balfour replied that having considered the matter carefully, he could not 'take the responsibility of finding the man a place as a boy's teacher ... Supposing there were again to be some mental lapse and something awful were to occur?' Much better, thought Balfour, to find him 'a job in a mining or trading company in some remote place'. The exchange could be taken from a Somerset Maugham story. In the end, the young man whose fortunate survival mirrored that of his country lived to an impressive age. John Fulljames died in Cardiff in February 2013.

CHAPTER THREE

Going Underground

If you share any DNA with the author, you will be wondering, at regular intervals, how you would have coped with the privations and problems of the period. But as your mind drifts off, bear in mind the words of Tom Hopkinson, wartime editor of *Picture Post* magazine. 'Ordinary people,' he wrote, 'were used to deprivation and lived every day with anxiety; so that side of the distress was not so much new as additional.' *London Can Take It* – just as it always has. Even so, the new conditions were capable – as we have seen – of pushing many beyond their limits. And the Blitz was not simply another period of economic hardship. It was far stranger and darker than that – which was why the poor law mentality had to be set aside – and it tested people of all ages and classes in unimagined ways.

Novelist and scientist C. P. Snow was the son of a shoe factory clerk whose drive and energy had propelled him to the High Table at Christ's College, Cambridge. Snow found to his horror that he was terrified by bombing. He later wrote:

When the bombs began to fall on London, I discovered that I was less brave than the average man. I was humiliated to find it so. I could just put some sort of face on it, but I dreaded the evening coming, could not sleep, was glad of an excuse to spend a night out of town. It was not always easy to accept one's nature. Somehow one expected the elementary human qualities. It was unpleasant to find them lacking.

Snow went on to describe how the apparent courage of those around him, including his landlady, made him feel worse. His admission is valuable as a reminder that we are never safe from ambush by our own sensibilities.

Viola Bawtree, a fifty-seven-year-old woman living in Sutton, shared her cellar shelter with various neighbours and members of her family. Her painfully honest diary entries paint a picture of base fear, and a struggle to retain religious faith. On 27 August 1940 she was undergoing 'stark terror' at the sound of the siren. She had to decide whether to stay in bed or go downstairs to the shelter where others were lying in deckchairs. She opted to stay in bed: 'Suddenly the searchlights started again and my heart started a furious pounding and I seemed to hear little sounds like distant bangs. I lay in abject terror.'

Viola went downstairs to the cellar, and took her place in a deckchair. 'Oh how welcome, for I feel I must be with someone,' she wrote. It is a sentence that might have come from *Mrs Miniver*, and it shows why 'Blitz Spirit' can never simply be dismissed as a myth: the scared and lonely were drawn into each other's company. Viola's nephew, Kenneth, and her neighbour, Ivan, were at the dark end of the cellar, where she joined them. In the diary she described her situation as 'comic' – but she was in no mood to appreciate the humour. As the others slept, Viola lay awake. 'Between 3 and 4 was the worst part,' she wrote, 'when my teeth chattered and I trembled violently.' After the All Clear sounded, she went up to bed, but sleep still would not come, and when the searchlights shone again, she crept back down to the cellar. She returned to her bed at dawn and finally grabbed an hour's sleep.

It is little wonder that for much of the Blitz, many people were in a state of near exhaustion. 'For some period,' says Ealing schoolboy Roy Bartlett, 'people were walking around like zombies.' And cellar life was providing Viola with a more basic form of existence than she had ever known: 'This morning something started falling from my hair. I thought it was my comb, but it was a huge spider, all legs! I want to tell someone, but mustn't.'

After a while, Viola – like millions of others across the country – began to adjust. 'Now that I'm more normal,' she wrote, 'I can think more of various advantages in all this.' These included using time in the cellar to write and mend things, and finding fun in 'trying to forestall Jerry'. She may have been clutching at straws, but the straws reflect a growing defiance.

On 7 September, the day of the first heavy bombing of London, Viola reflected that there was no real safety except 'to abide in His presence'. Until she could live a life of obedient faith, she would be afraid. That evening, as the sky above London glowed red, she called on God to frustrate the Germans. Later that night, she lay in despair thinking about all the people dying twelve miles away.

After reading newspaper accounts of the effects of the bombing, she wrote: 'I'm in danger of losing God . . . Oh, I can't write for tears – I feel as though nothing matters any more, and prayer seems utterly futile . . . I'm cut off from Him now in a nightmare world.'

By the following afternoon, she had found an explanation for His indifference: 'I think that possibly God allowed such horrors so that men and women should realise to the full that this sort of thing must be abolished for all time.'

Here is a vivid example of how an ordinary person was able to make sense of extraordinary events. The human spirit, it seems, is truly pragmatic and resourceful. But despite her deeply felt and intensely expressed emotions, Viola had not herself experienced any bombing.

The first bomb fell on Sutton on 10 September, and two days

later, after many more had fallen, Viola was able to congratulate her home town on having 'saved London a lot of bombs'. A sense of pride in being bombed is common in Blitz diaries and memories, and in Viola's case, it seems to have helped to displace fear. In some way, she was now 'doing her bit', no longer a voyeur but a full participant.

Certainly, a change in her attitude became noticeable once the bombing had become routine. On 22 September she wrote that while the sound of the siren could still trigger nerves, 'normally I think I can see it all more as an adventure'. Perhaps because danger can be easier to bear than the fear of danger, perhaps because normality breeds acceptance, Viola's diary became a bolder affair as September wore on.

Viola Bawtree and C. P. Snow were brave to record their fears – but they were certainly not alone in experiencing them. The consensus allows for the existence of fear – if only to acknowledge how successfully it was overcome. Yet fear was the dominant emotion of the Blitz. The Church Army acknowledged this in its shelter booklet, packed with prayers like – 'Let not your heart be troubled, neither let it be afraid.' Fear made people try to seem fearless. As the sirens wail in Marghanita Laski's *To Bed with Grand Music*, restaurant diners continue their conversations: 'It was conventional to ignore the noise, to flout precautions, to die in the middle of a carefully prepared epigram.'

Fear drove and shaped the country, and it tested the very idea of civilisation. It sent people underground against government advice, and kept them there, free of the sound of bombs and guns, oblivious to the stench and filth. And as people reacted viscerally, freeing themselves from the trappings of society, so they inspired others. The artist Henry Moore, for example, found himself excited and engaged by the primal sight of underground dwellers.

Moore is associated in the public mind with his reclining figures – human forms reduced to their pre-cultural and pre-civilised origins.

But these sculptures – as well as Moore's exalted reputation – would never have existed had it not been for a chance trip on the London Underground in September 1940. Moore had recently turned down an offer from Sir Kenneth Clark, chairman of the War Artists' Advisory Committee, to become an official war artist. He had no interest in becoming involved in propaganda; he wanted to concentrate on his own work, specifically with moving his sculpture in an abstract direction. But one night, Moore and his wife found themselves stuck inside Hampstead Underground Station. A raid was taking place above ground and they were ordered to stay where they were. In an interview with journalist and author Leonard Mosley, Moore described how, irritated and trapped, he began to look around:

> I could see what have since been called Henry Moore reclining figures. I just stood there, watching them – the lonely old men and women, the family groups, the chatterers and the withdrawn. When they announced that the All Clear had sounded and we could go up to the surface, I went reluctantly.

The next night Moore returned to the tube station with notebooks in his pocket, and he began drawing. As the weeks went by, his routine barely changed. He tucked himself into a corner of an exit, making himself as unobtrusive as possible, and he sketched people. He was fascinated by the distance of the people from the war – even as the war could be traced on their faces. And he was engrossed by their retreat from civilisation, by the elemental chaos and disorder. In a world of primal motivations, nothing remained but bare human essence.

When the authorities started to organise life in the tubes, Moore lost interest in them. His attention turned to shelters where the chaos lived on, such as the notorious Tilbury Shelter in Stepney, a massive goods yard packed with Eastenders. He also spent rapt hours inside an unfinished railway tunnel at Stratford Broadway. This shelter was visited, and described, by Superintendent Reginald Smith of the Metropolitan Police 'K' Division:

> The first thing I heard was the great hollow hubbub, a sort of soughing and wailing, as if there were animals down there moaning and crying. And then, as we went, it hit me, this terrible stench. It was worse than dead bodies, hot and thick and so foetid that I gagged and then I was sick. Ahead of me, I could see faces peering towards me lit by candles and lanterns, and it was like a painting of hell.

To Moore the tunnel was a unique prospect, to Smith it was Dante's seventh circle. Once again we see the Blitz as a time of extremes – in all directions.

If Henry Moore was inspired to action by the visceral, elemental world of the tube shelters, so was a Mass-Observation diarist who went by the name 'Rosemary Black'. But where Moore was professionally excited by what he saw, Black was overcome by emotional horror. A woman of independent means from St John's Wood in north London, her world was privileged and placid. She had understood from the newspapers that conditions in tube shelters were civilised – and she rarely doubted anything she read.

The epiphany of 'Rosemary Black' began one wintery night in London's West End. The blackout was in force, and she turned on her torch to look where she was going. The light caught the attention of a policeman who shouted, 'Put that light out!' She fumbled with the torch, failed to turn it off, and shoved it into her coat pocket. But the light continued to glow through the pocket. The policeman placed his hands on her shoulders, and pushed her down the stairs of Piccadilly Circus tube station. 'Don't you know there's a war on?' he barked, his conversation apparently limited to Blitz clichés. Once down in the station, Black was appalled by what she saw. Every corridor and platform was crowded three deep. The people seemed to her like worms in a tin. She was overwhelmed by the heat, the smell, the haggard faces, the crying of babies. She stared at a woman lying with her head on the bare platform, her face an inch from a huge gob of spit.

Shaken by the experience, Black spent the following day flipping between guilt and self-pity:

> God must surely have it in for me in my future life that I am granted all this underserved good fortune here and now ... I sometimes feel I'd be happier if I were bombed out of house and home instead of always being 'one of the lucky ones'.

Angry and helpless, she became resolved to *do* something. She went out and tried to find work as a war volunteer. After a series of rejections (as we have seen, it was not always easy to find such work) she was accepted as a tea and sandwich dispenser for the YMCA Mobile Canteen Service. Her journey is testament to the words of journalist Ritchie Calder in his 1941 book *Carry On London*. This book, written in the eye of the storm, reflected popular sentiment even as it tried to influence it. Calder writes:

> In this war we are all in it together ... Yet, until this truth is driven home by the agony of experience, we are apt to cling to habits and ways of thought, living in the past, ignoring the present, and closing our minds to the implications of the future.

'Rosemary Black' underwent an 'agony of experience' despite being neither injured nor made homeless. She was confronted by an uncomfortable new reality with the result that her mind was opened. Her desire to help was a true manifestation of Blitz Spirit – and at the heart of the process was fear.

But what of the government? Where did the guardian of the

people sit in the chaos? We have seen in previous chapters that it could predict neither the extent, nor the effects of bombing. It is worth examining, in this period of shifting realities, how it attempted to protect its citizens, and whether it succeeded.

In the years before the war, the government's shelter policy focused on dispersal and household protection. Rather than bringing people together in large shelters where they might be killed en masse by a direct hit, fall prey to epidemics of fear and panic, or succumb to a 'shelter mentality' of inactivity which could prevent the country from functioning, it was felt that people should be spread out, either in their own houses, in garden shelters, or in small localised shelters. Life, in other words, should carry on as normally as possible.

The importance of strengthening the home was heavily stressed: a Home Office booklet – *The Protection of Your Home Against Air Raids* – recommended that one room in the house be turned into a 'refuge room', preferably a basement or cellar, and stocked full of

A government-endorsed refuge room.

essentials such as books, playing cards, quiet games and a gramo-phone. Viola Bawtree's cellar presumably qualified as a refuge room.

J. B. S. Haldane – a distinguished biochemist and geneticist who had examined the problem of sheltering in Spain during the Civil War – took issue with the policy of dispersal. It was, he declared, worthless. It was true, he admitted, that large numbers would be killed if a large shelter was directly hit, but the chance of that happening was small. If people were sheltering separately, on the other hand, then 'almost every bomb would find a human target of some kind'. The government's desire for a dispersal policy, Haldane believed, resulted mainly from its unwillingness to pay for deep shelters. Not only that, but its emphasis on strengthening the home and building shelters in gardens shamefully ignored the needs of the slum- and tenement-dwelling working classes. In 1938 Haldane published a book called simply *ARP*, in which he set out his grand plan for miles of brick-lined tunnels sunk into the London clay with multiple entrances and a complex system of ventilation. The book received a mixed review in *The Times* – although the reviewer agreed that Haldane's faith in the value of deep shelters was sound.

In the same year that Haldane pounded the drum for deep shelters, Finsbury Borough Council in London commissioned an architectural firm (Tecton – which had been responsible for the elegant Penguin Pool at London Zoo) to come up with designs for a deep shelter capable of harbouring the entire population of the borough. Finsbury – the area south of Angel, east of Gray's Inn Road, north of Smithfield and west of the Barbican – was a crowded working-class area with an ambitious left-wing council keen to improve living conditions, and to provide the sort of protection dismissed by the Home Office. Tecton's designs, produced with the assistance of concrete engineer Ove Arup, consisted of fifteen circular tunnels capable of sheltering all 58,000 borough residents.

In answer to Haldane's criticisms and the Finsbury proposals, a government White Paper, 'Air Raid Shelters', was published in April 1939. It was the culmination of the Hailey Conference – a not-very-independent commission of experts which reported to Sir John Anderson, Lord Privy Seal and soon to become Home Secretary. In its conclusions, the White Paper unsurprisingly opposed the provision of deep shelters and defended the policy of dispersal. It endorsed the use of a corrugated steel garden shelter covered in earth (known as the Anderson Shelter – though named *not* for Sir John but for one of its designers, Dr David Anderson) as well as strengthened basements. The White Paper rejected Haldane's proposals on the basis that even working as quickly as possible, it would take two years to build sixteen miles of tunnels – and these

Finsbury had an unusually progressive borough council.
One of its developments was the provision of 'violet ray
treatment' for daylight-starved ARP workers.

would provide shelter for only 160,000 people. And it concluded that Finsbury Borough Council's deep shelters would not, in practice, allow sufficient time for the majority of citizens to reach safety. This could result in panic taking hold – particularly as people were likely to slow down, or even stop, once they had passed through the shelter entrance.

So it was that the Finsbury proposals and the principle of deep sheltering were officially rejected. Throughout its discussions and consultations, the government had been careful to acknowledge its responsibility to protect the public. It had no desire to alienate its people. It was keen, however, to immerse them in a warm bath of self-congratulation, and to that end, a sense of British moral superiority was embedded in the debate. A sober, sensible British man, it was implied, would rather sit calmly at home with his wife and children than cower among strangers in a communal funk-hole. As the war began, therefore, the government was free to pursue its existing policy. The bombing, however, had not yet begun . . .

By the time the White Paper was published, the government was hurrying along with its dispersal policy. In February 1939 two and a half million Anderson shelters had begun to be issued to households with gardens in vulnerable areas. Anybody earning less than £250 per year received a free shelter, or, if there was no outdoor space, the materials to strengthen a 'refuge room'. There were many people, as Haldane had reflected, with neither outdoor space nor a 'refuge room'. For these people and for those caught out during a raid, money was made available for the construction of communal street shelters with brick walls and concrete roofs.

Yet even people in tiny houses without gardens sometimes had a personal shelter. Margaret Vear was a Liverpool factory worker: 'We had back-to-back houses with a lane down the back,' she recalls, 'and they built shelters between the two walls so that when you walked down the lane you were walking through the shelters. You had a little gap, and then you walked through the next shelter.'

Under the Civil Defence Act, 1939, meanwhile, employers became legally bound to provide shelter for their workers, and new powers were granted to local authorities to requisition buildings for use as shelters.*

Despite these efforts, however, the government was facing criticism. In a House of Commons debate in April 1939, Herbert Morrison, who would become Home Secretary eighteen months later, expressed his deep concern about 'the absence of a shelter policy on the part of the Government'. In the same debate Arthur Greenwood, also to become a member of Churchill's War Cabinet, echoed Morrison, declaring that the people 'are deserving of a good deal more adequate protection'. These criticisms came in the very month that the White Paper was issued. And the fact is that five months later, at the outbreak of war, shelter provision was severely behind schedule. Yet throughout this period, there was one obvious source of shelter that was repeatedly overlooked – the London Underground. And it was a source that had been tapped before.

The First World War had seen aeroplanes turn from flimsy bird-cages dropping feather darts on enemy soldiers into heavy bombers dropping thousand-pound bombs on enemy cities. At first Zeppelin and Schütte-Lanz airships and then Gotha heavy bombers carried out attacks on Britain, killing over 1,400 citizens in the process. In

---

* Given these measures, it is interesting to look back over the first chapters of this book to examine how people were sheltering. Maisie Dance, for example, was entering her factory shelter when she was badly injured by a bomb. Ida and Joseph Rodway were in their garden Anderson shelter when a bomb damaged their house. Michael Bowyer and his parents took shelter in a secure room in the school opposite their home. Many of the residents of Vicarage Terrace were in bed when the bombs fell, but the members of the Unwin family (all of whom survived) were sheltering beneath the stairs. This was a popular place of shelter in houses across the country, as was the space underneath the kitchen table. So popular, in fact, that 'Morrison Shelters' went into production in January 1941. Named after Herbert Morrison, Home Secretary from October 1940, these were six-foot-long rectangular steel boxes which were used as kitchen tables by day and sleeping cages by night.

The world's safest table tennis table.

June 1917, 162 Londoners died in a single Gotha raid. Anticipating events of twenty-three years on, the bombs fell mainly on the East End docks and the City of London. Liverpool Street Station received a direct hit as did Upper North Street School in Poplar where a bomb exploded in the infants' classroom while the children were busy making paper chains.

The British authorities feared that panic from these raids might weaken national resolve to the point where the country would be forced to sue for peace. This worry gave way to other concerns. In a House of Commons debate, Evelyn Cecil, member for Aston Manor, noted that while he was sure there was no element of panic among the people, 'there is a very strong feeling of want of confidence in the general management'. Cecil was simply anticipating Herbert Morrison's 1940 observation that the government lacked a coherent policy. And the people's reaction to events in 1917 is revealed in a letter written by Bernard Rice, a Royal Flying Corps pilot at home on leave, in which he describes the beginning of a Gotha raid on London: 'First came the bobbies, pedalling round on bikes with a

"Take Cover" sign and continuous ringing bell attached. The streets cleared instantly. The tubes were thronged.'

The people of London were taking shelter in the London Underground. And while Rice's letter describes a daylight raid, people had begun congregating in the tubes overnight. In 1917 the London Electric Railway Company (having consulted Scotland Yard) began placing night staff in eighty-one tube stations to provide 'shelter facilities' to Londoners. LERC figures indicate that Hampstead Station – where Henry Moore would be inspired – held up to 3,000 shelterers, while Piccadilly Circus – where 'Rosemary Black' would have her dark epiphany – contained space for 5,000.

Yet, despite this clear precedent, the government and the London Passenger Transport Board (as the LERC had become) made up their minds in the mid-1930s that, in the event of another war, the tube would be closed to the public, and used exclusively as a transport system for government traffic. This idea fell from favour as war approached – and the minutes of relevant meetings reveal great confusion as to what role the tube would eventually play.

In January 1939 Lord Ashfield, the chairman of LPTB, argued that the Underground should be closed altogether and not used for any purpose. Thomas Gardiner, the Home Office Secretary responsible for ARP, disagreed, saying that the tube ought to be used as normal – but could be adapted into a shelter for 'refugees' (as shelterers were known) if the network broke down as a result of bombing. Sir Philip Game, the Commissioner of the Metropolitan Police, suggested having soldiers placed at his disposal to keep people out of the stations by force. The possibility was thus raised of British troops firing on women and children fleeing the bombs. Thankfully, Game admitted 'serious misgivings' about his own suggestion. The only common thread that can be drawn from the discussion is that the police, Home Office and transport authority did not want the tube being used as a shelter – unless it became absolutely necessary.

Several months later, the Minister of Transport, Euan Wallace,

asserted that tube stations would be open to ticket holders only and
not to refugees. Sir Philip Game questioned this policy. The police,
after all, would be responsible for enforcing the rules. How, Game
wondered, could they be expected to differentiate between travellers
and refugees? If stations were kept open, he insisted, they would end
up full of refugees, and there was nothing that the police – or anybody else – could do about it. Though hardly a solution to the
problem, it was agreed that a broadcast should be prepared announc-
ing that the tubes were essential to the war effort, and not available
as air raid shelters.

In the end, the government's approach to the problem was to
avoid the problem. Its aim was to prevent the tubes being used as
shelters. This was partly to avoid fostering a 'shelter mentality'
among citizens, and partly because the functioning of the tube was
essential to the functioning of London. But who was pointing out
that the current shelter provision was inadequate, and that the
tubes *should* be used to alleviate the problem? Who was proposing
that the tube might work adequately as a shelter by night and a
transport system by day? Who was suggesting that fear was a perfectly normal reaction to bombing, and that 'refugees' might remain
fully-functioning members of society? Ignoring the example of the
Great War, the authorities were simply hoping that the problem did
not arise.

It did arise. On the evening of 8 September 1940, the day after the
first heavy bombing of London, a huge group attempted to gain
access to Liverpool Street Station. The station entrance was being
guarded by police and LPTB staff. Bernard Kops, a fourteen year-old-
boy who had been bombed out of his Stepney home the previous day,
was in the throng with the rest of his family. With policemen barring
the entrance, he thought he was going to be crushed to death.
Screaming, he was swept along in the surge. The crowd was clearly not
going to give way, and nor, it seemed, were the police. Suddenly, 'a
great yell went up and the gates were opened and my mother threw

her hands together and clutched them towards the sky'. The people had won. The government, says Kops, had been made to acquiesce.

Three nights later, on 11 September, 2,000 people rushed down the stairs at Holborn Station before going to sleep on platforms and in corridors. Giddy with victory, the special correspondent of the *Daily Worker* (the Communist Party newspaper), wrote:

> On previous nights when a few groups of people had attempted to use the station as a shelter, officials turned them away. Now in the face of the determination of thousands of people to secure real shelter from bombs, the London Passenger Transport Board officers seem to have given up the attempt to keep them out.

On 14 September Phil Piratin, a thirty-three-year-old designer of hats and the Communist councillor for Spitalfields East, carried out a publicity stunt to bring attention to the tube situation. Together with seventy-seven associates from Stepney, Piratin invaded the Savoy Hotel shelter and refused to leave until the All Clear had sounded. The police soon arrived, and Piratin tried to explain his position. He pointed to a woman from Stepney with four children whose husband was in the army. 'What would you do,' he asked the police inspector, 'if your wife were put in the position of that woman over there?' Piratin says that the inspector expressed sympathy – although he proceeded to take the name and address of every Stepney intruder. After a while, waiters began serving cups of tea – for which Piratin insisted on paying. The price was agreed at tuppence a cup, the amount charged by a Lyons Corner House. When the All Clear eventually sounded, the occupation ended. 'Everyone left elated,' says Piratin, 'and there was publicity in the Sunday papers.' One paper was rather sombre in its tone, however. The *Daily Worker* predicted that 'One day the pent up fury of the workers will burst forth in all its majesty and might. And then woe betide the denizens of the Savoy.'

Before that day, however, there was a Blitz to struggle through, and by the night of 18 September, almost every functioning tube station was in use as an air raid shelter. At Hampstead, people were queuing outside the station at 2.30 in the afternoon. Across the network stations were filling up throughout the evening – and many were having to turn people away. Yet the following day, in the spirit of Canute, the government issued an urgent appeal to the public in the national newspapers. Under the heading 'No Sheltering In The Tubes', it urged people 'to refrain from using tube stations as air raid shelters except in case of urgent necessity'. The problem was that the government had one definition of 'urgent necessity' – while a scared and lonely pensioner with no Anderson shelter or refuge room had another.

It may come as a surprise, while reading of a battle between the government and its people, to discover that the head of that government – Winston Churchill – was actually in favour of using the tubes as shelters. (This also seems inconsistent given that Churchill had recently expressed strong disapproval of the Finsbury Borough Council scheme – but Churchill had never been shy of reviewing a situation in the name of pragmatism.) More surprising is that Churchill was ignorant of the problem until 21 September. On that day, he asked Sir John Anderson to prepare him a précis of the issue. The Home Secretary's note explained that the public had been sheltering in the tube since 'the intensified air attack' and that the authorities had found it impossible to keep them out. This could only be done with the use of military assistance – and public opinion would not allow this. 'The decision regarding the use of the tubes for shelter purposes,' explained Anderson, 'was thus breached and we were faced with a fait accompli.'

The government had lost the Battle of the London Underground and it tacitly admitted the fact when the decision was taken to turn the Holborn to Aldwych branch of the Piccadilly Line into a public shelter. (This branch line had sheltered the War Cabinet during the First World War, and was currently being used to shelter the Elgin

Marbles and other British Museum treasures.) On 25 September the government conceded public defeat with the issue of a declaration to the press which began: 'The use of tube stations as shelters has now been officially recognised.'

A leader article in *The Times* on the same day drew attention to the Home Secretary's admission that the provision of shelters across the country, and particularly in London, had been insufficient, and that 'urgent and large-scale action' was needed to remedy the problem. That action, argued *The Times*, should involve striking a balance between the policies of dispersal and deep sheltering: good use must now be made of all available deep shelters.

When assessing the performance of the government – and asking whether it did a good job for its people – we must first remind ourselves that the Blitz amounted to an unknown – and unknowable – prospect. Just as the government was having to guess at the size of the death toll and the number of psychological casualties, so it was imagining the rise of lawless troglodyte communities in deep shelters under the ground. And while this prospect may sound far-fetched, bear in mind the excitement felt by Henry Moore as he sat, night after night, sketching people in their primeval state as though evolution had reversed itself. He could not have hoped to encounter this scene in any other place at any other time. Perhaps the government was not being entirely fanciful. And there existed, too, a fear of the anti-authoritarian and egalitarian spirit which was thought to be brewing underground. 'Those under the ground instilled an element of fear in those who remained above it,' writes Peter Ackroyd. 'It is the fear of the depths.'

A more prosaic government concern related to the cost and construction of deep shelters. The Hailey Conference dismissed J. B. S. Haldane's proposals on the grounds that they would take too long to build. But while the conference clearly lacked objectivity, its concerns may have been valid. In November 1940, after Herbert Morrison became Home Secretary, construction began on ten deep-level shelters in London, each attached to an Underground station. Just eight were completed, all behind schedule, at a cost of almost three times the original estimate. They were only opened to the public in 1944.* The deep shelters proposed by Haldane and by Finsbury Borough Council might well have suffered the same fate.

The government also feared that large concentrations of people sheltering together would lead to instances of mass slaughter – and this was borne out by events. On 14 October 1940, for example, an armour piercing bomb forced its way through the earth above Balham Underground Station and exploded over a passage between the two platforms. Sixty-six people were killed. On 11 January 1941 a bomb fell on the booking hall of Bank Station. The force of the blast shot down the escalators and through the tunnels, killing fifty-one people. And on 3 May 1941 a bomb penetrated the basement shelter of Wilkinson's Lemonade factory in North Shields. One hundred and seven people – more than half of those in the shelter – were killed. The people killed in these raids probably believed themselves safe. Colin Perry, an eighteen-year-old from Tooting, who witnessed the aftermath of the Balham bomb, wrote in his diary, 'They had gone to the Tubes for safety, instead they found worse than bombs, they found the unknown, terror.'

Another government concern was that fear and panic would spread and breed in a crowd. An event which took place almost two years after the end of the Blitz suggests that this belief, too, had validity. On 3 March 1943, as a crowd of shelterers was entering Bethnal Green Station, the unfamiliar sound of a new type of anti-aircraft rocket in nearby Victoria Park caused a surge. It seems that a woman holding a child tripped at the bottom of the stairs leading from the street to the booking hall, and the surge quickly turned into a crush,

---

* The entrances to these shelters, at stations such as Belsize Park, Goodge Street and Clapham Common, are still identifiable by heavy concrete structures intended to shield the stairs from bomb blasts.

The surface damage caused by the Balham Underground bomb.

in which 172 people were killed at the scene. Another person died later in hospital. One of the policemen called upon was James Morten, who recalls, 'There were dead bodies piled up from the ground to the roof. It was simply a result of the panic by people coming in from behind.'

And beyond the government's concerns, it seems that dispersal appealed to the majority of the population. Even when deep shelter was at hand, many preferred to remain closer to the home, either inside the house or in an Anderson shelter in the garden. Only about four per cent of the population of London actually used the tube for sheltering. Perhaps this reflected a British tradition of self-containment, of lives led alongside, but never interfering with, the neighbours. Or perhaps it simply offered a less disrupted existence. Either way, the Anderson shelter undoubtedly proved effective from a psychological point of view: millions of citizens spent nine months

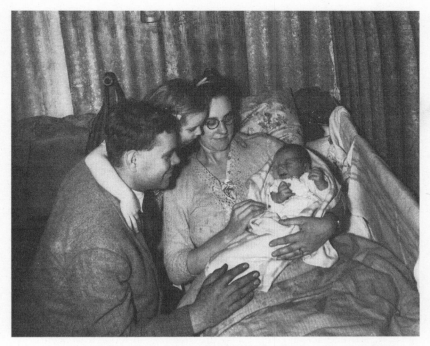

During a September 1940 raid, Mrs Winifred Roderick gave birth
to a son in her family shelter. The boy was named
Peter John ANDERSON Roderick . . .

in its womb-like safety before emerging into the world in the early
summer of 1941.*

And it stood up very well to bomb damage – though not, of course,
from a direct hit. The Anderson's chief problem was a lack of basic
comfort. It was small, cold and dark, and difficult for a family of four
(or perhaps even six) to bear over long winter nights. As the Blitz
wore on, many started to desert their Andersons for the relative comfort of the house. 'A lot of the shelters got waterlogged,' says Betty
Brown, a factory worker from Chingford, 'and we decided that we'd

---

* The British Psychological Society did not approve, however. At its general meeting on
26 July 1941, it was agreed that 'the presence of crowds and shelter officials reduced
anxiety' and that 'the provision of communal shelters rather than individual ones is, in
general, the best policy'.

sleep inside.' John Fowles, a schoolboy in Hackney, speaks for many when he says, 'We had an Anderson shelter in the garden but we felt we stood as much chance in the house.' The decision to stay indoors was taken by John's father, whose Great War service afforded him total authority on such matters. This was a common theme across the country. Elsie Glendinning's father had been a proud 'Old Contemptible' – one of the original British soldiers in France in August 1914. As Elsie and her mother sheltered inside their Anderson, Elsie's father stood to attention beside it. 'He wouldn't go into the shelter,' explains Elsie, 'because he'd been in the First World War.'

Yet while the policy of dispersal was rational in theory, and both convenient and acceptable to many, what about those with no access to an Anderson or a refuge room? By dismissing the option of deep shelters and by initially refusing to make the tubes available, the government was consciously placing a sizeable section of the population at risk. While the months of relative inactivity of the 'Phoney War' allowed shelter provision to be accelerated (although it remained behind schedule) there was still many, across Britain, whose only protection was feeble brick shelters in the streets and parks. These are not fondly remembered. 'Surface shelters,' says Metropolitan policeman Walter Marshall, 'were mostly used by ladies of easy virtue or by people needing to relieve themselves. You had to be careful what you trod in.' Nor were they very safe. 'The roofs of the shelters in Hull,' says fireman John Cooper, 'were not tied into the walls at the top so they weren't effective against lateral blast. The walls would be blown in – or in some cases outwards and the whole roof would come down in one solid piece.'

One of the few defenders of the surface shelter was Home Secretary Herbert Morrison, who describes it, in his autobiography, as 'the safest of the lot'. And so it is interesting to note that when the roofs of surface shelters caved in, the resulting mess was often known as a 'Morrison Sandwich' – the filling consisting of shelter occupants. Wartime investigations revealed that rogue builders and penny-pinching local authorities were frequently substituting sand for

The shelterers inside this Anderson were unhurt,
despite widespread damage.

concrete in the shelters' construction – so that, in London alone, at least 5,000 faulty shelters were erected. But there were still plenty of people spending the nights in these unhappy death traps. For six months, London secretary Alda Ravera slept in one, bedding down each evening, alongside her family, on a copy of the *Evening Standard*. It is hard to argue with Tom Hopkinson's observation that the people of Britain were hardened to deprivation. And if anything could prove his point, it was the large-scale tendency of people in towns across Britain to avoid the bombing by the extreme measure of 'trekking'.

Trekking was the daily rush of people from the towns to the countryside in search of a place to shelter for the night. Trekkers were sometimes invited into people's homes, but more often they ended up sleeping in barns and churches, under hedges, and in fields, before returning the next morning. The phenomenon took place in towns and cities that experienced heavy bombing, and it was viewed by the government as a sign of weakened morale. According to Richard Titmuss, the official historian of social policy, the government was so anxious that nothing should be done to encourage trekking that 'no specific provision was to be made for the people taking part'. It was treated, in other words, as though it wasn't happening. The press mentioned nothing, and no assistance was offered to the trekkers. Just as Londoners had reacted spontaneously to the bombing by occupying the tubes, people around the country were heading out of town – and the government was choosing to ignore them in the hope that they would go away.

Gwen Hughes was a young mother from Southampton. On the night of Saturday 30 November, she was buried alive by a bomb blast in one of the town's shelters. It took several hours to dig her out, but her injuries were only minor. The following night her brother drove her out of Southampton to a recently built house six miles away. Gwen remembers:

> Every evening my brother would drive around the town picking up strangers, and he'd drive them into the country. To escape the bombs. Mr and Mrs Hutchins's wooden bungalow was made open to anyone. They were very good people. And people would shelter in this room, all sitting around the floor and lying wherever they could, just to be out of the danger of the town. The only time I agreed to go was on the Sunday – I couldn't stand any more!

There are no figures for the numbers who would trek out of Southampton every evening, but a Mass-Observation estimate suggests that by 10 December, 'twenty per cent or less of the normal resident population' was sleeping in the old parts of the city.

After exceptionally heavy raids on Plymouth in the spring of 1941, around 30,000 people were trekking out of the city each day. On 24

April, after the city had been attacked over three consecutive nights, the figure may have reached 50,000. The following night, according to a Society of Friends report, a YMCA mobile canteen stopped near Yelverton on Dartmoor. The moor seemed deserted – but people soon began to appear 'from among the ditches and heather'. A week later, the Luftwaffe bombed Merseyside for seven nights, and the town of Bootle suffered terribly. Up to 5,000 houses were destroyed, and every rest centre barring one was put out of action. An estimated half of the population trekked out of the town on 8 May, the last night of the bombing. These people were not cowards. They were ordinary citizens doing what they could to keep going in terrible circumstances. Clearly the authorities had not anticipated trekking, and so closed their eyes to it. It was rigid and unsympathetic leadership, demonstrating, in the words of Tom Harrisson, 'an inability to understand the needs of ordinary people in extraordinary times'. Indeed, the fact that people were willing to walk for miles, sleep in ditches, and still arrive at work the next morning hardly demonstrates a lack of morale. It shows, on the contrary, supreme determination. Rather than trekking, perhaps it should be described as extreme commuting. And it confirms, once again, that Tom Hopkinson was correct to stress the underlying toughness of ordinary British men and women. What were a few nights on the moors to people who had lived their whole lives in hardship?

Yet despite their mistakes we should not be too critical of the government. Not only was it dealing with an unknown quantity in enemy bombing, it was also facing unfamiliar problems concerning its own role. The population was (or else soon would be) told what to wear, what to eat, where to live and where to work. Politicians and civil servants were devising plans for most of the people most of the time – and sheltering in the tubes and sleeping on the moors (or with Mr and Mrs Hutchins) did not constitute any part of those plans. And while it was arrogant to disregard deep shelter, short sighted to close the tubes, and unfeeling to ignore the trekkers, the government was having to adapt to new conditions just as the people were. It was feeling its way on these and many other issues. Particularly alarming to the authorities was the realisation that the people would have to be rewarded for their efforts and sacrifices.

British citizens were, after all, being asked to volunteer on an unprecedented scale, as ARP, AFS, WVS, firewatchers, firemen, policemen, Home Guard and in countless other roles. Their work in the factories kept the war effort going. They made up the armed forces. And they were in daily physical danger from enemy bombs. This amounted to far greater responsibility than they had ever been asked to bear, and it was why, in the end, the government couldn't keep them out of the tubes, and it was why deep shelters began to be constructed – and it was why trekking was finally acknowledged in May 1941 (the government being forced to accept that its previous position had been wrongheaded). It was also why down-to-earth policeman's son Herbert Morrison became Home Secretary and Minister for Home Security in place of the more distant Sir John Anderson. 'It's essential that the man for the job should understand the people,' Churchill told Morrison when he was appointed. Within days, Morrison was allocating new funds for shelters. 'What does money matter?' he asked. 'There are thousands of lives at stake!' In Britain, during the Blitz, a lot of relationships started changing. The loveless marriage between government and people was only one of them.

CHAPTER FOUR

Shelter Life

Roy Bartlett was an ordinary boy living an ordinary life in west London. He had a cat called Stripey, he attended Little Ealing School, and his parents ran a hardware shop in South Ealing. But as war approached, his life became a little less ordinary. He was issued with a gas mask that scared him so much that it made him cry. He was glad when it misted up, because the mist hid his tears. He started laughing, though, when one of his friends discovered that the mask made a rude noise when he blew out, and soon the whole class was competing, like an obscene dawn chorus, to make the best mask-fart. And when war arrived, life became less ordinary still. Roy was evacuated twenty-four miles – though it felt like hundreds – to the farming community of Wooburn Green in Buckinghamshire.

In the village hall, Roy and the other children were paraded before the locals. The biggest boys were picked first: they would be useful on the farms. Then the girls were taken: they were less likely to cause trouble. Roy was among the leftovers – so he was bundled into a car and touted around the village. 'Don't he look pale?' said one woman. 'What funny accents!' said another. Eventually a nice young couple said, 'Would you like to come and stay with us?' In the modern world of Child Services and Emergency Protection Orders, it is strange to consider that, not very long ago, children were being handed out as casually as gas masks. And the results could be tragic. In April 1940 the chairman of a bench of Sussex magistrates was almost in tears, according to the *Daily Mirror*, as he sentenced Edith and Ruth Sills, a mother and daughter from Hailsham, who had beaten a four-year-old boy sixty-four times with a stick. The unnamed boy had, apparently, stolen biscuits from the larder. His 'whole life might be affected by this brutal chastisement', said the magistrate, and he urged the boy's mother, who lived in London, 'to give him the tenderest care to help him forget'. Roy's evacuation tale, fortunately, was very different to this. His foster couple, Bill and Connie, proved to be exceptionally kind, and he remained close friends with them until Connie died in 2006, aged ninety-four.

Roy returned to Ealing in May 1940. London was not, at this point, any more dangerous than Buckinghamshire. In the meantime, however, the cellar beneath his parents' shop had been converted into a public air raid shelter. The roof had been strengthened, pillars were added, and a street entrance built. An Elsan chemical toilet, screened off by hessian curtains, stood in the corner. The shelter could accommodate fifteen people, sleeping in double bunks. Little Ealing School, meanwhile, now had large shelters of its own, in the form of twin tunnels under the playground, lit by hanging hurricane lamps.

In August the sirens began sounding and life in the school was disrupted by endless trips back and forth to the shelters. As this became increasingly tiresome for the teachers, the children were kept at their desks until an unfamiliar noise suggested that danger might actually be close. Inside the shelter, the children sat on benches singing and chatting, until the teachers decided that some simulacrum of education should be attempted, and the children were given quizzes and puzzles. But there were no lessons in the shelter, and Roy and his classmates were having a good time.

On 7 September 1940, when the daylight bombing of London

started, Roy was in his parents' hardware shop. The sirens sounded – and, as was usual by now – no one moved. But then Roy, his father and his mother heard the heavy droning of aircraft. This was new – and they went to the top floor of the house to see what was happening. The drone became louder, ack-ack guns began to fire, and the family ran down to the cellar shelter where they were joined by customers and a few passers-by. Everybody was scared. No one knew what to expect. For several hours, this random grouping huddled in the shelter. When they emerged in the dark, Roy's family went back to the top of the house to look out over London. Fires were burning everywhere, and a black cloud was forming. They returned to the shelter later that night when the bombers came back, and every night for the next fifty-six nights. Life was changed utterly.

Rules and customs were soon imposed on shelter life. When people across the country went to the shelters they carried cases with savings certificates, cheque books, property deeds and wills. In Roy's shelter it became silently understood that good toilet etiquette involved waiting for the drone of an aircraft or a burst of ack-ack before getting down to business. If one's timing was good, any embarrassment would be spared. And though the shelter was cold, damp and musty, and though the smell of carbolic disinfectant from the Elsan was overpowering, life was bearable. People brought in bits of curtain to give their bunks some privacy, and pictures of relatives in the armed forces (not behind glass, of course) provided comfort. One day Roy's father fetched some distemper from the shop, and painted everything light blue, though the consensus was that this made the atmosphere cold. Everybody liked listening to the wireless. Tommy Handley's *ITMA* had been on air in early 1940 and would be again in mid-1941. Featuring depressed laundrywoman Mona Lott ('It's being so cheerful as keeps me going!') and other wartime archetypes, it kept bores around the country supplied with catchphrases. As the bombs began falling, comedy programme *Hi-Gang!* – with Vic Oliver (Churchill's barely tolerated son-in-law), Ben Lyon and Bebe

Daniels – was popular. Roy's shelter also had an old wind-up gramo-phone, but it proved impossible to find new needles. After a while, every record began to sound like sizzling fat.

One night, a bomber passed low overhead, releasing bombs which came down whistling. Instinctively, everybody left their bunks and came together on the floor. One man said aloud what everyone else was thinking: 'This is bloody dangerous!' The bombs fell harmlessly two or three miles away. Later on, a bomb fell three hundred yards away – and the shelterers learned what a near-miss really felt like – the pressure in the shelter changed suddenly, causing a vacuum in the ears. The bomb made a huge crater behind a nearby block of shops, damaging five houses beyond repair.

As the weeks passed, Roy started to learn a new skill – knitting. He was taught by a seventeen-year-old girl who had been injured by a landmine. (Though known as 'landmines', these were, in truth, huge magnetic anti-shipping mines with adapted detonators. They para-chuted down, causing huge devastation on landing.) This girl had been at a local dance when planes were spotted. The dance stopped briefly but the decision was taken to carry on as the aircraft seemed to have passed over. But as the music was restarting, a landmine floated gently down, exploding with devastating effect. The dance hall's plate glass windows shattered, lacerating the girl's arms. Time had passed, and she was now spending her evenings with Roy. They were unravelling old jumpers, and transforming the wool into bunk bed covers.

Roy had, in the meantime, become known as 'Wee Willie Winkie' to a twelve-year-old girl who shared the shelter, and, for a long time, he had no idea why. Whereas everyone else there walked around in dirty old clothes or siren suits (these were one-piece jumpsuits pop-ularised by Churchill – one of whose siren suits sold for £30,000 in 2002), Roy's mother made sure that he was always correctly dressed in pyjamas. One night, Roy stood up, carefully undressed, and began sleepwalking across the shelter, before climbing the stairs to his bedroom. He was followed by his mother, whispering, 'No, we won't sleep upstairs tonight. Let's sleep downstairs in the shelter.' Eventually, Roy turned round, and made his way slowly back to his shelter bunk. The twelve-year-old girl was watching him, giggling, and when he woke up the next morning, he had a mysterious new nickname.

Siren suits were available in all sizes.

Shelter life involved all kinds of new experiences. One night, Roy woke with a sense that his head was hurting. He opened his eyes and found himself on the floor. A thick fog of dust filled the cellar, and he felt as though he was choking. He could see nothing. When he tried to stand up, his leg hurt. In confusion, he could make out shapes. There seemed to be others on the floor. After a while, the shelterers began to collect their thoughts, and a group – including two soldiers who had missed the last train back to barracks – headed outside to find out what was going on. In the street they were confronted by a red glow. The house next door was on fire. Walking through rubble and broken glass, they made out the gable end of the next row of shops – and then nothing. All seven shops were missing. On the other side of the road, a large house was destroyed, and the fire station next door was damaged, its pumps mangled. Roy, meanwhile, was relieved to find that his parents were safe. His mother had been in the shelter, while his father had been sitting in an armchair in the kitchen upstairs. He had been listening to aircraft and ack-ack guns, and then heard what he described as 'an exploding roar like Dante's Inferno'. The kitchen windows came in, there was rubble and dust everywhere. But he was unhurt.

The blast was caused by a landmine. It seems that it had dropped on the butcher's in the middle of the row of vanished shops. Seven people in those buildings were killed, twelve badly injured – and the butcher and his family were never found. Meanwhile, the house next door to the shelter was burning to the ground – though this blaze had been started by a small incendiary bomb. At first, it was thought that the owner of the house was missing – she usually sheltered under the stairs – but she had behaved differently that night. Her son, home from the navy on leave, had persuaded her to spend the night else-where. And in spite of the shock, the shelterers had escaped serious injury. The only casualty was Roy – his right foot had been slammed against the wall, crushing his cartilage. The house and shop, however, were in a pitiful state. The windows were gone, the frames were loose, and every room was filled with rubble, dust, and bits of glass. There was glass in the larder, and this created a dilemma, acted out all over the country. While official advice was not to eat from a bombed house as slivers of glass could infiltrate food, waste was unthinkable in straitened times. And so, at every meal over the coming weeks, as food was served up, Roy's mother would say, 'Look at it, chew it slowly, don't gulp it!'

The morning after the blast, Roy's father took him to Mattock Lane Hospital. The roadway was full of rubble, so Roy hung on to his father's arm, and hopped until they reached the first working bus stop. When they arrived at the hospital, it was crowded and chaotic. The area had suffered badly during the night, and Roy saw trolleys dripping with blood; his injury seemed very minor relative to others. When he was finally treated, the hospital had run out of plaster, so his foot was dressed in a mess of sticky bandages. The emergency services, meanwhile, had spent the day removing bodies from the wreckage. By the afternoon, the road had been cleared – and expressing a mood of defiance, Roy's father decided to open his shop. It was already open, Roy's mother said, seeing as it didn't have windows or a front door. A few customers appeared, more out of prurience than anything else. One lady, who lived a hundred yards away, marched in carrying a paraffin oil stove with a 'Bartlett's Hardware' label tied to it. She said that she had found it in her garden, and despite its long flight, it had only a small dent in it.

A few weeks after the blast, Roy came home from school to find the local handyman, George, clearing a blockage on the roof. A drain was overflowing, and Roy, being a nosy child, watched closely as George climbed the ladder. Suddenly, George ran back down and was violently sick in the gutter. Roy was eager to know why, but was quickly ushered away by the adults. George, he figured, must have spent lunchtime down the pub. But he was wrong. As George was clearing the drain, he had pulled out a mane of long black hair. Attached to it was a scalp. It must have belonged to the butcher's wife from down the road.

Roy's story is important because it offers a genuine picture of shelter life, untarnished by the consensus. It involved changes in the way people lived, and in the way they viewed and treated each other. It brought periods of genuine fear and danger, it brought sudden, intensely lived experiences, but it also brought mundane experiences and sometimes a feeling that life was on hold. All of this is present in Roy's memories. And the landmine that landed on South Ealing also brought him an unwanted souvenir. His ankle injury – insignificant at the time – became more troublesome as he grew older. An x-ray revealed that he had no cartilage left in the joint, and years of limping resulted in having to have both hips replaced. But as he reminds himself, 'There were plenty of other people worse off. It was one of those things.' It is worth noting, however, that Roy received his injury while asleep in a strengthened shelter. His father, who was sitting in an unprotected kitchen above ground, was unhurt. A shelter was no guarantee of safety – as Gwen Hughes could testify.

When Southampton was heavily attacked on the night of 30 November 1940, twenty-seven-year-old Gwen was in a public shelter at the bottom of High Street, together with her children, four-year-old Gloria and three-year-old Anthony, as well as her dogs, Pronto and Peggy, and a litter of newborn puppies. The shelter was really a large medieval cellar, divided into three chambers by modern brick walls. There was wooden seating around the sides, but Gwen and her husband Monty, a fireman, had brought a bedstead down, which they placed in a corner reinforced by the modern walls.

That evening, the siren sounded and the sky was lit up with parachute flares. Down in the shelter, Gloria and Anthony, dressed in siren suits, sat under a ledge built into the corner, while their mother

The Southampton cellar in which Gwen, Gloria and Anthony sheltered.
Photographed in 2014.

stood beside them. Gwen announced to the shelter that she had only one cigarette, and apologised that she couldn't hand any round. She asked whether anybody had a light. A man named Pat Powell walked over, stood in front of her, and struck a match. Sitting nearby were local sweetshop owners, Mr and Mrs May, and their thirteen-year-old daughter. They had recently returned to Southampton after a time away, escaping the bombs. 'Oh, why did we come back, why?' moaned Mrs May. 'The business, my dear, the business . . .' said her husband. As he spoke, the wall in front of Gwen caved in. Pat Powell, shielding her, was killed instantly. A bomb had exploded on the pavement above and to the side of the shelter. A moment later, another bomb fell into the shelter from the restaurant above. It landed on the May family. And it brought the upper floors crashing down into the cellar.

For a while, Gwen wasn't sure whether she was alive or dead. She could hear screams coming from all around her, but she couldn't move her head. All she could do was dribble dirt out of her mouth. She realised that that she was buried. Then she heard her daughter's voice, calling out, calmly, 'Mummy! Mummy! Are you all right, Mummy?' She couldn't answer. At some point, she remembers her husband Monty – who was on duty as a fireman – shouting from above, 'Gwen, Gwen, are you all right?' before calling to someone, 'Come and help me! My family's under there!' and receiving the answer, 'No good going down there, mate! They're all finished!' Ignoring this advice, Monty fetched volunteers to start digging. Gwen, meanwhile, could hear her son screaming. He was alongside her, his head beneath one of her hands. She now knew that he was alive – but after a while, he became quiet.

As Monty and his helpers were digging, the raid intensified. A hundred and twenty-eight German bombers dropped bombs on the city that night. Most of High Street and the main shopping centre were destroyed. All communications were cut off, and so many fires were started that their glow was visible from the French coast. Water from a severed main, meanwhile, had started seeping into the shelter. Gwen heard her husband say, 'What are we going to do if we can't get them out?' She also heard the reply: they should be shot to save them the misery of drowning.

As the water level rose, Gwen finally found her voice. 'How are the children?' she asked. 'Gloria's all right,' said Monty, 'but I'm not sure about Anthony. I think he's finished.' Gwen began to lose consciousness – and when she eventually came round, she received the news that both children had been pulled from the rubble safely. She asked Monty whether he could help Mr and Mrs May. 'It's no good, my love, there's nothing we can do for them.' Gwen remained trapped by a wooden post across her legs, and as the rescuers scraped away the last layers of rubble, she was struck in the leg by a pick-axe. When she was freed after five hours of digging, the water level in the shelter had risen to her chest.

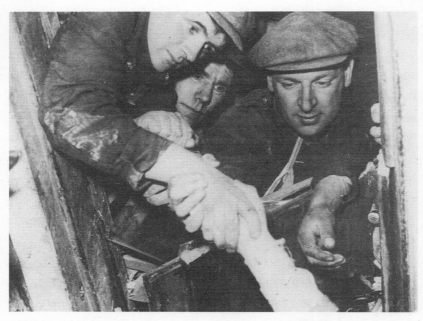

A photographer captured this rescue scenario – similar to Gwen's – in a wrecked London pub. Like Gwen, the trapped woman survived.

Gwen felt reborn as she was carried hurriedly up High Street – but the Luftwaffe was still coming over, and a bomb exploded fifty yards away. Everybody fell to the ground, but no one was injured. Her memory of Southampton's main thoroughfare, at that moment, is of two solid walls of flame on either side of the road. She was eventually brought to a shelter on the harbour front where she was reunited with her children, who were both alive and well, although badly shocked. (The dogs and puppies were not so lucky. They were all killed.) Once the All Clear had sounded, Gwen and the children were taken in a private car to South Hants Hospital, which was itself damaged. A rumour was rife – and it was quite possibly true – that the hospital had only been saved by a quick-thinking porter extinguishing an incendiary bomb on the roof earlier that night.

Remarkably, Gwen had suffered only minor injuries. Her foot was broken, and her hand had been hurt by a falling piece of cement. This hand had been resting over her son's head – and it probably saved his life. She was frozen stiff after five hours in water and rubble, and she would be haunted by the sounds of cries and screams for many years – but at least she and the children were alive. Of the twenty-eight people in the shelter that night, they were the only survivors.

Southampton was heavily bombed again the following night, this time by 123 aircraft. Over the two nights, 137 people were killed – 96 of whom were in shelters. Some were in Andersons, others were in public shelters underground, but the result was the same; contemplation of the human reality of that night makes the dispersal versus deep shelter debate seem as fatuous as the boiled egg dispute in *Gulliver's Travels*.

Bombing was not the only danger offered by shelter life, however. Accidents in shelters were common, resulting in an odd abundance of civil claims. The Blitz, it appears, gave rise to its own 'compensation culture'. In an April 1941 memorandum, Wandsworth Council drew up a long list of payments made to claimants. These ranged from £526 (for falling down the stairs of a shelter on Putney High

Street) to £4 (for 'walking into an air raid shelter'). In a letter to the London Civil Defence Administrator, the town clerk explained that 'owing to the magnitude of the council's task and the speed with which it had necessarily to be performed, such "negligence" as has given rise to many of the claims must necessarily be claimed by the council to have been unavoidable'. This translates into English as: 'It isn't our fault.' The reality, of course, was that an insurance company was paying out.

This trend was repeated across the country. A typical case concerned a Mrs Buckingham from Bexleyheath. On the afternoon of 28 January 1941, as she hurried down the steps of No. 1 Shelter in Danson Park, Mrs Buckingham was passed by two cleaners coming up the other way. She ran into the shelter, and stepped onto what she believed were waterlogged floorboards. In fact, the cleaners had just removed the floorboards, and were in the process of fetching buckets to bail water from the sump underneath the boards. Mrs Buckingham received a huge surprise when she stepped, not onto solid wood as she was expecting, but into a large watery hole. As a result, she received cuts to her leg, and a doctor was called.

A few days later, Mrs Buckingham's husband wrote to Bexleyheath Council's town clerk, setting out her version of events. He described his wife's injury as 'a terribly lacerated leg from knee to ankle' although the need for only four stitches possibly undermines his words. On 20 February the borough engineer submitted a report, stating that Mrs Buckingham had dashed so quickly past the cleaners that she gave them no chance to warn her that the floorboards were missing. In his opinion the incident was caused by Mrs Buckingham's own carelessness, and not that of the cleaners. On this basis, the town clerk wrote to Mr Buckingham denying liability. Mr Buckingham wrote back saying that, in his view, the council was entirely responsible for the negligence of the cleaners who had simply left a gaping hole unattended. He threatened legal action unless an offer was forthcoming. In the end, the council seems to have agreed to pay the doctor's fees while continuing to deny any negligence – and the matter was left there.

Aware of a growing problem, the Court of Appeal tried to ease the burden on local authorities – or, more accurately, on their insurance companies. The case of Jelly v Ilford Corporation involved a claim brought against Ilford Council by a woman who was injured during the blackout when she stumbled over a sandbag outside the entrance to a shelter. The woman claimed that the council was negligent in failing to draw her attention to the sandbag. The court found for the council. The local authority was entirely within its rights to place a sandbag outside a shelter entrance, and the woman should have been paying more attention. This was the judicial equivalent of: *Don't you know there's a war on?* The court was urging the people of Britain to start taking more responsibility for themselves, while in the process trying to nip the 'compensation culture' in the bud.

But there were, it was becoming plain, plenty of ways to be harmed in shelters other than by bombs. Sixty-two-year-old Quillian Simpson, for instance, died in a Birmingham shelter after inhaling noxious fumes from a stove. A woman present told the coroner's inquest that she had almost been suffocated, and that others had been so ill that they were unable to work the following day. The coroner officially warned the public of 'the danger of improvised heating in shelters without expert supervision'.

There were many instances of violence and disorder in shelters. Sometimes it was because the shelter was full, entry had been refused, and tempers flared. In September 1940 a professional wrestler called Christos Ptonopoulos was fined at Marlborough Street Magistrates Court for 'shouting, gesticulating and threatening a warden' after being refused entry to Soho Square shelter.* There was

---

* The shelter in Soho Square still exists and can be accessed through the mock Tudor gardener's house in the centre of the square. In January 2015 it went on sale through a local estate agent for £175,000. There was talk in the media about the possibility of opening a restaurant inside.

also plenty of rowdy behaviour for its own sake. In October John Sumner, a railway goods loader, was sentenced to a month's hard labour for kicking a shelter marshal in the jaw. 'He is the leader of a group of youths who have been persistently annoying people in the shelter and refusing to obey rules,' the shelter marshal told Clerkenwell Magistrates Court.

Some cases had darker overtones. In September a thirty-year-old labourer from Dartford, Percy Clark, called an ambulance, saying that his wife was hurt. An ambulance driver and a nurse arrived to find Irene Clark lying unconscious on the floor of the family's Anderson shelter with a head wound. The couple's three children were asleep beside her. Percy Clark accompanied her to hospital in the ambulance – before being charged with her attempted murder. In his police statement, he said: 'Before it got light we had a quarrel because I asked her to let me go into lodgings and have a separation. I lost my temper. I struck her on the head with my fist. I then hit her two or three more times on the head with my fist. She fell back as though she was unconscious.'

Irene was operated on in hospital. Her surgeon reported that she had every chance of making a full recovery – yet, shortly afterwards, she was killed by a bomb blast when her hospital ward received a direct hit. This is a bleak train of events that tells much about the period: the extremity of life leading to domestic trouble, the intensity of the shelter magnifying tensions, and the arbitrary death of a woman who had already survived so much.

The case of James Miller is equally illustrative of the period. Miller was a rescue and demolition worker from Bethnal Green whose wife and children were evacuated away. On 18 October, after six weeks of continuous raids, and an endless round of gruesome sights and demoralising jobs, he walked into Old Street Police Station and told an officer, 'You had better take me in, guv'nor. I have just done the old woman in.' By 'the old woman' he meant his seventy-five-year-old mother, Ann, whom he had strangled with a piece of cord. She had, he said, told him that 'she could not stand it much longer'. Each night she was sleeping in different tube stations where she always had to sit on the stairs because she wasn't a regular, and she had lost her attaché case containing her valuable documents. Miller strangled her, he explained calmly, in order to relieve her suffering.

James Miller's case has much in common with that of Ida Rodway. Both were driven by intense and unfamiliar stress to behave as they did. Both believed they were doing the right thing by their loved ones. And both were sent to Broadmoor after being found 'Guilty but Insane' at the Old Bailey. Ann Miller found shelter life hard to bear, but she died because her son found rescue work harder still. They, like the Rodways, were tragic victims of the Blitz.

James Burnham, meanwhile, was a victim of an element of the Blitz that many found exciting: the public shelter's ability to bring strangers together. Twenty-one-year-old Burnham was a trooper in the Lancers. During a period of leave he returned home to Dalston where he became rather too friendly with his brother's wife, Phyllis. (His brother was serving with the army in Palestine.) Burnham and Phyllis spent a week together. When he returned to his unit, they continued to 'write to each other in endearing terms'. Phyllis said she was never going back to Burnham's brother and they agreed to live together when the war was over.

When Burnham returned on leave six months later, Phyllis had moved to a new address and Burnham heard rumours that she had been 'carrying on' with another man. When he tracked her down to a flat in Leyton, she admitted that she *had* been out with someone else, but denied sleeping with him. She and Burnham lay together on her bed for an hour, and arranged to meet up the following evening in the Ritz Hotel where she was working.

The next night, Burnham waited at the Ritz for three hours, but saw nothing of Phyllis. He went to a nearby pub and drank four half-pints. He then travelled to her local shelter and found her asleep on a mattress, lying next to a man. Burnham sat nearby, talking to strangers, until the All Clear sounded when he walked up to Phyllis. Groggy with sleep, she asked him what he was doing there. 'You know what I am doing here,' said Burnham. The man lying next to Phyllis – William Sullivan, a fireman from Islington – said, 'It's all clear, let's go up.' 'He's not going up there, is he?' asked Burnham. 'Yes,' said Phyllis. Burnham picked up his service rifle, and walked smartly out of the back entrance, before running around to the front, and confronting Phyllis and Sullivan as they came out. He fired two shots. Sullivan fell down and Phyllis screamed. Then Phyllis fell too.

In his subsequent police interview, Burnham said that he had grabbed his rifle and opened fire 'because I was jealous'. He described how he then ran back into the shelter to ask if there was a doctor there, before charging down the road, shouting 'Doctor!' and 'Ambulance!' He eventually ran into two policemen, and asked to be arrested. Although he didn't know it at the time, his bullets had caused relatively little damage. One struck Sullivan in the arm, causing a compound fracture. The other missed entirely.

At Burnham's Old Bailey sentencing, an army officer, called as a character witness, described him as a promising young soldier due for promotion. His unit, said the officer, was anxious to have him back. Sentencing Burnham to a year in prison, the judge described the case as miserable: 'I hate to send a young soldier to prison,' he explained, 'but I cannot allow it to go forth that soldiers can return on leave with their rifles and go shooting people of whom they are jealous. It is only by the mercy of Providence that you are not guilty of murder.'

The judge was concerned about guns being introduced into everyday situations. When the officer said that soldiers were under a duty to carry their rifles while on leave, the judge lamented the number of cases coming before him of soldiers 'shooting while on leave'. The fact is that had Burnham not had a rifle, an argument would have taken place, perhaps a fist fight, the usual consequences of passion and betrayal. But when emotional young men have access to guns, as the case of John Fulljames has already demonstrated, the consequences are very different. It is a lesson as relevant today as it was seventy-five years ago.

But this case is interesting in other ways. Shelter life undoubtedly encouraged liaisons. What else could be expected when people were lying alongside each other in the dark for long periods, alternately scared and bored? But shelter life was also opening up private worlds to public exposure. Had it not been for the war, Phyllis *might not* have started a relationship with Burnham. Had it not been for the Blitz, she *might not* have been playing around with Sullivan. But had it not been for public shelters, she would *definitely not* have been caught by the former in bed with the latter. Lives were increasingly on show for all to see.

The issue of sex in shelters is not quite so clear. We should not imagine that they were steamy caverns of carnal incontinence – although their reputation was along those lines. Humorist and author Caryl Brahms overheard the following exchange in a public shelter:

Warden – 'Are there any expectant mothers in this shelter?'
Woman – 'Give us a chance! We've only been here ten minutes!'

In November 1940 an outraged probation officer at Southwark Juvenile Court spoke of seeing 'youngsters in their teens, of mixed sexes, making up their beds together on the floors of public shelters, even under their parents' eyes'. The Public Morality Council, meanwhile, a prurient collection of church groups determined to stamp out vice wherever it lurked, reported a marshal in a central London shelter as saying, 'This shelter is nothing more than a brothel!' before admitting that he had never actually caught anybody 'at it'. A Mass-Observation report from one of London's largest shelters asserted that 'prolonged observation, night after night' has revealed only 'a certain amount of necking among young couples' and the occasional glimpse of 'a couple engaged in intercourse in the dark area'. (One can almost feel the disappointment of the investigator.) Yet even these slim pickings probably amounted to more sexual behaviour than prolonged observation in a public place would have revealed before the war.

And it is interesting to note a reader's letter published in a freely available – and highly unusual – weekly wartime publication called *London Life*. A 'lifestyle magazine' before such a thing existed, *London Life* contained features on popular history and the latest movies – but with a particular focus on what it coyly described as 'fads'. These included – from a randomly selected issue – body piercing, dressing in rubber, transvestism, and something called human-pony-riding.

The letter, written by someone calling himself 'Shelterer', records that he had recently been sitting in a shelter with a young actress who was reading a copy of *London Life*. Others gathered round, and began admiring its photographs and articles relating to fetishism. This led a few people to start discussing their personal pleasures – shoes, underwear, corsets – and as a result, others started buying the magazine and bringing it into the shelter. One night, a group was so deep in discussions about the current issue that they failed to react to a bomb exploding nearby. When a warden ran in to find out whether everyone was all right, somebody said that they had been too busy talking to pay any attention. The warden asked what could have been so interesting, and they showed him *London Life*. This was funny, said the warden, because during the last war, he and his friends had visited a club in Paris named 'Fétiche', where people wore corsetry and long gloves and rubber costumes. The conversation took off again, and the group decided that they would host a special evening in the shelter where everyone would dress according to their own particular pleasure.

It is safe to say that the majority of public shelters were not planning fetish evenings. But nor were most people as well protected as singer and comic actress Florence Desmond. In a popular song, she explained to a gentleman why he should spend the night with her:

I've got a room for two, a radio that's new,
An alarm clock that won't let you down,
And I've got central heat, but to make it complete,
I've got the deepest shelter in town.

Florence invokes the Home Secretary in her effort to win over the gentleman:

Now Mr Morrison says he's getting things done,
And he's a man of the greatest renown,
But before it gets wrecked, I hope you'll come and inspect
The deepest shelter in town.

The popularity of 'The Deepest Shelter in Town' gives a sense of a country able to laugh at its situation – but the fabled British sense of humour was not impervious to the stresses of the period. With a distinct lack of levity, magistrates sent fifty-three-year-old George Hall to prison for fourteen days – for snoring in a public shelter. Having snored and been woken several times, George began using abusive language to those who continued to wake him. These people were, depending on one's point of view, either attempting to maintain peace in the shelter, or denying a tired man some rest. Eventually, Hall threatened to hit a shelter marshal who was ordering him to stop snoring, and a policeman was called. Hall was found guilty of wilfully disturbing persons in the proper use of an air raid shelter under Rule 3(a) of Regulation 23 (A-B) of the Defence Regulations 1939. It is not recorded whether Hall returned to the shelter following his release from prison. Perhaps he preferred to take his chances at home in bed.

Across the country, people objected to their shelter-mates for all manner of reasons. Elizabeth Robson remembers a difficulty in her cellar: 'We had two Irish maids with us, and my brother in law, all sitting in the basement. "Mary Mother of God", "Mary Mother of God",

"Mary Mother of God". It went on all night. My brother in law eventually said, "I'm terribly sorry, I can't stand that."'

Others were less judgemental. Inside Piccadilly Circus tube station, Vera Reid sat watching people. She watched a tiny baby grow until it could sit up. She watched an old man learning to knit until he could make a pair of gloves. And she watched a young woman who wrote endlessly every night. A diarist herself, Vera was fascinated. What was this woman writing? 'I think it's letters. But what can she find to say? For whether I go home early or late there she is always writing away as if her life depended on it.'

Vera took pleasure in these characters, and a touching pride in their achievements. But while she was merely casting an eye around, Mass-Observation investigators were spending long periods in the tube, scrutinising their subjects like subterranean ornithologists, filing careful reports on everything they saw and heard. Two particular reports on life in the tube shelters cast vivid light on the reality of the time, uncoloured by the consensus.

The first report opened at 2.30 p.m. on 24 October 1940, with the investigator standing in a queue outside a west London tube station together with about a hundred others, all waiting to stake their claim once the doors opened. These were mostly middle-aged and elderly women, along with a number of children, and a few men who looked particularly shabby. Most people had prams or handcarts full of bedding ready to place down. It seemed to the observer that little interest was being taken in appearance: women wore curlers and bedding was stained and torn. Real lives were on show. Fear was clearly visible beneath talk of last night's raids. 'What was that?' asked a woman suddenly. 'Car, that was,' someone said. 'Funny the things you think you hear, isn't it?' said the woman, trying to retain her pride. 'Can't hear a leaf falling without giving a jump, can you?'

At 3.30 someone shouted, 'They're opening!' and the cry went up along the queue. People began to surge forward. The police were supposed to be in charge of the process, but people stampeded through the doors, and it took a while before some order was imposed. Loud complaints then began about queue barging: 'Some of them have only just come! We've been here since six o'clock in the morning!' A woman carrying a baby and a roll of bedding was overtaken by a puffy-faced man. 'What time did you get here, you sod?' she yelled at him as he passed.

By the time the investigator arrived downstairs, all the spaces on the platforms and lower passageways had been claimed, mostly reserved by blankets rolled into strips. An eight-year-old girl was keeping places for her family at the platform entrance. She told the observer that she had been queuing since six o'clock in the morning. It was all right on the platforms, she said, but it was too cold by the stairs. While the investigator was speaking to her, an argument broke out further along the platform. A little boy had arrived in the queue at half-past-six to reserve places for his family. But as soon as he had set out his blankets, a station porter came along, pushed them out of the way, and gave the spot to an elderly mother and daughter. According to the unofficial rules of conduct that were beginning to assert themselves, this was a clear breach. The boy was in tears, and four or five women were arguing loudly on his behalf.

'It's wicked to do a thing like that!' said one. 'Freddie started waiting before it was light this morning. He was up there with the guns going and all, before any of us!'

'He has that place every night!' her friend pointed out. 'They've no right to do a thing like that!'

'You wait 'til that young man [the porter] comes back. I'll tell him . . .'

The mother and daughter were embarrassed, but the women, it was clear, were not angry with them. This was the porter's fault. He would be taken to task. But when he returned, his voice rose above everyone else's. 'That place wasn't taken! If I gave that place to anyone, then that's their place! I'm not going to hear any more about it!'

The porter walked away, and disappeared through a door into the mysterious backroom world of the London Underground. The women had lost the battle, but not the war. 'Never mind dearie,' said one. 'They shan't get your place tomorrow! I'll keep it for you if I have to take my skirt off to put it down!'

In this account, tensions are close to the surface. This is, in part, because it focuses on the early part of the day as people competed for the best places. But the 1943 Mass-Observation file report, from which it is taken, cites it as evidence that tube shelter life, in the early months, was 'chaotic and undisciplined' with frequent outbreaks of 'rowdyism and squabbling'. 'Again and again,' writes the anonymous author, 'investigators report fights and quarrels in the shelters.' The author gives examples, including a report of two family fights in the same shelter:

> First was a girl, shouting and screaming at her mother. In the end they were separated by force, and led away from each other, struggling and screaming. The other case was of a man and his wife. The wife wanted him to sit down, the husband wanted to walk about. She became very excited, and a crowd of 'rubberers' formed round them. She bit his ear and tore out his hair. He smacked her face and threw her to the ground.

The author suggests that this 'disorderly behaviour', which occasionally called 'for police intervention', caused the public to think that tube shelterers were 'a rough, low type'. But this was not the case:

> The real explanation seems to lie not so much in the character of the individuals as in the complete novelty of the social set-up ... People who in their ordinary, familiar surroundings were models of respectability might easily lose some of their inhibitions when in totally new surroundings, for which no accepted standards of behaviour had yet been evolved.

And from this early chaos, states the author, order was established. This was mainly due to unwritten laws which came to govern conduct, and to natural leaders who could enforce it. And so, over time, 'each shelter became more and more a self-sufficient community, with its own leaders, traditions and laws'. Indeed, by April 1943, according to the author, investigators were routinely reporting 'a pleasant, social atmosphere' that shelterers were finding difficult to leave.

This is a revealing story. Published before the consensus had fully crystallised, it both challenges and confirms what we have come to understand. On the one hand, tube shelters had been chaotic and ill-disciplined, riven with rowdyism and squabbling. This is not part of the consensus. Yet they grew into happy, self-governing communities without any guiding hand from the authorities. This is the consensus in its purest form.

The second account comes from another Mass-Observation investigator, observing a different tube station on 25 September. It covers the period later in the evening, once the reserved places were taken up by families and working people. By seven o'clock, in this station, most small children were tucked up, and many of the adults were eating sandwiches, chocolate and fruit, and drinking tea or beer. The acoustics of the curved platform roof made the limited amount of conversation – mainly about the effects of raids – sound louder and more widespread than it was. Interest was occasionally injected when somebody went upstairs for air, and returned with news of conditions above ground. There was a card game taking place on one platform, but other than this, the investigator noted almost no 'occupation' or 'amusements' taking place. Nobody read a book, and 'the majority just sit doing nothing'.

The investigator heard plenty of grumbling through the evening. The chief complaint was the belief that places on the station platform were being bought, and that members of the station staff were accepting bribes. Evidently these were recognised problems. On 1 November, the *Daily Express* reported:

Racketeers now plant members of their gangs in all the favoured Underground shelters. These stooges take up as many as twenty-five places on one platform. Then, when Mrs Brown, of Stepney, arrives with her two children, having been crowded out from one station to another all along the line from Liverpool Street to the City, they catch her in her desperation and say: 'I was keeping this place for a pal of mine, but you can have it – for a couple of bob.'

The stooges, known as 'droppers', were using ingenious methods to jump the queues. One dropper told tube staff that he had just been released from hospital, and that standing in the queue might 'loosen his stitches'. His story was believed, and he was allowed to enter the station before anybody else. Droppers tended to charge more for the deeper stations, which were considered safer. A place at Holborn could cost half a crown, while a spot in a less popular station – such as Charing Cross – could be yours for just sixpence.

Cards and stares. People packed onto a tube platform in late September 1940.

While this particular grumble was a genuine irritant, others were the product of sheer frustration. The investigator listened as a woman complained to a policeman that she had a right to sit blocking the stairs having failed to find another spot in the station. 'I'm a ratepayer,' she said, 'I pay my rates as good as anyone else, I can sit where I like!' Eventually, she got up, without the policeman having to say a word. The investigator heard only one other argument during the night. A woman on the stairs was being repeatedly woken by people passing her to use the toilet. She complained loudly that 'Seventy-eight people want to go to the lavatory!' and another woman shouted back, 'Can't you shut up, you bleeding little hypocrite?' The argument was over as soon as it had begun.

The night ended quietly. The first to get up were people on early shifts. Families began leaving at about 5.15 a.m., often to catch some sleep at home before the day began. But the ack-ack guns were still firing above ground, so people came back down, causing a blockage on the stairs, exacerbated by the fact that some were still asleep at the edges. The All Clear sounded at 5.40 a.m., shortly before the next night's queue started forming, and by seven o'clock the platform was empty of people, and cleared of rubbish by the porters. The station had begun its day job.

Taken together, the two accounts paint a rich and complex picture of a world adjusting to new circumstances in which all manner of human behaviour could be found. There was – of course – no single picture.

A fascinating example of tube shelter life occurred towards the end of 1940. Flight Lieutenant Guy Gibson, later to lead the Dambusters raid, was, at this period, flying night fighters with 29 Squadron. One night, unable to find a cheap hotel room in London, he made his way down to a shelter, and walked past rows of bodies, trying to find a space. As he went, he noticed the atmosphere turning hostile around him. Suddenly a woman yelled, 'Why don't you get up there and fight those bastards?' Gibson's uniform was conspicuous – and the shelterers were furious at the inability of the RAF to prevent German bombers from wreaking havoc on London. Gibson, more nervous of the London mob than of the Luftwaffe, turned and fled. He did not wish, he later wrote, to be torn limb from limb. It seems extraordinary that such fury could exist so soon after the RAF's huge popularity in August and September. (It also seems harsh on Gibson given that he *was* getting up there and fighting the bastards.) But events were moving quickly, and past successes counted for little while fear was dictating emotions.

As volatile as tube shelters could be, it is worth noting that they caused the police very few problems. Reported incidents over the first few weeks of heavy bombing included a twenty-five-year-old man sentenced to three months for indecently assaulting two boys at Colliers Wood, a man of seventy-eight fined ten shillings (£20 in 2015) for using insulting words and behaviour at St John's Wood, and a number of people ejected from stations for distributing communist material. And yet by 23 October, only sixteen incidents had been reported across the entire tube network despite the vast numbers taking shelter (the tube population on a single night in later September was estimated at 177,000). This is an almost negligible level of crime – and some, of course, will cite it as proof that tube shelter behaviour was exemplary. Others, meanwhile, will see the first Mass-Observation report as evidence that morale among shelterers was disintegrating. They will all be wrong.

It is worth looking again at an observation made by the second investigator who wrote that the majority in the tube 'just sit doing nothing, staring into space'. Mass-Observation carried out a very careful study of Tilbury Shelter, the enormous goods yard in Stepney, holding about 6,000 people each night, and notorious for its appalling conditions and bad behaviour. Journalist Ritchie Calder was not enchanted by the atmosphere at Tilbury, writing in the *Daily Herald*:

When ships docked, seamen would come to roister for a few hours. Scotland Yard would know where to look for criminals bombed out of Hells' Kitchen. Prostitutes paraded there. Hawkers peddled greasy, cold fish which cloyed the already foul atmosphere. Free fights had to be broken up by police.

Yet after two months of close scrutiny, a Mass-Observation report concluded that it was not bad behaviour that characterised Tilbury Shelter, but 'the extreme vagueness and lack of plan' of the shelterers. There was 'an enormous amount of simply sitting about with no occupation of any kind'.

A typical case study was a middle-aged woman who entered the shelter slowly at 4 p.m. before unfolding her rug, sitting down, and staring ahead without expression. An hour later, a man sat down beside her without speaking, and he, too, sat doing nothing, before slowly untying one of his boots. Pausing, he said, 'What you got there, Mum?' The woman said nothing, but reached slowly down into a basket and pulled out a newspaper parcel, a bottle of cold tea and a china cup. In silence, the man ate half of the sandwich and then continued to untie his boot. Two hours later, the man and the woman had a nap under an eiderdown. They went to sleep for the night by 10 p.m. In the meantime, they had been joined by a younger red-haired woman, but they shared little conversation and no activity or amusement.

Only an organisation such as Mass-Observation, dedicated to long periods of scrutiny, could faithfully record how much disengagement took place among those affected by the Blitz. Lack of activity, after all, fails to catch the attention of a casual observer, and is unlikely to form the basis of a readable memoir. Yet while arguments rage over the levels of unity and spirit or dissent and misbehaviour, something important is being overlooked. Beyond *Thunder Rock* enthusiasm, Ida Rodway desperation, or self-seeking opportunism was a quieter extreme populated by disengaged individuals. A truly untold (though very easily conveyed) story of the Blitz, is that for a surprising number of people, almost nothing happened at all.

'The Tube: October 1940' by Feliks Topolski.

CHAPTER FIVE

The Klondyke of the Midlands

Terror came suddenly to Coventry. 'I heard this terrific noise,' wrote Joan Thornton to a friend. 'I cannot describe it, it was deafening and made us all jump. I shouted, "My, what's that?" and dashed into the street.' Joan was horrified by what she saw. 'I have never experienced anything like it, absolute chaos. The falling glass did more damage than anything . . . all those people dead and injured.' Joan described the fate of a fourteen-year-old girl caught by the blast:

> The surgeons say it's a miracle she's alive. The bomb blew a hole in one of her feet, on Sunday she had a 2" piece of metal removed from one of her legs. The doctors say she will not be a cripple but will have some disability. I think it is shocking for a child on the brink of life and such a nice girl – her clothes were blown to rags.

Joan then changed tone to enquire about the friend's recent holiday in Skegness. The letter is dated 1 September 1939 – two days before Neville Chamberlain declared war on Germany.

Joan Thornton was writing about the 'Broadgate Bomb', planted by the IRA in Coventry's city centre, which exploded in the early afternoon of Friday 25 August. The homemade bomb had been left in a bicycle basket near such high street familiars as Boots, Burton and H. Samuel. This was part of what the IRA called its 'S' Plan, a sabotage campaign against economic and military targets – yet it had killed five civilians and wounded seventy others. Revulsion was widespread at the time, but today, it is little remembered, papered over by memories of the war.

Coventry was an obvious target for the IRA because of its economic and industrial vitality. Previously a car manufacturing centre, its factories were now building tanks and aircraft, and workers were pouring in from across the country. The accents of Somerset, Scotland and Sunderland could all be heard in the 'Klondyke of the Midlands'.

In May 1940 Anthony Hern visited Coventry for *Tribune* magazine, and was impressed by what he saw. Only three small shops were available to let in the city centre. Registered unemployment figures totalled just 600 men and 500 women – and these were 'casually' unemployed, without work for two or three days at most. The Coventry Co-Operative Society was the biggest store in town. And although a slump in menswear sales had been noted, this was because male workers were engaged in twelve-hour shifts. A solution, suggested Hern, was staggered opening hours. In a wartime economy, state-planned underwear shopping was a possibility.

Hern also noted a side of Coventry that is hard to imagine today – the picturesque medieval city with its alleyways, courts, and passages. (According to Pevsner's *Buildings of England*, Coventry had been Britain's fourth city in the fourteenth century, after London, York and Bristol.) But what really excited Hern was Coventry's progressive spirit, with its cheap bus and tram fares, its female bus conductors, and its public library lending 40,000 books every month, many to unskilled and semi-skilled workers looking to educate themselves. And even if cinema and music-hall attendances were low (a twelve-hour shift left little time or energy for leisure), Hern compared the city's mood favourably with London, where 'To Let' notices were a common sight.

People were arriving in Coventry en masse to take up the opportunities it offered. The population had grown from 90,000 in 1931 to almost 250,000 in May 1940, with tens of thousands of newcomers expected in the next twelve months. And as was common with boom towns, sudden expansion was straining its seams. Accommodation was so limited that strangers were sharing beds in dubious hostels and boarding houses. The *Midland Daily Telegraph* painted a picture of 'filthy beds huddled together' and 'double beds shared by two and even three men' while *Tribune* warned of 'inadequate and even unhealthy accommodation'. But the city's economic migrants seemed willing to accept the conditions – so long as well-paid factory work remained available.

Accommodation problems aside, there were advantages to becoming a Coventrian. All essential services – water, electricity, gas, transport – were council-run, and while the council itself had a Labour majority, the mayor was Conservative, as the role was regularly alternated between the two main parties. The overall result was a progressive municipality, with a unified outlook. And there were ambitious plans to redesign the city. Coventry's streets had been built to ferry a fraction of the traffic they were now carrying. Taking inspiration from models as diverse as Paris and Welwyn Garden City, architect Donald Gibson had drawn up proposals for a modern, spacious, grid-designed city. With a central park (described as a 'pedestrianised gardenway'), a modern shopping centre, an impressive town hall, an art gallery, a swimming baths and library complex, all surrounded by a ring road, Gibson's redesigned Coventry would, he believed, comfortably service a fast-growing population with rising expectations. And as a concession to those who valued the beautiful medieval and Tudor city centre, his plan spared some of the most significant buildings. In June 1940 Gibson staged an exhibition of his plans. But he was a pragmatist, and he doubted whether such a formidable project would ever be realised. Large parts of the city would have to be demolished – and such a thing was hardly likely to happen.

Here, then, is a snapshot of the upwardly mobile, overcrowded, ambitious city of Coventry as the Luftwaffe was beginning its England-War. And just as people often have a misconceived idea of the city, so they sometimes suppose that Coventry's experience of war consisted only of one hateful night, or that 14 November 1940 was the city's first taste of horror. In fact, Coventry, like Cambridge and many other towns and cities, was being attacked before the Blitz is supposed to have begun. A single aircraft dropped the first bombs soon after midnight on 18 August, demolishing houses in Canley Road and Cannon Hill Road. Optimists who had suggested that the city would avoid serious damage because it sat in a natural 'bowl' of mist and fog, were soon put right by further raids. And a joke began that the air raid siren was serving more usefully as the All Clear.

On 25 August the state-of-the-art Rex Cinema was destroyed by a direct hit. It was empty at the time – and due to show *Gone With The Wind* the following day. On 16 September a Junkers 88 lost its bearings and dropped its bombs on Wallace Road, killing twelve people. The aircraft then collided with a balloon cable and crashed. Raids on 12 and 14 October resulted in the deaths of over fifty people. The roof of the fourteenth-century cathedral was damaged, while the Owen Owen department store and Ford's Hospital, a set of beautiful half-timbered Tudor almshouses, also suffered. The nineteenth of October saw the first of three consecutive nights of bombing, as well as the machine-gunning of the Coventry bypass by a daylight raider.

By now, ARP services were coming under pressure, and changes in behaviour were beginning to be observed. Trekking had begun each night, out to villages in the countryside. Some people were taken in by strangers, others slept in their cars or in the open. There were further nights of raids, and then the first royal visit – from the Duchess of Gloucester – on 13 November. The next night's raid, however, would raise the royal stakes, bringing King George VI to the city. It would also add neologisms to both the German and English languages – *koventrieren* and 'to coventrate' – meaning to raze to the ground or devastate by heavy bombing. Some allege that the word was coined by Hitler's most devoted minister, Josef Goebbels, while a German High Command communiqué attributes it to the British. Either way, on the night of Thursday 14 November 1940, Coventry received the most intense aerial attack yet mounted on a centre of population.

Chief Officer Cartwright of the Coventry Fire Brigade reported that the raid began in brilliant moonlight – appropriate for an operation code-named *Mondscheinsonate* – Moonlight Sonata. The industrial centre that produced aircraft, tanks, engines, tyres, parachutes, radio sets and countless other armaments and instruments was defended by twenty-four 3.7 inch anti-aircraft guns, twelve 40mm Bofors guns, fifty-odd barrage balloons at various heights, 124 night fighters, and a parade of other guns stretching from Merseyside in the north to the Isle of Wight in the south. Yet despite the deployment of all these agents of interception against more than 500 German bombers, only one was destroyed, a Dornier struck by anti-aircraft fire that crashed near Loughborough. And for all of their combined hours in the air, the RAF fighters stumbled upon just two German aircraft all night. Richard Mitchell, a Hurricane pilot with 229 Squadron, was on his first night fighter sortie. He flew all the way from Northolt to the south coast with a bomber supposedly off his starboard wing-tip. He never saw it. 'The air was full of bombers,' he says, 'but without a radar set-up, it was like looking for a needle in a haystack.' In effect, the attackers had a free hand – and for eleven hours they took advantage of their opportunity.

On the ground, events moved uncomfortably quickly. Chief Officer Cartwright noted that the Yellow Warning was received at 7.05 p.m., while the Red Warning came five minutes later, triggering the public sirens.* The first outbreak of fire was reported at 7.24, and over the next half-hour, seventy-one emergency calls were received. Fires were usually concentrated in one district, but these calls were coming from numerous different areas. And a central gas main was hit – which glowed like a beacon for the bombers that followed. It was clear to Cartwright that something unusual was underway.

Guy Burn, a soldier in the Royal Warwickshire Regiment, was at a dance twenty-five miles from Coventry when the lights suddenly went out, causing 'some confusion and not a little pleasure'. From his vantage point, above Coventry, he watched the city 'being set on fire – and gradually destroyed. In the end, the whole city was ablaze. It was a terrifying sight.' Accounts from those inside Coventry describe how a series of small fires gradually merged into one single conflagration. Most people headed for shelters or tried to escape the central areas. Some, however, were going the other way. Jack Miller of the King's Own Royal Regiment was in barracks twenty miles outside of Coventry when the raid started. Just after midnight, his company was brought into the city:

> We were walking through Coventry as a platoon, singing, and there were people weeping. We reached where the Cathedral was, and the sergeant said to me, 'Dusty, get on the wall and see what's over the wall.' I got on the wall, but I couldn't stand up well, and he said, 'I see you're not a builder, come on, get down!' Someone else got up, and said, 'Yes, there's three or four bodies there.' They sent some chaps over, and we dragged over three dead firemen. It was a ghastly sight. Their faces almost seemed sand-encrusted.

---

* The Yellow Warning was a preliminary message, issued to official personnel (such as members of the fire brigade) who were to take 'preparatory and unobtrusive measures' for a raid within the next twenty minutes. This was followed by the Red Warning, at which point the sirens would sound to alert the public of raiders five to ten minutes away.

There were many others with jobs to do that night. By day, John Sargent was a machine operator, making shell cases on a twelve-hour shift. At night, he worked as an ambulance driver, usually on call between 8 p.m. and 5 a.m. And at the weekends, he taught first aid to Home Guard and civil defence personnel. There can be no better example of the volunteer spirit gripping the country. But on this night, John encountered his biggest task.

At some time after seven o'clock, John made his way to Silver Street where a poorly built surface shelter had collapsed. The walls had blown down – creating a potential 'Morrison Sandwich'. About thirty people were trapped inside. John drove back to the Coventry and Warwickshire Hospital, and returned with a nursing sister. Crawling through a small gap, he passed morphine to whomever he could reach. No one was dead at this stage, but it would take time for rescue equipment to arrive. In the meantime, the roof was jammed, the raid raged on, and John had other work to do. He never discovered if anybody died, that night, in the surface shelter.

Back at the hospital, where 200 casualties were being attended by three doctors and a team of nurses, John and his partner, Doug Henderson, were told to start assessing patients. A little girl was brought in. She seemed in perfect physical condition, her features were unscathed apart from slight puffiness in her cheeks – but she was dead. The air pressure of a bomb had burst her lungs. She looked eerily like John's little sister who had died at a similar age.

By nine o'clock, John found himself cleaning the eyes of patients with saline solution, and helping with blood transfusions. He was then sent to the operating theatre to assist with amputations. He marvelled at the calm of the surgeons and sisters as the floor shook beneath them. By midnight, large numbers of injured firemen, soldiers and volunteer workers were being brought into the hospital. Telephone and wireless lines were down. At 3 a.m. the hospital boiler was hit, and the heating went off. The senior doctor told John to start evacuating patients. The nearest available hospital, it was decided, was in Warwick.

As John drove through Coventry, he came across one blocked road after another. St Michael's Cathedral was on fire, and driving onto Little Park Street, he found houses ablaze on both sides. The heat was so ferocious that had anything blocked the road, John and his patients would have baked to death. A fire engine came alongside and asked whether he had room for an injured fireman. The ambulance was full; but the man was squeezed onto the step in front of the doors. John was hugely relieved when he reached the Kenilworth Road, clear of danger, on his way to Warwick.

On arrival, the Warwick hospital staff were not aware that Coventry was being raided. And they were surprised to learn that they were about to start receiving the contents of Coventry and Warwickshire Hospital. As soon as his ambulance was empty, he turned around and repeated the journey. John and the other drivers also ferried patients to hospitals in Stratford and Leamington. The Coventry and Warwickshire was hit by a succession of bombs that night. Some were direct hits, others smashed windows. But through-out the mayhem, the operating theatre continued to function.

At some point during the day, John found the time to telegraph his brother to say that he was safe. His brother was in the army, ten miles away, and he, too, was entirely unaware that a huge raid had taken place. It is difficult, in our modern world, to imagine a time when news travelled slowly. Earlier in the Blitz, a lot of news had not trav-elled at all. The press had initially been prohibited from naming bombed towns and cities. By November, this unnecessary restriction had been lifted, and the national papers were able to report the attack on Coventry in their Saturday morning editions.

Once John and his partner Doug had made their last evacuation run, they fought their way into the ruined hospital kitchen where they found a loaf of bread and some cheese, blew the dust off, and made a couple of sandwiches. (Strictly speaking, this was an act of looting – which was punishable by death. Happily, neither man was charged . . .) John had now been awake for thirty hours, and he went home for an hour before returning to the nearest first aid station, his own having been bombed. There was, after all, still work to do. By Saturday afternoon, every patient had been evacuated.

John's story may be inspirational – but it is not unique. Many similar accounts could be recounted of that November night. The list of courageous deeds performed by the Stoke Division, ARP Wardens, as recorded by Divisional Warden Lowe, soon blurs into one:

> **Barham** – Crawled right under a demolished house, working for several hours and succeeded in rescuing a mother and two children. At one time he had to work head downwards – suspended by his feet – for over an hour . . .
>
> **Jones** – Worked until exhausted in extricating trapped persons with great success while bombs were dropping all around . . .
>
> **Enstone** – Displayed great courage when H.E. Bomb struck Anderson Shelter and worked for long period trying to rescue the trapped persons until absolutely exhausted . . .

These are just three out of twenty-four names on the list. The divisional warden felt unable a single out any individual to be recommended for the George Cross or George Medal 'owing to the fact that so many of my Wardens did work of equal merit'. He did ask, however, for some form of higher recognition for the head warden, A. E. Alcock, a gearbox fitter, who began his evening by fighting a fire with a stirrup pump while balanced on a ladder. He saw the job through – even though a bomb fell on the next-door house. His subsequent adventures that night included the dousing of another fire, and the rescue of fifteen people from a shelter. 'His utter disregard of personal danger in the service of the public,' wrote the divisional warden, 'and his devotion to duty in most trying circumstances have worthily upheld British traditions.'

Out of a population of 242,000, 568 had been killed and 863 seriously injured during the raid. Many more were treated for minor injuries – or never treated at all. About 30,000 incendiary bombs, 1,000 high-explosive bombs, 300 delay-fuse bombs and 50 landmines were dropped. By the morning, Coventry had ceased to function as a city. Water, gas and electricity were cut off, sewers were damaged, houses were destroyed or uninhabitable, food was scarce, and most roads were cut off or locked down by delay-fuse bombs. St Michael's Cathedral, according to journalist Ritchie Calder, had been 'left like the fretwork walls of a film set', while the city centre had been 'trampled into mash'. From the mayor and his officials downwards, people were dazed, confused, and nervous that the bombers would return the following night. Many began trekking early in the day, some through fear, others because their homes had disappeared and the city's four undestroyed rest centres were full. 'There began an exodus which was like the flood of refugees in Belgium and France,' wrote Calder. 'They carried the few belongings they had or piled them on perambulators or hand-carts or the wrecks of cars.'

But as people were leaving, vehicles were coming into town, passing through the police road blocks. In a Salvation Army mobile canteen were young Sydney Higgins and his father. Sydney remembers:

> The really unforgettable memory was the smell of burning. We stopped at what must have been a clothing shop where nothing had survived but glowing embers and what appeared to be the distorted remains of mannequins. The smell was disgustingly pungent. In alarm, I looked at my father. He pulled me away by the hand, and said, 'That, son, is the smell of death.'

Daily Express journalist Hilde Marchant arrived in Coventry that morning from Birmingham. As she drove into the city, charred bits of wood flew in through her car window. She was struck by 'a heavy, stifling smell that bit into your throat and lungs'. The fires had raised the temperature; it was 'as warm as a spring day', and the sky was darkened by fog and soot. In the worst affected area, an open plain

The city centre on the morning of 15 November 1940.

stretched for half a mile 'broken only by an occasional girder that poked through the ruins like a broken rib'. Hours after the bombers had passed over, metal was still red hot.

Reginald King was a member of a rescue party that spent the day searching for survivors. Informed that people were trapped in a basement shelter in Greyfriars Green, the party dug through debris, reaching a wall. From the other side, a voice shouted that twelve people were trapped inside. 'Please come and get us out!' But minutes later, a policeman ordered the party out. Two unexploded bombs had been found nearby. There was no option; the rescue had to be abandoned. Three days later, when the bombs had been made safe, a rescue was finally attempted. Only one old man was still alive. 'We had been close enough to speak to them,' Reginald says, 'but could do nothing to help.'

Mass-Observation sent a team of experienced investigators into Coventry on that day. Its initial impression was of a city – of a people – in shock:

The overwhelmingly dominant feeling on Friday was the feeling of utter helplessness. The tremendous impact of the previous night had left people practically speechless in many cases. And it made them feel impotent. There was no role for the civilian. Ordinary people had no idea what they should do.

The investigators reported 'signs of suppressed panic' among citizens – such as crying, trembling, and fainting in the street, as well as hearing phrases such as 'Coventry is finished' and 'Coventry is dead'. And given the circumstances, it would have been surprising had they not. After eleven hours of unimagined brutality, the people of Coventry had emerged into a world of nothingness. Shock, anguish, sleepless disbelief – these raw reactions were bound to produce the sorts of behaviour observed by the investigators.

Yet, as might be expected, the Mass-Observation report has served as fuel for those keen to reduce the story of the Blitz to a neatly packaged cliché. On the one hand, after the report was quoted in a *Sunday Times* article in May 1972, furious correspondence was sent both to that newspaper and to the *Coventry Evening Telegraph*, protesting that morale in Coventry had never wavered. On the other hand, the report is cited in *1940, Myth and Reality*, a book by ex-civil servant and writer Clive Ponting, as part of his contention that morale across the country was consistently poor.

Both of these reactions are insulting. The first to the investigators who reported in good faith from a city in shock. The second to the people of that city, for whom the issue of morale, as they staggered around their dark new Jerusalem, was meaningless. Only once the bomb dust had settled, only once people like Reginald King had done their jobs, could any meaningful assessment be made of whether Coventry *could take it*.

And the fact is that is most workers went into their factories that day, and many found themselves helping with repairs. A Daimler employee, Mr Harrison, arrived at the works in Browns Lane, three miles from the city centre, and spent the morning stretching lengths of tarpaulin across the shattered glass roof of the machine shop. During these pre-welfare state days, wage-earners had to work – or face not getting paid. Quite apart from considerations of morale, spirit and patriotism, there was a strong financial incentive to 'keep on' through the darkest times.

Twenty-four hours seemed to make a great difference to the city. On the Friday night the bombers did not return. (The Luftwaffe ignored Coventry for almost five months, and never sent as many air-craft over a provincial town or city again.) On Saturday morning the Mass-Observation investigators reported that 'Coventry people were looking calmer and more purposeful'. They detected a spirit starting to foster among the ruins – and an absence of scapegoating. The anti-aircraft gunners were not blamed for failing to protect the city, and it was not the firemen's fault that water had run short during the night. And nor were the authorities being blamed: events had been so unprecedented, so unexpected, that it seemed likely that *everybody* had been taken by surprise. In the ensuing vacuum, rumour provided a different sort of target. Traitors, it was said, had been caught sig-nalling to the bombers. A swastika, drawn in smoke, had been spotted in the sky before the raid. Its purpose, apparently, had been to warn Nazi sympathisers to leave the city.

A sense of unity began to grow. The sheer scale of the disaster was a unifying factor – everybody was affected. St Michael's Cathedral had belonged to all – so all had lost it. And a sense of pride arose. *We have suffered the country's greatest disaster – and made it through!* Pride was bolstered by the surge of interest coming from elsewhere. On Saturday Dilwyn Evans, a Red Cross worker, was busy carrying out rescue work. She had been working day and night, helping to release people trapped beneath the debris. She was in the process of recov-ering a dead body on the High Street, when she was tapped on the shoulder:

I turned round – it was the Mayor of Coventry. He said, 'Excuse me, I've got someone here who would like to have a word with you.' I got up and looked and there was King George VI in full field marshal's uniform. He just put his hand out and thanked me for what we were doing.

Herbert Morrison and Lord Beaverbrook were also in Coventry on Saturday. As Minister of Aircraft Production, Beaverbrook was keen to learn the extent of damage to the twenty-one factories – twelve of which were concerned with aircraft production – that had been badly hit. The following day he sent a telegram to the mayor pledging his offer 'to help with any resources I can mobilise for your service'.* And telegrams of support were pouring in from all manner of individuals, cities and organisations. The Salvation Army's cable praised the spirit of the people who have 'risen courageously from this tragedy'. The National Union of Railwaymen congratulated the mayor on 'remarks in the press that you intend to stick it out'. 'If we can help, let us know,' wrote London County Council. Tel Aviv sent its sympathies. Coventry was becoming a name on the world map, and an example to others.

As the city tried to heal its wounds, and those of its people, it experienced similar problems to those that had befallen London. While casualty services and clear-up operations had been carefully planned, for example, little thought had been given to the plight of the homeless. But this was ultimately less of a problem in Coventry – thanks to people trekking to outlying villages. According to a Home Office estimate, between 70,000 and 100,000 people began sleeping outside of the city and commuting in to Coventry to work. On Saturday

* Beaverbrook also wrote that though 'a very substantial fighter force contributed to the defence of Coventry . . . unhappily the results were not satisfactory'. Two months later, Beaverbrook's son, Max Aitken, a decorated Battle of Britain pilot, would take over a night fighter squadron, flying Bristol Blenheims out of Catterick.

afternoon a Mass-Observation investigator visited the village of Kenilworth, six miles south of Coventry. The Parochial Hall, the hotel ballroom, the school and the Wesleyan Chapel had all been given over to trekkers, while four rest centres were open, and all available rooms in private houses had been taken. Kenilworth had suddenly gained hundreds of new residents, as had many other villages. By the New Year, according to the Home Office, about eighty per cent of the trekkers had returned to their homes in Coventry.

One reason why so many were trekking was the time taken for houses to be repaired. The head of the department responsible was Donald Gibson – the architect with ambitious plans to rebuild the city. According to Gibson, one bomb was likely to demolish a single house, seriously damage three or four others, and knock out the windows and roof tiles of up to a hundred more. His department was faced with an onerous task that winter. Gibson began importing carpenters, joiners, roofers, slaters and tilers from other Midlands towns and cities, and in December the unit of builders specially released from the army was called in. Even with the increased manpower, however, repairers were often unable to gain access to houses because the owners were out of the city. At one point, in a public-spirited undertaking, repair materials were made available on the streets for people to help themselves – though it seems that this measure was discontinued. Perhaps material temptation overcame community spirit.

So far as everyday essentials were concerned, volunteers stepped into the breach, just as they had in London. The most celebrated was local Women's Voluntary Service chief Pearl Hyde. Already something of a celebrity, Mrs Hyde had recently told the *Yorkshire Post*, 'Whatever they ask us to do, we do it, cutting all bunkum and red tape.' And so when the Coventry chief constable, as head of the local ARP, came to her and said, 'Feed the people ... it is the only way to steady them,' she went to work straight away.

Mrs Hyde began by organising mobile canteens. These started

arriving in Coventry at half-nine on Friday morning. They were met at the Central Fire Station by a WVS team, and dispatched around the city. Some fed rescue workers, police and firemen, others focused on the public in shelters, rest centres, and on the streets. For eight days, this food – mainly cheese or corned beef sandwiches and a bowl of soup – was provided without charge. Famously, she ran her 'Devil's Kitchen' from an underground room at the Central Police Station, in which volunteers – many high born – worked tirelessly. Lady Mary Lygon – on whom Evelyn Waugh was to base Lady Julia Flyte in his novel *Brideshead Revisited* – was seen cooking spinach on a primus stove, while the Duchess of Marlborough accepted a delivery of bully beef in the canteen.

Pearl Hyde became the public embodiment of the WVS, a one-woman emergency service taking delivery of water carts, boilers, field kitchens and anything else the city needed. Her fame grew following her role in *Heart of Britain*, a 1941 documentary film about the role of women in wartime which became so popular in the United States that a recreation of 'Devil's Kitchen' was built in New York. A newspaper feature, syndicated across the United States in 1943, spread the legend of Pearl Hyde, and offered an almost biblical account of her feeding of '75,000 persons, homeless, dazed, hurt and sick'.

All of this is further evidence of how volunteerism allowed the country to function – while quietly altering the relationship between government and people. Collectivism may have been encouraged by the state, but it was taking root organically, and it was sowing the seeds of the post-war world. And when it was given a charismatic figurehead like Pearl Hyde, it offered excellent propaganda opportunities, both in Britain and the United States.

As the days passed after the raid, Mass-Observation investigators noticed a slow edge towards 'something like normality'. Certainly, by 25 November the investigators were observing a returning sense of 'purposeful demeanour' alongside a thankfulness 'nearer to joy'. It had taken some time for people to come to terms with the reality of their survival – and the Luftwaffe's failure to exploit the situation was contributing to a city-wide sense of relief. People had begun to return from outlying villages, and a commercial traveller who came regularly to the city noted in his diary that while Coventrians had felt 'helpless at first ... having got over the initial shock I think they are now prepared to stand anything.' Harold Holttum remembers the city a fortnight after the raid: 'It was astonishing. On that open ground were wooden huts – Barclays Bank, Coventry Co-op, Boots the Chemist, Freeman Hardy and Willis, business as usual in wooden huts! With the original layout still there! Astonishing!'

Yet alongside mild euphoria came a growing dissatisfaction with the authorities' inability to restore essential services such as utilities and public transport. This might indicate a genuine drop in morale; more likely it reflected the low-level grumbling of everyday British life – and a return to normality. But it is important to note that the mood was not – never was – black and white.

Certainly the factories were returning to work. Some were barely affected, while production at those hit worst was resumed within a few weeks. It appears that eighty per cent of the Coventry workforce was back on the shop floor within a month. Any delays were attributable to the lack of power and water; the workers were keen to start earning again.

It seems, therefore, that necessity was a key factor in forging a spirit of community, both emotional and physical, in the people of Coventry. This spirit was certainly present in the large-scale burials that took place after the raid. During a council meeting on 16 November, it was explained that resources did not exist to allow for individual burials. The lack of gravediggers, electricity and transport effectively precluded the possibility. It had been decided, therefore, that a mass burial would take place at 11 a.m. on the morning of 20 November at the Coventry Cemetery. The cost of the burials would be met by the council, and ministers of various denominations would be present. The next day, the plan was modified. Offers of assistance from neighbouring towns and cities now allowed for each of the 'fallen' to receive a coffin. And it was conceded that private burials would be allowed so long as arrangements were made by relatives who could meet the cost. In the event, 172 people were buried on that Wednesday, with another 250 laid to rest three days later. At the first service, the Bishop of Coventry said in his address:

> This evil air raid has brought us together in a great bond. In this city we have been better friends and neighbours than we have ever been before. As we stand here, let us vow before God that we will go on being better friends and neighbours for ever . . .

The bishop's words and the mode of burial may have reflected a growing collectivism, but there were still plenty of issues dividing Coventrians. Perhaps the most pressing was the city's lack of accommodation. While huge numbers of houses were uninhabitable, many undamaged houses lay empty, their owners away from the city. In June 1941 a member of the council's billeting department came before the city treasurer, requesting that some of these houses be requisitioned. The department was coming under 'severe criticism' from homeless people who wanted to take over unused houses, and from householders who were being asked to take in lodgers while perfectly good houses stood empty. The other side of the argument was presented by a homeowner who was frightened to leave the city, lest her home be requisitioned. How long, she wanted to know, could she stay away before her house was commandeered? The city treasurer gave unsatisfactory answers to both questioners.

And while it is generally understood that the Blitz was a time when British people were content to 'make do' in a common cause, it is interesting to read a report prepared by a committee investigating Coventry's 'war problems'. One of these problems was that working women no longer had time to prepare meals. The result was a new demand 'for ready-prepared types of food (e.g. meat pies, cooked meats, meat products, cakes and similar foods)'. And as the women were relatively well-paid, they could now afford more than the rationed staples. They wanted 'packeted breakfast cereals, sauces, pickles, jellies, blancmange powders, coffee essence, cakes, sweet biscuits, chocolate and sugar confectionary' as well as 'supplies of cooked meats and manufactured meat products'. In short, the time-poor female workers of Coventry wanted modern convenience foods. It is clear where the (non-organic) seeds of the late twentieth-century diet were sown.

But whereas the Coventry local authority was keen that war workers should receive their treats, the government was not. The town clerk wrote to the Board of Trade in London, requesting that the number of 'essential shops' in Coventry be increased, adding that 'a reasonable number of "luxury" shops would do no harm'. In reply, the Board of Trade wrote that the building of shops would be allowed 'if it can definitely be shown that they are essential' – but that luxury, or semi-luxury shops 'cannot be allowed'. Clearly there was a limit to the rewards the government was willing to offer its people in return for their efforts and sacrifices.

But for all the social, economic and emotional effects that the Blitz had on Coventry, the most obvious was the physical change it brought to the landscape. In June 1940, readers will remember, Donald Gibson exhibited his architectural plans for the redesign of the city. He had doubted that the project would ever be realised, as it called for the large-scale demolition of much of the city centre. The Luftwaffe removed his doubts.

A week after the raid, the *Manchester Guardian* declared, 'There is a great opportunity here for the rebuilding of Britain to begin', and it promoted Gibson's proposal for Coventry as 'a plan for a hundred years instead of tomorrow'. Shortly afterwards, Gibson – simultaneously in charge of housing repairs – gave a talk, in which he said: 'In one night the entire site is cleared ready for this regeneration, and it rests with the fortunes of war and the desires of a great people to see it accomplished.'

A city redevelopment committee, headed by the mayor, formally adopted the scheme in February 1941 (over a more conservative proposal which abided by the existing street patterns) and Gibson set out his plans in some detail on a BBC Home Service programme in November 1943. He painted a picture of a world fit for citizen heroes. His utopia would boast an indoor shopping centre 'with no buses or cars which could splash mud or endanger children', where 'people can do all their shopping in comfort without an umbrella if it rains'. He enthused about a crèche – which he described as 'a nursery where the children can play together if the parents don't want to take them around the shops'. The central train station would contain a café and restaurant, while the new ring road would 'wipe out transport headaches'. Newly built residential areas would have their own schools and health clinics. Families would live in houses with good-sized gardens, sunlit on all sides, while 'grownups living as single people' would live in flats. There would be excellent municipal facilities, such as a gym, tennis courts, swimming baths, library – and an Adult Education building, because 'education doesn't stop when you leave school . . .'

When one considers that London's first indoor shopping centre (at Elephant and Castle) was not built until 1965, Gibson's ideas more than deserved their title – 'Coventry of Tomorrow'. And the fact is that comfortable housing with modern amenities and opportunities was exactly what people wanted. According to *Flashman* author and wartime soldier, George Macdonald Fraser, his fellow soldiers were fighting above all for 'jobs, and security, and a better future for their children than they had'. They had lived through the thirties, the dole queues and the poverty, and they now wanted comfort and security. Donald Gibson's plans seemed to offer this modest and achievable dream. He understood the people he served.

In 1949 Gibson's plans were finally approved by the government – but in a compromised form, the result of spending restrictions and a shortage of materials. Three areas were built: the central district, and

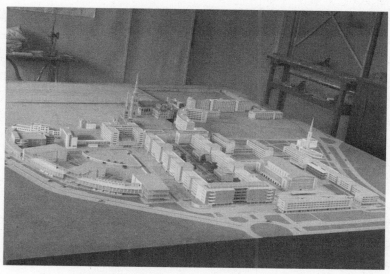

Donald Gibson's plans for post-war Coventry laid out
on a scale model in his office.

two residential districts. The modern St Michael's Cathedral, designed
by Basil Spence, stands in the city centre alongside the skeletal ruins
of the old cathedral. Together they represent loss and renewal, the
death and resurrection of Christ, the rebuilding of a city. The zig-zag
walls, punctuated by full-length windows, make St Michael's feel
gothic and modern at the same time. It is a beautiful and painful
memorial to an astonishing story.

Out of terror came shock, anger, helplessness, pride, frustration,
determination – and finally the demand that things get better. And
though it had been terrible, if you looked hard enough, there was
beauty to be found in the horror. J. B. Shelton, a draying contractor,
found it where few others could. Interviewed by Pulitzer Prize winning
journalist Ernie Pyle, for the *Boston Globe*, Mr Shelton was an amateur
archaeologist. 'Not very young, except in enthusiasm', he had recently
found some wonderful Roman coins and artefacts – all unearthed by
the Luftwaffe. And he was the only man allowed to poke around
among the ruins without fear of being arrested for looting.

Mr Shelton told Ernie Pyle that he had spent the night of 14 November trying to save his horses, taking them out two at a time, ready to place sacks over the heads of any who panicked. 'Sparks were falling just like rain,' he said. 'See those holes in my old coat? That's where sparks fell on me. I'll never see anything like it again in my lifetime.' And then Mr Shelton surprised Ernie Pyle. 'I wouldn't have missed it for anything,' he said. 'It was wonderful.'

CHAPTER SIX

Striking Oil in Sherwood Forest

The manner in which the Blitz was weathered, it seems to this author, harks back to the medieval tradition of misrule. There may be little, outwardly, to link wild pagan-style revels with the struggle to endure high-explosive bombs – but consider how, in both cases, the usual order of things was set aside, the status of ordinary people was raised, odd rituals became accepted as normal, and a return to the status quo was expected once everything was over. And while there were countless odd rituals adopted during the Blitz (sheltering, firewatching, talking to strangers . . .), one of the oddest was adopted by the government, and it resulted from the need to keep the struggle going. At any other time it would not have been attempted, but this was a time for extreme measures. Fifty-six miles north of Coventry, in the heart of Sherwood Forest, a massive effort was underway to pump oil out of the ground – an operation once described by Churchill as 'the greatest secret of the war'.

The importance of oil during the war cannot be overstated. To people on the Home Front, it meant heat, light, comfort and food, as well as hospitals, life-saving equipment and clean water. To the military establishment, it was the source of toluene for explosives, of synthetic rubber for tyres, of wax for packaging, and of petroleum, the magic ingredient in modern warfare. In May 1940 supplies of an improved form of petroleum, 100 octane fuel – the result of a process known as catalytic cracking – had begun arriving in Britain, giving an instant boost to the power rating of Fighter Command's Spitfires and Hurricanes. British pilots were surprised by increased speeds, and enhanced rates of climb and acceleration; such a sudden improvement in performance contributed greatly to their success during the Battle of Britain.

The oil supply could not be taken for granted, however. The country was sustained by tankers, but German U-Boats, hunting in packs, were causing huge problems. Between September 1939 and February 1941, seventy-nine British or British-controlled tankers were sunk with the loss of over 630,000 tons of oil. Oil stocks were soon two million barrels below normal safety reserves, sufficient for only two months' supply, even as military requirements were increasing. And not only were the U-Boats picking off tankers, but the Luftwaffe was destroying hundreds of thousands of barrels in dock areas. As a result, the Secretary for Petroleum, Geoffrey Lloyd, called an emergency meeting of the Oil Control Board. The impending crisis was discussed in predictable terms until Philip Southwell, a senior Anglo-Iranian Oil engineer, stood up to speak. His words caused a sensation. The most pressing matter regarding Britain's oil requirements, he said, was the increased exploitation of Britain's own oilfields. His listeners were amazed. *What oilfields?* Even the Oil Control Board was unaware of what was going on in Will Scarlet's back yard.

The impetus had come from Lord Cadman, the government's oil adviser. Cadman had been at the forefront of oil and petroleum technology for almost forty years, and as war approached, he led a nationwide search for deposits. In June 1939 reserves were discovered near Eakring in Sherwood Forest, and Cadman hammered home the need to start drilling immediately. D'Arcy Exploration Co. was assigned to work the oilfield, and specialist drillers were summoned to Eakring. Sandy Ross, an Anglo-Iranian driller, was on leave from Iran when his telephone rang. Without explanation, he was told to report to Newark railway station – and for the next five years, he worked as a driller in Sherwood Forest. But men were needed in numbers, and the first raw recruits were Nottinghamshire coal-miners deemed unfit for work underground. The labour exchange was called upon to provide the rest of the workforce, with the result that unskilled men, some of whom had never even worked outside, found themselves training to become members of drilling crews. Jack Clarke had been a miner at Ollerton Colliery before starting work at Eakring. He remembers tiny country roads jammed with double decker buses ferrying oilfield workers to and from the wells. 'The lanes were so busy,' he says, 'that local people used to avoid travelling along them.'

Wells were being drilled at depths of between 2,380 and 2,500 feet, producing on average 700 barrels of oil per day, but sometimes up to a thousand. And just as Lord Cadman had urged oil exploration, so he began to press his old friend Winston Churchill to create a government Petroleum Department. His wish was granted, and the department's Inspector of Drilling, Richard Stallard, was sent to Eakring in October 1940 to witness the calibration of vast new storage tanks, each with a capacity of 100,000 gallons. From these tanks, Eakring's oil was transported by rail to Pumpherston refinery near Edinburgh to be processed.

And so a national oil industry was built up from scratch – a massive undertaking – at a time when the country was unsure of its own survival, and weakened under daily onslaughts. The oilfield itself, with its derricks and pumps, seemed unlikely to be targeted by the Luftwaffe, hidden away in Sherwood Forest among the oak, birch and hawthorn trees.* And it turned out that the crude oil coming out of

---

* All the same, it appears odd that the derricks were painted light blue and the drilling engines orange with no apparent effort being made to camouflage them.

the ground was of an astonishingly high quality, purer than anything being produced in Europe or the Middle East. This made it ideal for the high octane fuel used by Spitfires and Hurricanes.

In 1941, as supplies of Iranian oil were running short and not being replaced, the Petroleum Department urged an increase in production, stating that 'in the present emergency every ton of oil produced in this country is a direct contribution to the national war effort'. The department's target was a fourfold increase in production. The oilfield was immediately extended – but more needed to be done. This was why Philip Southwell went before the emergency meeting of the Oil Control Board.

The problems Southwell laid out were the lack of skilled labour and the difficulty in obtaining materials and equipment. The drilling rigs currently in use had been designed for deep-drilling operations in Iran, and were not appropriate for the shallower Eakring reserves. They were large and complicated to erect and move, resulting in a lot of time being wasted. Denis Sheffield, working at Eakring in 1941, remembers the effort required. 'This heavy equipment would be pulled by hand and jacked by a gang onto a lorry,' he says, 'and they would literally manhandle it up at the next site.' Smaller and more mobile American rigs were needed. Given the equipment, and the men to operate it, it was hoped that a hundred new wells could become operational within a year.

The United States, it was agreed, was producing the most modern equipment in the world – so Philip Southwell flew to Washington to meet American officials. Flying across the Atlantic was no easy task mid-war.* Once in Washington, he set out Britain's requirements: he

* For most of the war, BOAC flew commercial flights between Bristol and neutral Lisbon, using Dutch aircraft and aircrew. (One of these flights was attacked by the Luftwaffe in June 1943, killing everybody on board including the actor Leslie Howard.) From Lisbon, Southwell would probably have flown to the Azores, then to Bermuda, and finally to the United States.

wanted to buy the latest rotary drilling rigs, drill pipe and rotary rock bits. But the transaction was not straightforward. United States law, it seemed, would not allow drilling equipment to be sold to a foreigner. With some lateral thinking, a solution was found. The equipment would be sold to an American employed to carry out operations in the United Kingdom. And so Southwell asked Samuel Lloyd Noble, the president of the Noble Drilling Corporation of Oklahoma, to purchase the equipment on his behalf – and to recruit experienced men to come to Sherwood Forest to operate it. Noble agreed to the deal, and to forgo any profit from the operation.

The Noble Drilling Corporation immediately set about engaging forty-two oil workers on year-long contracts. They were from Oklahoma and other oil states, and they would work in crews of four, each crew consisting of a driller, a derrick man, a motorman and a helper. It was felt important that the Americans should be billeted together, to combat homesickness, and to make them easier to control, and the billet ultimately chosen for them was in a working Anglican monastery in the Nottinghamshire village of Kelham. The monastery was large and well appointed (and bears a striking resemblance to St Pancras Station in London, having been designed by Sir Gilbert Scott in a similar style to his masterpiece), but how suited was it to the sudden arrival of dozens of boisterous oil drillers plucked from another world? Eugene Rosser, the Noble Drilling Corporation representative who would be looking after the men in England, was keen to reassure the anxious monks. 'I'm figuring,' he said, 'that not many of them is going to feel like a lot of hell-raising and whoring around in their spare time.'

One of these men was Lewis Dugger from Louisiana. He had taken the job over the draft: it paid $29 a day compared with $50 a month in the army. 'I said yes straightaway,' he says, 'and I had no idea where it was going to be.' The oil workers met each other in New York before sailing for Britain, and one man was fired – for getting drunk and running wild – before they had even boarded the ship. When they disembarked, they all went pub crawling together, and played a trick that night in the hotel. Lewis remembers: 'We were mischievous. The people at this hotel put their shoes out at night to be shined. We thought we'd mess this up real good. We didn't steal the shoes, but we mixed them all up. It was a prank. We got a kick out of it.'

Kelham Hall Monastery was clearly in for a surprise. The 'roughnecks' – as oil workers were known – arrived at the monastery on 18 March 1943, carrying banjos as well as bags. The next day, they were taken to Newark, where they mistook the ruins of Newark Castle for war damage. In the town, they spoke happily to locals, bought bicycles, and stood out in the crowd. One local woman remembered their Stetson hats, colourful shirts, and cowboy boots – an unreal sight against their monochrome English backdrop. So incongruous did the men seem, that a rumour spread that they were in Britain to make a film.

Soon after arrival, one of the oil workers tried to place a telephone call to his family in the small town of Stroud, Oklahoma. After a long discussion, the operator placed his call through to Stroud, Gloucestershire. The roughneck had never heard of *that* Stroud, the operator had never heard of the other, and he shouted down the line, 'Hell, no, honey! I want Stroud America! Not Stroud England, or Stroud South Africa or Stroud Australia!' Meanwhile, in the Fox pub, the men, accustomed to Budweiser and Schlitz, were unimpressed by the local beer. They started drinking whisky instead, but the supply quickly ran out, and they were soon reduced to adding salt to pints of bitter and mild in a desperate attempt to improve the taste.

The roughnecks' accommodation was in one wing of the monastery, two men to a room. The roommates worked different shifts, twelve hours on, twelve hours off, so they barely saw each other. Lewis Dugger, on afternoon shift, shared with Spanky Hemphill on morning shift. Their room, according to Lewis, was spacious and warmed by a fireplace, and nearby was a recreation room with a snooker table. There were also excellent washing facilities – unusual for the time but important for men who spent their days in filthy conditions. There were six cooks and stewards (all soldiers recently released from hospital) and while Lewis appreciated their efforts, he was not keen on the food they prepared. 'It was either Brussels sprouts, or mutton, or potatoes fried in mutton grease,' he says. One particular steward has lodged in his memory: 'His name was Percy, and when one of the roughnecks got ticked off at him and said, "Kiss my ass," he said, "I'd love to do that." I think he was a homosexual.'

Once the roughnecks were settled, Eugene Rosser set them their target. 'Guys, we want to get after it! We want to drill a hundred wells in a year!' And they were soon showing their worth. After the first twelve-hour shift on an existing Anglo-Iranian rig, the Americans reported 1,010 feet. The works manager refused to believe that this was possible, or that if it was, the roughnecks must be wrecking the equipment. But there was no mistake; the American drillers worked much quicker than their British counterparts. The British practice had been to change the drill bit every four to five hundred feet; the roughnecks were simply continuing with the same drill bit until it was worn. The saving in time and effort was enormous.

In April the new American rigs started to arrive, and were soon ready to go into operation.* By the beginning of June, the Americans had completed forty-two wells, at an average of one a week per crew; the British crews had been taking up to eight weeks to complete a well. The Anglo-Iranian Oil Company was astounded by this pace, and arranged for its representatives to meet Eugene Rosser for an explanation of how it was done. In front of Sir William Fraser, chairman of Anglo-Iranian, and a room full of experts, Rosser explained that the English wasted too much time changing rock bits when the bit was still doing a good job. He also said that the Americans saved

---

* These were National 50 rigs capable of drilling 5,000 feet with a 4.5-inch drill pipe. They were pulled by two diesel engines. The 87-foot-high mast was capable of assembly in four hours.

time by drilling with water, rather than with chemically-prepared mud, and that the English had been waiting far too long for cement to set on their wells. Above all, Rosser asserted that the English drillers were too rigid in their application of rules, when they should have been reacting to circumstances as they arose. The experts listened, and decided that American practices should be adopted. It was also felt that a British worker should, in future, be placed with each American crew.

Lewis Dugger is blunter than Eugene Rosser in his assessment of British drillers, their methods, and the Eakring working conditions. His complaints offer a vivid snapshot of the British–American wartime cultural divide. Surprised to learn that an operation carried out mechanically by the Americans (laying down a drill collar) was done manually by the British, Lewis asked a British driller how they did it. 'We get about fifteen men round,' he was told, 'and we push the bugger!' He was not impressed – and his description of most British drillers as 'military rejects' gives an indication of his feelings.

Lewis was equally unimpressed by British social conventions. 'I had one Englishman working for me,' he says, 'and he told me one of his duties – he had to shine the boots of the driller.' The problem, he decides, is that the British have a 'caste system'. And he recalls being positively amazed when he met an Englishman in his twenties with a full set of dentures. American contempt for badly maintained British teeth stretches back a surprisingly long way.

Nor did Lewis always appreciate working conditions. To keep warm, every drilling crew had a pot-bellied stove in a small shed beside the derrick. One day, Lewis was told that his crew would be allowed no more coal for their stove; they had used up their ration for the week. But instead of accepting the situation, Lewis started burning diesel meant for the drilling engine. When the D'Arcy office discovered how their precious diesel was being used, a bag of coal was sent straight over. 'You do what you gotta do,' Lewis says.

Though he is critical of much of the Eakring set-up (which was, it should be remembered, entirely new and operating under difficult wartime conditions), he was clearly enthusiastic about the job itself, saying, 'I felt like I had an obligation, and I wanted to do it to the best of my ability.' He also enjoyed the small amount of leisure time he received. When his crew was excused a shift after a casing had been set, they would take the train into Nottingham for an evening's dancing. And he is happy to praise the younger British workers whom he trained. 'The English roughnecks weren't skilled when they started to work,' he says, 'but we taught them what to do and they're quick learners.'

One of the British oil workers who learned under the Americans was Ivan Mitchell. Ivan was a local boy recruited through the labour exchange. Attracted by the money – '£3 more than I was getting' – he cycled through the forest to attend an interview at the oilfield. His first job, at the age of seventeen, was tidying up the yard, but he was soon assigned to a drilling crew. His attitude toward the Americans is revealing: 'They were crackers, the way they fly about. Crackers. When they first came, the way that they performed, people were scared of them. Those jack-knife drilling rigs, God, they were terrifying compared to the old rigs we had here. On the deck, everything was like lightning.'

The British, according to Ivan, copied the American ways, and began to improve. 'We went the same way eventually,' he says. In Ivan's case, this included dressing like them, in their cast-off clothes.

And it wasn't just oil workers gaining knowledge at Eakring. The director of the British Geological Survey, Sir Edward Bailey, wrote to the chairman of Anglo-Iranian Oil, pointing out that Eakring's activities were offering unprecedented scientific opportunity. Well 146, he wrote, 'had recently passed through a very thick breccia-conglomerate series', and he asked for the chance to drill another 200 feet in search of fossils. 'Such an opportunity cannot be expected to repeat itself in the next fifty years.' The chairman agreed to Bailey's request – though the operation was described in Anglo-Iranian records, with a marked lack of enthusiasm, as 'coring in old rocks'. The war took many forms in many places, but surely only here was it used to advance knowledge of prehistoric carboniferous rock formations.

Despite their initial rate of progress, and the impression they made on the locals, the Americans were beginning to experience problems as the weeks passed. Mistakes crept in, levels of drinking increased, and the mood turned darker. The problem, it became clear, was lack of food. The roughnecks were used to a varied diet of red meat and fresh fruit and vegetables. They were not conditioned to an English diet, and certainly not to an English wartime diet where many foods were rationed, and others were simply unavailable. Working twelve hour days, seven days a week, the men were losing weight alarmingly. 'It was food for an office worker,' says Lewis Dugger.

To make matters worse, American soldiers were receiving excellent rations. The roughnecks were made fully aware of this when an army visitor arrived with forty thick steaks, one for each of them. Motorman Ray Hileman tried to help the situation by growing his own vegetables in an allotment behind the monastery. Offered the use of a local family's greenhouse, he began cultivating tomatoes, peppers and celery – but he overstepped the mark when he borrowed a shotgun and bagged a brace of pheasants. Somebody arrived at the monastery to warn him that poaching was a crime – and that local farmers had heard the gunshots. Hileman quickly returned the gun, and decided to concentrate on keeping chickens, rabbits and bees on his allotment.

Another means of augmenting rations was the black market. Talking to a farmer one day, Lewis agreed to trade five gallons of petrol for a dozen eggs. At 2015 prices, this works out at about £2 per egg, but as Lewis points out, 'Money don't mean nothing when you can't get stuff.' Food matters came to a head one morning, when a steward announced that breakfast would consist of warmed-up Brussels sprouts from the previous night's dinner. Fed up and hungry, the roughnecks announced that that they would work another month – but that if the food had not improved by the end of that month, they would be returning to America.

Deeply concerned, and aware of the army's abundant food supply, Eugene Rosser travelled to London to speak to the Petroleum Attaché at the United States Embassy. He was sent to see Major General John C. H. Lee, chief of supply of services, who, in turn, wrote to his chief quartermaster, Brigadier General Robert Littlejohn, ordering him to issue military rations to the oilfield workers. After a few days, however, nothing had happened so Rosser went in person to Littlejohn's headquarters – where it became clear that the brigadier general was not prepared to see him. Littlejohn was a plain-speaking man with a huge logistical task on his hands – and no interest whatsoever in civilian oil drillers.

Unwilling to return meekly to Kelham Hall, Rosser plucked up courage and barged into Littlejohn's office. The astonished quartermaster began shouting at him – until the situation was saved by a timely telephone call from Major General Lee, confirming his order. The seething Littlejohn had no choice but to do as he was told, and the roughnecks were soon receiving increased rations – including an extra meal at midnight as the day and night shifts crossed over. 'We could eat great,' says Lewis, 'sugar, pork luncheon meat, sliced pineapple, sliced peaches . . .'The mood improved immediately – as did the standard of work.

Even with extra rations, however, oil drilling was a dangerous occupation. Richard Stallard, the government drilling inspector, visited Eakring regularly to check on safety precautions, and to report on accidents – which were common. One man's arm was broken by a spinning rope, another caught his hand in a motor clutch. And in November the inspector was sent to report on the death of derrickman Herman Douthit. The twenty-nine-year-old Texan had fallen from a platform fifty-five feet above the ground. His boots, it seems, were covered in clay and his gloves were wet. As he climbed down a ladder, he placed his foot on a platform rail, slipped, and fell, suffering

head injuries. An ambulance arrived quickly, but Douthit was pro-
nounced dead on arrival at the United States Military Hospital at
Sutton-in-Ashfield. 'To sum up,' the inspector concluded his report,
'the accident was just one of those unfortunate occurrences that
cannot be prevented by any safety regulations.'

Lewis Dugger had worked with Douthit in Louisiana before they
came to England. He remembers him as a popular man with a taste for
bright flowery shirts, but also as a good worker with a huge amount of
drilling experience. The incident did not affect the roughnecks' morale,
Lewis claims, although it probably made everyone a little more careful. It was, after all, a reminder 'that your life could be over at any time
you went out there.' Douthit's funeral was held in the small church
attached to the monastery. The coffin was draped in an American flag
that was sent to his widow in Texas, along with the proceeds of a collection taken by local people. Today, Herman Douthit is the only civilian
buried in the United States Military Cemetery near Cambridge.

By the end of the Americans' year in Sherwood Forest, they had
drilled 106 wells, from which 'nodding donkeys' pumped nearly a
million barrels of fine crude oil. In the days that followed, D'Arcy
Exploration Co. offered the roughnecks the chance to carry on
working at Eakring (albeit at lower wages) but they all went back to
America. In fact, four men had already gone back: one had been
injured, another was homesick, and two had been fired – the first
for drunken fighting and the second for helping a local farmer when
he was meant to be sick in bed. When the time came for the rest to
leave they went quietly. 'We disappeared without any fanfare,' says
Lewis. But before they left the country, they were taken to London
where they were shown around the city by Philip Southwell. It was,
believes Lewis, a mark of appreciation for what they had done.

They sailed home on *Mauretania*, having achieved Southwell's
objective of a hundred wells. They had helped to ease the national
petroleum shortage, and they had passed on their knowledge to local
men, many of whom would have long careers as oil drillers around

the world. At its peak, the Sherwood Forest oilfield employed 1,200 people, and by the end of the war, it had stretched across nine miles of countryside, and produced over 300,000 tons of high-grade oil, equivalent to two and a quarter million barrels from 170 nodding donkeys. It had become a genuine commercial proposition, with a life that was to extend into the mid-1960s.

A reminder of Sherwood Forest's forgotten oil industry. This pump – known as a 'nodding donkey' – was photographed in 2014.

After the war, Father Gregory, the prior of the monastery, wrote about his American tenants in *NAFT*, the in-house magazine of the Anglo-Iranian Oil Company. He admitted that initially, the monks had been alarmed by the prospect of the roughnecks' arrival, but that 'the assurances about quiet were fully realised in practice. I hope we have disturbed them as little as they have disturbed us.' Father Gregory then revealed himself to be a movie lover, who could not have been happier had Gary Cooper come to stay:

It really is most interesting, and at times almost uncanny, to see how like the films they are. For one thing, like the people on the films, they dress well and seem to justify the boast that you cannot tell a man's social status from his clothes. Bright coloured suits, broad-brimmed hats, or caps with peaks pointing to heaven, and high-heeled boots seem to be the favourite dress when not working. But where I scored most heavily was in the manner of speech, for they talk the language of the films perfectly. I felt I knew them well at once; there is nothing odd about them, I had seen and heard them often before.

A visit to the area reveals that they have never quite gone away. Their names are still carved into the bark of old beech trees. Their image is visible in a bronze statue in Duke's Wood nature reserve. And perhaps, one day, they will sit beside the Merry Men as figures of Sherwood Forest legend – outlaws and roughnecks together. But, for our story, they represent the ambition of a nation that was having to change its beliefs and assumptions. The British oil industry was the oddest ritual of a period of misrule, and it was an acknowledgement that oil was no longer something that simply came from abroad. As the people of Britain were making do and mending – so was the land itself.

CHAPTER SEVEN

The Germans Are Coming

Since transparent justice is often said to be the cornerstone of a democratic society, it came as a surprise to learn, in June 2014, that the British government was attempting to conduct an Old Bailey terrorism trial in total secrecy. The Court of Appeal ruled that parts of the trial had to be heard in public. Commenting afterwards, the Lord Chief Justice, Lord Thomas, said, 'I really passionately believe in open justice. Justice that is not open is not good justice.' In reporting the case, the *Daily Telegraph* wrote that a secret trial 'would have been unprecedented in British legal history'. Many other newspapers and television networks made the same point, and repeated the same word: *unprecedented*. But they were all wrong. A series of entirely secret trials took place in Britain during a period far more extreme than our own.

The first, and most remarkable, of these cases was heard in November 1940 at the Old Bailey. It concerned three Nazi spies, charged with treachery, who had landed in September on the south coast of England. They had been sent as the advance guard of the German invasion – and just as the Court of Appeal expressed its democratic concerns in 2014, so Sir Alexander Maxwell, Permanent

Under Secretary at the Home Office, wrote to the Home Defence (Security) Executive in 1940, expressing his department's disapproval of the concept of secret trials. 'Public opinion and public criticism,' wrote Maxwell, 'is the most important safeguard for the proper administration of justice.' In his reply, Lord Swinton justified the secrecy:

> I want to make it plain that there is much more in this than keeping the enemy in doubt as to the fate of his agents. The combined work of all the services has built up, and is continually adding to, a great structure of intelligence and counter espionage; and a single disclosure, affecting one individual, might send the whole building toppling. I have no love for unnecessary secrecy; but in this matter we cannot afford to take any avoidable risk.

The 'great structure' was MI5's network of double agents whom the Germans trusted as loyal spies. (A double agent is someone who pretends to spy for one side when he or she is really under the control of the other.) MI5 had all sorts of plans for these double agents, a number of whom were Nazi spies who had been sent to Britain, captured, and presented with a stark choice – either serve the British or face execution. But not every captured spy became a double agent. Many were not considered suitable, and were sent for trial instead. And MI5 was brutally aware that a single piece of information from one of these trials had the potential to expose the entire 'double cross' system. The Home Office's scruples about secret trials were both admirable and reassuring, but democracy was going to take a sabbatical to ensure its own survival.

This particular trial was the culmination of a chain of events set in motion by General Alfred Jodl, the Chief of Operations Staff at Wehrmacht High Command. In July 1940 Jodl was responsible for formulating the preliminary plan for the German invasion of Britain. He envisaged an invasion front stretching from Weymouth to

Margate, and an assault force of forty-one divisions – including the SS Totenkopf Division, responsible just weeks earlier for the murder of almost a hundred British prisoners-of-war outside a barn at Le Paradis in France. As part of his planning, Jodl spoke to Admiral Wilhelm Canaris, chief of the Abwehr (the German Intelligence Service), explaining that a network of spies was needed in Britain to serve as scouts in advance of the invasion. These spies, said Jodl, would identify suitable landing grounds, provide detailed information about defences, and guide the invading troops once they had fought their way off the beaches.

Less than a week after Jodl's preliminary plan had been delivered, Adolf Hitler issued his Führer Directive No. 16, bringing Operation *Sea Lion*, as the invasion was codenamed, into official being. *Sea Lion's* ultimate objective, according to the directive, was to occupy Britain 'should it become necessary'. Hitler was not yet committed to an invasion. Given Germany's inexorable military advance, his respect for the Anglo-Saxon people, and his desire to turn his attention eastwards, he remained confident that Britain would sue for peace.

When no approach had arrived by 19 July, Hitler addressed the Reichstag in uncharacteristically measured tones. It almost caused him pain, he told the assembly, to be responsible for bringing down a great empire which he had no desire to harm. He could see no reason why this war had to go on. His offer of peace reached Britain – and three days later, it was flatly rejected by the Foreign Secretary, Lord Halifax. When printed copies of the offer, headed *A Last Appeal to Reason*, were dropped over Britain by the Luftwaffe, a Pathé newsreel showed a grinning Englishman holding a copy of the offer and tearing it into squares. Nowadays this man would happily tell the cameras – in some detail – what he was intending to do with the squares. In the coy style of the 1940s the newsreel suggested that he was preparing 'shaving papers'.

Preparations for the invasion intensified. Almost two thousand cargo barges were adapted to carry troops, artillery and tanks. Soldiers were trained to scale the cliffs of Kent and Sussex. Amphibious tanks were developed to emerge from the sea onto English beaches. The most pressing preliminary objective, however, was the destruction of the Royal Air Force, so that it could not threaten the invasion force as it crossed the Channel. The resulting 'Great Air Offensive', the responsibility of the Luftwaffe, became the successive phases of the Battle of Britain and the Blitz.

As time passed, disagreements between the commanders-in-chief of the army and navy resulted in a compromise plan being agreed. This involved an assault, in several waves, along a narrow front between Worthing and Ramsgate, building towards the encirclement of London in a pincer movement. The attack would begin in the middle of September – so it was important that Canaris's spies were in place to guide the attackers. The operation to send them to Britain, codenamed *Lena*, was allocated to Major Nikolaus Ritter of the Abwehr's Hamburg sub-office . A shortlist of candidates was selected by Walter Praetorius, a man known as 'The Pied Piper'. He began searching for recruits in Belgium and Holland. This made sense: refugees from recently occupied countries were arriving in Britain in numbers. From the list Praetorius drew up, Ritter chose his favourites.

The chosen few would be expected to report back on coastal troop positions, frequency of patrols, locations of landmines, and weather conditions – but their training proved to be woefully inadequate. They received a month of sketchy instruction in Morse and cryptology, they were shown how to use their transmitters, and they were given a few perfunctory lectures about the structure of the British army. They were not told how to behave when they landed, nor were they provided with identity papers. Such neglectful preparation might, perhaps, be the result of the speed with which they had to be turned into spies. But as MI5's Guy Liddell observed in his wartime diary, it was diffi-cult 'to believe that they [the Abwehr] could have been so stupid, as having sent these men over without having schooled them properly and worked out plans by which they could be really effective.'

This begs a question – was the Abwehr stupid, overstretched, or had it deliberately neglected the men's selection and training? The answer may turn on the fact that the Abwehr was not slavishly loyal to the Nazis. Wilhelm Canaris, although personally appointed by Hitler, was never a member of the Nazi party. He was, in fact, a consistent – albeit careful – opponent of Hitler and Nazism, who filled key positions in the Abwehr with like-minded associates. And even those officers who were not actively anti-Nazi were often unconcerned by the quality of their work. In a post-war memo, the historian Hugh Trevor-Roper, at the time a counter-intelligence officer, wrote:

> The operational officers of the Abwehr sat in Paris and Athens, in Biarritz and Estoril, enjoying the opportunities for self-indulgence provided by these resorts, undisturbed so long as a quota of reports was sent in. Whether these reports were true or false was unimportant, since there was no centralised evaluation.

Canaris once told a fellow intelligence officer* that he did not care if every German agent in Britain was under control so long as he could tell German High Command that he had agents in Britain reporting regularly. The success of *Lena* may have been irrelevant to the Abwehr so long as it could show that it was dutifully sending spies across the Channel. But, to go a stage further, it is not impossible that the choice of spies and their pitiful training amounted to an act of internal sabotage by anti-Nazi members of the organisation. Nikolaus Ritter, the man responsible for *Lena*, was, after all, a trusted protégé of Wilhelm Canaris.

The first four *Lena* spies were certainly a motley band. Charles van den Kieboom was a half-Dutch, half-Japanese YMCA receptionist. Carl Meier was a failed medical student who spoke English with an American accent. Sjoerd Pons was an unemployed Dutch ex-army

---

* Johann Jebsen, an officer who attempted to defect to the Allies in 1944, and was eventually murdered in Oranienberg Concentration Camp.

ambulance driver who could barely speak English, while Jose Waldberg was a French-born German who had no English at all. He was, however, a committed Nazi who had spied for the Abwehr in France before its fall. The others had no experience of spying and no obvious credentials for the job. Pons and van den Kieboom were not even willing volunteers; they had been blackmailed into spying. It is little wonder that among themselves, the spies described their mission as *Himmelfahrt* – 'the journey to heaven'.

The journey began with the men being brought to within a few miles of the English coast, placed in rowing boats, and pointed towards Kent. In one boat were Meier and Waldberg, in the other, Kieboom and Pons. The boats landed in the early hours of the morning of 3 September; one near Dungeness, the other by the Dymchurch Redoubt. They had with them binoculars, wireless transmitters, cases containing clothes, cigarettes and brandy, £30 in bank notes, and enough food for a fortnight, by which time, they had been assured, the German invasion force would have arrived.

Only Waldberg had the makings of a decent spy. In his twenty-four hours of freedom on the Kent coast, he managed to make wireless contact with his German handlers. The other three men were truly hopeless. Meier gave himself away by knocking on the door of the Rising Sun pub at Lydd at nine in the morning and asking the landlady for a champagne cider, and a hot bath. Lydd was no hub of cosmopolitan activity in 1940, and Meier with his foreign accent and ignorance of pub etiquette did not blend in easily. The landlady explained to him that a bath was not on offer, and asked him to call back later. On his way out he smacked his head on light fitting. When he returned, he spoke to an air raid warden who asked to see his identity card. He replied that he had no card, and said, '*We* arrived here last night,' revealing the existence of his fellow spies. Two members of the public stepped up to arrest him. 'You've caught me, I guess,' Maier told them, 'and I don't mind what happens to me, but I don't want to go back to Germany!'

Carl Meier with his American fiancée.

By the time of Meier's arrest, Kieboom was already in custody. His beached dinghy had been noticed by a patrolling soldier in the early morning gloom, and he was spotted minutes later. 'I am a Dutch refugee,' he shouted, 'and if I can see one of your officers, I can explain the situation!' Pons, meanwhile, was spotted by a soldier in a nearby field. When he was challenged, he shouted, 'I am a Dutchman!' and tried to explain, in broken English, that he had lost his companion. Early the next morning, Waldberg was noticed by a policeman as he walked along a railway line.

Brought together again, the men were sent to Britain's wartime spy prison situated on the edge of Richmond Park. Latchmere House, known as Camp 020, was run by Colonel Robin Stephens, known behind his back as 'Tin-Eye' for his ever-present monocle. Stephens's role was to interrogate his prisoners, and to decide whether they could be used as double agents against their German masters. Stephens enjoyed his job – Christopher Harmer, an MI5 officer, remembers him rubbing his hands with glee on hearing that a fresh spy had been caught. But before a prisoner could be used as a double agent, he or she had to confess to being a spy. Stephens used his own carefully crafted methods of extracting confessions. One tactic, which he called 'blow-hot/blow-cold', will be familiar to viewers of modern police dramas. Stephens would begin by behaving ferociously towards the prisoner. A calm officer would intervene, apparently trying to pacify Stephens. The kindly officer would take the prisoner aside and explain gently that it would be better if he confessed, because Stephens could become very angry indeed.

Stephens also invented 'Cell 14'. Just as George Orwell's Room 101 contained the worst thing in the world, so Cell 14 was created to conjure up the prisoner's darkest fears. It was a perfectly ordinary cell around which a tale of death and madness was spun. The prisoner was told that the previous occupant had committed suicide, that it was opposite the mortuary, that he would remain locked up without human contact until he confessed – or until he was taken away 'for the very last time'. Fear and vulnerability often prompted a quick confession. Perhaps surprisingly, Stephens would never allow physical violence to be used against his prisoners. But this had less to do with progressive thinking than with an understanding that confessions gained by torture were rarely reliable.

While in Stephens's custody, Waldberg confirmed that he had been a willing German agent – but the others denied being spies. Sjoerd Pons claimed that he had intended to give himself up as soon as he arrived: 'I want to take it all to you,' he said, 'I want to tell the police and take him my apparatus under my arm.' Pons was asked whether he would be willing to become a double agent. 'It is difficult,' he answered. 'Difficult, is it?' replied Stephens, 'Why? You love Germany, do you?' Regardless of his feelings for Germany, Pons was facing a dilemma. On the one hand, he believed that the Germans would arrive in Britain shortly, and he did not want to risk betraying them. On the other hand, if he refused the British offer, he might be executed before the Germans arrived. He asked Stephens whether he could be sent to America, where, he claimed, he had wanted to go all along. The answer, unsurprisingly, was 'no'.

It did not take long for Stephens to conclude that the men could

Sjoerd Pons.

not be used as double agents. For one thing, three of them continued to deny being spies. For another, their arrests had been locally observed and discussed. News of this might have filtered back to the Germans. Another factor was that Waldberg had made wireless contact with his German handlers. It was one of Stephens's rules that the initial contact between a double agent and his enemy handlers must be made under British supervision. Waldberg might, after all, have warned his handlers of his imminent capture, in which case they would now use him as a triple agent. And so the 'Four Men in a Boat' were sent for trial at the Old Bailey – with the exception of Waldberg who pleaded guilty, firm in his belief that the Germans would shortly arrive to release him from his cell.

The trial, held in Court One before Mr Justice Wrottesley, began on 19 November 1940. The three men were charged with the new offence of treachery, introduced to fill a loophole as the existing crime of treason only covered British subjects. The trial was held in total secret, with jury members being told by the judge to 'Make up some story if you are asked what you are trying.' Mr Justice Wrottesley also told them to keep 'an open mind' – but at a time when spies were feared and hated, when Britain was expecting an invasion, when cities were being coventrated, and when Britain and its dominions were fighting without Russian or American help – an 'open mind' was an extremely tall order. Rarely can a jury have approached a trial in a more prejudiced frame of mind. Which makes what was about to happen all the more remarkable.

Section 1 of the Treachery Act reads:

If, with intent to help the enemy, any person does, or attempts or conspires with any other person to do any act which is designed or likely to give assistance to the naval, military or air operations of the enemy, to impede such operations of His Majesty's forces, or to endanger life, he shall be guilty of felony and shall on conviction suffer death.

The penalty was death and the stakes were high. In his examination-in-chief, Pons told his festively named counsel, Christmas Humphreys, that he and Kieboom had been caught by the Nazis smuggling jewels between Holland and Germany. He said they had then been given a choice – either agree to spy for Germany in England, or be sent to a concentration camp. They had agreed to spy, said Pons, but had decided that they would hand themselves in to the police as soon as they came ashore. Pons preferred, he assured his counsel, England over Germany.

Once he was ashore, Pons said, he had decided to wet his wireless set to make it unusable before surrendering it to the police. 'I found a ditch, there was an inch of water in it. I pressed it down into water and mud. That was the best I could do,' said Pons. 'What is wrong with the sea?' asked the judge. 'There is a lot of water there, you know . . .' 'I could not find it again,' said Pons. 'Yes, you could,' said the judge. Pons then told Humphreys that having left his wireless set in the ditch, he had seen two men in the distance, and had walked towards them. These were the soldiers who arrested him. One of them had called out to him. 'Did you mean to help the Germans when you got to England?' Humphreys asked. 'No, sir!' Pons replied. He was attempting to convince the jury that he had done nothing, in the wording of the Act, 'likely to give assistance to the enemy'.

During his cross-examination, Pons was asked by the judge why he had not come ashore waving a white handkerchief. 'We had all these incriminating things with us,' Pons replied. 'Why not throw them overboard and come ashore waving a handkerchief?' asked the judge. 'I have not thought of it,' said Pons.

In his closing speech, Sir William Jowitt, counsel for the prosecution, urged the jury to convict with these stirring words: 'If you have no doubt, do like thousands of other Britons younger than yourselves are doing today – do your duty!' In his summing up, Mr Justice Wrottesley offered his view of the defence case:

Had they [the defendants] gone to the first person they had seen and told the whole story, they had everything which was needed to establish beyond any doubt that their story was true: the boat, the brand new wireless set. Do you think that intelligent persons would have feared anything if they had taken that course? But instead of adopting a course like that, the course which they have adopted is one of hiding themselves so long as they could, the equipment so long as they could – it is a difficult course of conduct to reconcile with innocence.

Referring specifically to Sjoerd Pons's defence, the judge went further. 'You may think,' he said, 'that that is a cock and bull story.'

The jury retired to consider its verdict halfway through the third day of the trial – and an hour later it came back with a question. What should they do, the foreman asked, if they thought that one of the defendants had originally conspired with the others to spy for Germany – but that 'when he arrived in England he decided that he would not do anything to help the enemy but he would make a clean breast of it here'. Sir William Jowitt stood and said that would be a verdict of not guilty. Minutes later, the jury returned with a not guilty verdict for Sjoerd Pons, and guilty verdicts for Kieboom and Meier.

In Jowitt's view, expressed after the trial, Pons was acquitted because the jury was not keen to see him executed. Pons seems to have cut a more sympathetic figure than Kieboom or Maier, and it is certainly not unknown for juries to decide cases on emotion rather than logic. But on the facts as presented, Kieboom and Meier had made clear attempts to hide their equipment and conceal their identities, while Pons had been relatively co-operative after arrest. The jury may, therefore, have decided that Pons's actions revealed a genuine desire to surrender once in England.

Pons was released, and immediately rearrested by MI5 as he left the dock, and interned as an enemy alien. The other three men, Waldberg, Meier and Kieboom were hanged at Pentonville Prison in

December. After the executions, the veil of secrecy was set aside, and the public was informed that three men had been convicted of treachery, and executed. A photo of Waldberg's radio transmitter even appeared in *The Times* and *Picture Post*. But the public was never told that a fourth man had been acquitted. The existence of Sjoerd Pons had to remain a secret.

Pons was described, during his five-and-a-half-year internment, as 'a difficult, dangerous and surly customer', who 'expressed anti-semitic views as well as admiration for German efficiency'. This assessment jars depressingly with the jury's impression of a victimised Anglophile. (One wonders how his respect for German efficiency had survived his abominable spy training.) Pons was deported to Holland in July 1946 on a flight from Hendon alongside other Dutch internees. He was taken into custody in Holland, but released two months later. He divorced his wife, married a French woman, and died in Spain in 1983. When considering his fate, it is worth thinking back to John Fulljames, another young man whose life was spared by outrageous fortune, who passed the war in captivity, and who was given the chance to make a fresh start after its end.

A search through the case files reveals letters that Meier, Kieboom and Waldberg wrote to their loved ones the night before their executions. They died believing that these letters had been sent via the Red Cross – but they never were. Carl Meier wrote to his American fiancée, Margaret Moseley. The letter's last paragraph reads:

> Darling, keep your chin up! Say goodbye to all our friends from me and here's all the love that my last thoughts will convey. I'm not going to say goodbye, because there must be something after this. Darling. XXXX So long! Carl.

But the letter also includes a section which gives an insight into Meier's true state of mind, rather different from anything he had told the jury:

I went into this with both my eyes open, telling myself that a man who has an ideal must be willing to sacrifice everything for it or else the ideal isn't an ideal at all, or the man isn't a man at all, but a humble creature who deserves only pity.

The story of the four invasion spies is not simply an episode of *Dad's Army* recast by the German Intelligence Service. It represents a secret trial held during a war fought, ironically, to preserve liberties such as open justice. The justification for secrecy was that transparency would have offered an unthinkable advantage to an enemy of unparalleled evil. Hindsight cannot dispute this – but will *R v. Meier, Kieboom and Pons* ever be cited as the precedent for a future – and less justifiable – secret trial?

The story also casts light on the Abwehr, that crucial cog in the Nazi machine, whose anti-Nazi leader, Willhelm Canaris, managed to maintain a quiet resistance to Adolf Hitler until his arrest in 1944. The 'Four Men in a Boat' owe their contrasting fates to the shadowy workings of Canaris's conflicted organisation.

And most importantly, this story reveals a jury's extraordinary courage at a moment of national uncertainty. Whether its verdict was right or wrong is a moot point – it had resisted its prejudice and acted according to its conscience. Only weeks earlier, Sir Malcolm Hilbury, High Court Judge and Treasurer of Gray's Inn, had complained of 'the extravagance of the jury system in wartime', but the right to a fair hearing was clearly still available. In his closing speech Sir William Jowitt (Solicitor General in the coalition government as well as prosecuting counsel in the case) said, 'Although the Germans may bomb this building brick by brick they will never succeed in destroying the heritage we have had handed down to us and will hand on of British fairness and justice.' Whenever the right to trial by jury is discussed, this case deserves to be invoked. As a nation, we should remember it with pride.

And we should not forget that this story represents the only part of the German invasion actually to arrive in Britain. Viewed as con-firmation that enemy forces were about to cross the Channel, it prompted an invasion scare on the evening of Saturday 7 September. A number of factors came together that night to suggest the moment had come. As well as the spies' arrival, reconnaissance photographs of the invasion force were arousing concern. A full harvest moon and high tides were coinciding to create ideal assault conditions. Meanwhile, the first day of heavy bombing of London was inter-preted as a softening-up before invasion – just as Great War 'pushes' had been preceded by artillery barrages. And given the sheer number of attacking aircraft, the General Staff seems to have concluded that some were likely to contain parachute troops.

As a result, just after eight o'clock in the evening, the codeword 'Cromwell' was issued to Southern, Eastern and Western Commands by GHQ Home Forces. 'Cromwell' was actually meant to indicate imminent danger from airborne landings. But not only was this threat non-existent in reality, the codeword was widely miscon-strued as an alert that the invasion had actually begun. Soldiers were recalled to their barracks, Home Guard commanders rang church bells to summon their men, and news of an invasion spread – along with rumours of enemy sightings. A Southern Command officer remembers:

> The great word 'Cromwell' was received and everyone thought that the time had come to fight to the last man and the last round of ammunition, with reports coming in that parachutists were drop-ping in the South Midland and Bristol areas. The reports on further investigation were found to have been whiffs of cloud. When the scare was over, it was then found that we had no codeword for 'stand down'.

In London's East End, in the midst of the falling bombs, fire fighters and ARP men were warned to look out for paratroopers and traitors.

"'Ow the 'ell d'you recognise friend from foe,' a London fireman was heard to ask, 'when we're all covered with the same shit?'

Michael Bowyer was a fourteen-year old boy living in Cambridge on 7 September. He was fascinated by the Germans – and remembers hoping that they would come in the daytime so that he could see them. That night, a Home Guard sergeant rushed round to the house he shared with his mother and father. 'It's Cromwell!' said the sergeant. Michael and his father had about a hundred corked beer bottles, filled with petrol, as well as strips of torn-up wincyette pjamas. 'Dad and I were going to stuff these things in, set fire to the wincyette, and throw them at the Germans. We were really ready for it!'

Less ready was Kenneth Johnstone, an officer in the Durham Light Infantry. He and his men were stationed in a house in the Devon countryside. When the codeword arrived from battalion headquarters, he was lying in a large four-poster bed, while his men were asleep in the stables. To signal a turnout, Johnstone was supposed to pull a tattered bell rope beside the bed as though summoning a servant. When he pulled it, the rope came away in his hand. He and his men finally responded to the invasion in two buses, two trucks, and a borrowed wedding car. The wedding car promptly got stuck in the gates. 'It really was like a film,' says Johnstone. 'It was absolute pandemonium. I think if Hitler had seen us, he would have had a good laugh.'

For much of 1940 and all of the following year, people in Britain were living under tense threat of invasion. Whether he truly intended to invade or not, it was certainly in Hitler's interest to keep the threat alive. His occupation of the Channel Islands at the end of June 1940 had this effect. And when examining the attitudes of the British people to the threat, it is instructive to start at the top with Winston Churchill.

In the summer of 1940, the Prime Minister did not seem to think – or perhaps did not *want* to think – that an invasion was likely. In a War Cabinet minute of 18 July, he found it 'difficult to believe' that the south coast was under serious threat of attack. The 'main danger', he conceded, was from 'Dutch and German harbours which bear principally upon the coast from Dover to the Wash', but he played down this threat as being dependent on the weather and compromised by limited air support. And even *were* the Germans to invade, he felt that 'the invaders' losses in transit would reduce the scale of attack' and that the army 'is already at a strength when it should be able to deal with such an invasion'. As a result, he spoke somewhat startlingly of his desire to bring entire divisions of troops away from defensive duties on the coast 'so that they may proceed in the highest forms of offensive warfare'. Churchill could always be relied upon to promote attack as the primary means of defence.

In the same minute the First Sea Lord, Sir Dudley Pound, gave his considered opinion that 100,000 invading troops would be able to reach the British coast without being intercepted by naval forces. 'I personally believe that the Admiralty will in fact be better than their word,' said Churchill. It was clearly difficult for the Prime Minister to acknowledge an opinion contrary to his own. In 1941 journalist James Lansdale Hodson wrote:

> I could wish Churchill was less arrogant ... The other day, Churchill, when at Broadcasting House, referred to three bombs dropped. His secretary said, 'No, sir, one bomb.' Churchill held up three fingers. 'Three bombs,' he said determinedly. He cannot be contradicted even on fact ... Lamentable.

The War Cabinet minute underlines this observation. The Prime Minister was prepared to contradict the head of the Royal Navy about his ability to counter a German invasion, and to suggest the removal of defensive troops from the coast at a time of unparalleled danger. Seventy-five years' worth of consensus have told us what to think about Winston Churchill – but if we take ourselves back to 1940, we may feel a measure of sympathy with those – mainly older – people who were horrified at the prospect of this political wild man leading the country.

And yet dangerous times often call for feral instincts. Oliver Lyttelton (later Lord Chandos), President of the Board of Trade, explains:

> Leadership is the power to dull the rational faculty. There are people much cleverer than Winston, with a much more balanced brain but you or I would not follow them up a glacier. Henry V never said, 'Now, gentlemen, I've been into the whole of this thing and the Channel is very tricky at the moment and we can't get the reinforcements, the bridgehead is too small and in short I feel there is nothing else but to launch an attack.' He said, 'Once more unto the breach, dear friends!' Churchill had that extraordinary power. He made you feel as though you were a great actor in great events. Leadership is dulling the rational faculty and substituting enthusiasm for it. In 1940, on a careful evaluation of the odds, nobody would have moved.

Attempting to dull the First Sea Lord's rational faculty might serve no obvious purpose, but Churchill's monumental – and frequently misplaced – self-belief, when directed at the population, had a role to play. Joan Seaman, a civilian in London, remembers her terrific fear as France was falling. 'I thought it was going to be us next,' she says. But when she heard Churchill speaking, the effect was transforming. She suddenly lost her fear. 'It was quite amazing,' she says. 'When people have decried Churchill, I've always said, "Yes, but he stopped me being afraid." Oliver Bernard, a schoolboy evacuated to Sussex, remembers listening to Churchill's 'On the Beaches' speech. 'That raised hairs on the back of one's neck,' he says, comparing Churchill's words with Macaulay's 'Horatius', in which three men defended the city of Rome against the entire Tuscan army. At a time when Britain had little to offer but blood, toil, tears and sweat, Churchill's exquisitely phrased determination was intoxicating. And his framing of the struggle as the preservation of freedom spoke effectively to Americans as well as to his own people. It is the folk memory of this period that has ensured Churchill's place in the consensus, reflected by his selection as 'The Greatest Briton of All Time' in a 2002 BBC poll, and his climactic appearance, played by actor Timothy Spall, in the closing ceremony of the 2012 London Olympics. We have Churchill to thank, the ceremony was suggesting, for a free Olympic Games in a free United Kingdom in a free world.

In a speech to the nation broadcast on 11 September 1940, a week after the spies' capture and four days after the invasion alert, Churchill said that an invasion could not be long delayed, and that the next week or two must be regarded 'as a very important period in our history'. Evoking Nelson at the Battle of Trafalgar, he said that 'Every man and woman will therefore prepare himself to do his duty, whatever it may be, with special pride and care.' His public tone was noticeably different from his Cabinet tone two months earlier. The country was being placed on notice, and the following morning's *Times* editorial pointed out that the people of Britain were now guarding 'the fate of humanity'.

'Why doesn't *he* come?' was, according to Ealing schoolboy Roy Bartlett, a defining expression of the period. One night during an air raid, Roy's family believed that he *had* come. Roy's sister looked out of her bedroom window and saw two parachutes in the sky. In a panic, she ran downstairs screaming, 'It's happening! It's happening!' The entire family waited, terrified, for gunfire in the street, or for church bells – but nothing came, and eventually the All Clear sounded. The parachutes had been carrying two members of a German bomber crew. 'We were so on tenterhooks already,' says Roy, 'that we were willing to believe that it was happening.' James Oates, a member of Dagenham Home Guard, heard the sound of invasion bells one evening, and set off with his rifle to meet the Germans, before it dawned on him that the sound he had heard was the pounding of metal at the nearby Ford motor works. 'It was a sound I heard every night,' he says, 'but why that particular night I thought they were church bells . . .'

Denis Warren remembers being handed a note one evening in early summer 1940, which read, 'Parachutists have landed at Bent Bridge'. Denis, a young Local Defence Volunteer in Lancashire, set off with nine others in a small Humber motor car. 'I was absolutely terrified,' he says, 'and when we got to the main road, a chap stepped out of the bushes with a stopwatch.' The 'invasion' had been a test to see how quickly the unit would react – and Denis's relief is palpable seventy-four years later. 'We would have had *no idea* what to do.'

Denis and his friends were not alone. There were large numbers of people across the country responsible for defending Britain against invasion with little real idea of what to do. The fact was that no centralised anti-invasion authority existed – so enthusiastic amateurs stepped in to take the lead. Just as volunteer groups steered Britain out of the Blitz crisis, so they led the line against invasion. Local 'invasion committees' sprang up across the country. Hilda Cripps was a member of an invasion committee in Essex. 'Your duty,' the local garrison commander told her, 'will be to provide the essential things for life. Do your best to prevent panic and keep some semblance of life going.' Hilda and her colleagues placed containers of survival rations in strategic points around the area, made an index of local livestock, and took delivery of hundreds of papier-mâché coffins. Given personal responsibility for the water supply, Hilda had nearby wells inspected, and earmarked farmers' carts to be sterilised and used for transporting water. Great stress was placed on secrecy – which made Hilda and her fellow members feel particularly important. 'The last thing we were told by the authorities,' she says, 'was that if the invasion did come, six of our committee would likely be shot by the Germans.' There is pride in her voice.

The plan for the Local Defence Volunteers was announced in May 1940 in a radio appeal by Secretary for War, Anthony Eden. Across the

Members of the LDV in early July 1940. These proud gentlemen were 'Old Contemptibles' who had served in France and Belgium in 1914.

country, the response was overwhelming. In Sutton, in Surrey, 1,400 men immediately enrolled and many others were turned away. Responsible for defending their area against the Wehrmacht and the SS, these Suttonians had no uniforms and a handful of rifles between them. They paraded in overalls, and carried broomsticks. As summer turned to autumn, weapons and uniforms began to appear, and the unit became 55th (Sutton and Cheam) Battalion Home Guard. Once the Blitz had started, part of 'B' Company was very nearly wiped out while guarding the local hospital. Standing on the roof, the men watched a paratrooper descending towards them. But as the parachute came closer, they realised that slung underneath was not a man, but a large black cylinder. This was their first encounter with a parachute mine. The mine was coming down directly on top of them when a gust of wind carried it up and away; it exploded some way off with terrifying force. Such was the line between life and death during the Blitz.

A Leicester Home Guard anti-tank section.

Stanley Brand, a Middlesbrough Home Guard, complained that all he was ever taught to do was march backwards and forwards:

> We didn't have training in house to house fighting – yet we would have had more of that than anything else. And Jerry was good at it! He'd had lots of experience in France. We were prepared to lean out of a bedroom window, light a piece of rag in the neck of a bottle and throw it at a tank. How long would we have survived?

Yet as though to illustrate the variety of people's experience, Stan Poole, a north London Home Guard, remembers taking part in precisely the sort of manoeuvres denied to Stanley Brand. In one exercise he crossed the Regent's Canal in a rubber dinghy, attempting to ambush 'the enemy' inside Camden Town tube station. 'Blokes finished up fighting each other with gun butts on the roof of the Aerated Bread Company,' he says. 'There were blokes riding past the roof on buses, throwing thunderflashes up, pretending they were hand grenades. It was very good fun.' Considerably more fun, one imagines, than the arrival of the SS Totenkopf Division would have proved.

The most clandestine anti-invasion force was another volunteer organisation whose members were picked from the ranks of the Home Guard. Concealed in carefully sited and camouflaged underground hideouts, the Auxiliary Units were to wait until the invaders had passed over, before emerging at night to carry out sabotage behind German lines. They were to be, in effect, the British Resistance. During training, George Pellet, a member of a unit in Kent, noticed somebody peeping at him from behind a tree as he entered his hideout. The snooper was quietly warned to keep his mouth shut – and one member of the unit was selected to shoot him as soon as the invasion arrived.

Auxiliaries were trained in methods of sabotage and combat. 'We would have booby-trapped German stores and vehicles,' says Percy Clark. 'We'd have stretched wires across roads to catch necks. We were trained to be silent killers.' The members were only expected to survive for the shortest of periods before being caught. 'One didn't really ask for anything very sophisticated,' says Peter Wilkinson, chief of staff to Colonel Colin Gubbins, the founder of the Auxiliary Units. 'All one hoped was to be able to survive the first fortnight of the invasion and prevent the bridgehead being enlarged.'

Volunteers were crucial to the defence of Britain. They filled the gap left by the lack of a centralised body, and stood alongside the sparsely equipped and badly bruised professional army. Thinking back to the autumn of 1940, Captain Kenneth Johnstone of the Durham Light Infantry remembers an officer being placed on a charge by the brigadier for not having his revolver, until it was explained that there was only one revolver in the battalion – and it hadn't been that officer's turn to wear it. Peter Vaux was second lieutenant in the Royal Tank Regiment. His squadron was equipped with a train specially

modified to carry his tank to wherever it was needed along the coast.
'The Germans would land,' Vaux says, 'the thinly spread-out infantry
on the beaches would withdraw and the Germans would establish a
beachhead. We had to get there with our tanks before they broke out.'
Just as Rommel became convinced, in 1944, that the Allied invasion
of Europe would have to be defeated before it could establish itself,
so the British understood, in 1940, that the Germans must be resisted at the earliest possible opportunity.

The strange hot summer of 1940.

But large-scale volunteerism served a purpose beyond the obvious: it kept people busy and involved, and free from complacency and dissatisfaction. The result was boosted morale. Cambridge schoolboy Michael Bowyer and his father could barely wait to collect their spades and shovels and set off to help to dig the anti-tank ditch which stretched across East Anglia. 'Every evening we were digging away,' he says. 'It was *Dig for Victory* with a different slant. *Dig for Survival!*' The fact is that while it suited Adolf Hitler to keep the threat of invasion alive, so it suited the British government to do precisely the same. At one period, in one respect, British and Nazi war aims can be said to have coincided.

But if some were fortified by Churchill's words, and others were galvanised by their responsibilities, public attitudes could still vary widely. Some fall wide of the consensus. In September 1940 an Ayrshire steelworker wrote, in a reply to a Mass-Observation directive, 'We wouldn't know there was a war on if we were not told.' And even those under the bombs did not necessarily fear invasion. Elsie Glendinning was a young woman living in Glasgow who was deeply affected by the war. She joined the WVS, and on the first night of the Clydebank Blitz, was terrified by the explosion of a nearby landmine. Yet the prospect of the Nazis arriving several hundred miles away made little impression on her. 'We didn't hear much of it, really,' she says. 'I think maybe people in the south felt more apprehensive than we did.' The truth, once again, is that there is no single truth. For some the reason for calm was geography, for others it was a question of understanding. A prep schoolboy remembers being called into the classroom by his headmaster to listen to the BBC news at the fall of France. As the headmaster gravely explained that the world would never be the same again, the boys could only think about their interrupted football match.

For some, though, anxiety gave rise to desperate plans. After consulting with her husband, Hilda Cripps bought a large bottle of aspirins. 'If the Germans came,' she says, 'we'd have dissolved them

in some milk and given them to our four-year-old to drink.' Alison
Wilson, a fifteen year-old girl in 1940, was later told a disturbing story.
'My mother said that she would have shot both my brother and me
if the Germans had invaded. She said she knew what these Germans
were capable of. And mother didn't make idle threats.'

A common reaction to the threat of invasion was defiance. Brenda
Winterbotham's father, manager of the Llandarcy oil refinery near
Swansea, wanted to send his twelve-year-old daughter to America to
pass the war in safety. A young girl with a highly developed sense of
duty, Brenda refused to go. 'I'm quite tough and he listened to what
I had to say.' Donald Browne's father, meanwhile, started teaching his
mother how to shoot an old Great War pistol. 'The lessons were not
successful,' says Donald, 'so the pistol was returned.' And when
Ronald Oates went round to a friend's house, he went to pick up
some carved wooden bellows. 'Don't touch them!' shouted the
friend's mother. 'Why not?' asked Ronald. 'They're full of pepper,' said
the mother. Her plan was to blow pepper at any invading troops who
came within range. 'I'm not going to let them get away with it easy!'
she told Ronald.

From some there was acceptance of a plain situation. When Walter
Miller said to his parents, 'We've lost the war, haven't we?' he was not
contradicted. Instead, he was told, 'You mustn't say that!' He took this
to be a tacit admission that the war, in his parents' eyes, was indeed
lost. And humour – which the consensus deems was so important at
this period – could amount to defiance or acceptance. Caryl Brahms
kept a Blitz diary full of observations. She records being cheerfully
greeted one morning by a warden with the words, 'Real invasion
weather!' and notes the following conversation with her close friend,
Jack Bergel:

In the evening, the Bergel told me that he had composed his speech
to the firing squad 'in case of invasion'. It was a good speech, he
said, not angry or bitter, but pitying. Suddenly a look of anxiety

settled on his face. 'Do you think they will understand English?' he asked. I planned to get him a German-English dictionary the next day, but in the morning the joke seemed a little too grim.

For Brahms and Bergel (who was killed a year later while serving with the Royal Air Force) a joke borne of defiance threatened to stray into acceptance.

A seemingly illogical – but common – reaction is noted by author Ronald Blythe. Fully aware of the corresponding strength and weakness of the British and German armed forces, Blythe expected an invasion. Yet – in the face of all evidence – he refused to believe that the Germans could win. Bernard Kregor was an ARP messenger boy in east London who would go on to serve valiantly with Bomber Command. As a Jew, he remembers fully understanding the implications of a German victory. 'We had no illusions,' he says, 'as to what would happen if we lost. No illusions at all.' But it never entered Bernard's mind that the British *could* lose. Such an outcome was simply *not a possibility* for Bernard Kregor. 'You ask me why I felt like it,' he says. 'I don't know. But I truly never believed it would happen.'

There are, of course, well-established psychological reasons why people might refuse to acknowedge a genuine danger. Freud identified *Verleugnung*: 'a specific mode of defence which consists in the subject's refusing to recognise the reality of a traumatic perception.' A modern pop-psychologist would call this *denial*. And the fact that it was so common suggests that it was crowded down the rabbit hole where rational faculties were replaced by optimism and blind enthusiasm. It was, as Oliver Lyttelton noted, Winston Churchill's rare skill to lead them there. And so a situation existed in which the government (through the mechanism of the Ministry of Information) was trying to provoke the people into a state of alertness by stressing the threat of invasion at a very real level, at which point the Prime Minister took them by the hand and reassured them that everything would be all right in the end.

One method by which the Ministry of Information was putting its invasion message across was through widely distributed leaflets. A June 1940 leaflet entitled 'If the Invader Comes' warned people that they 'must not be taken by surprise' and gave some basic rules for behaviour once the Germans had arrived. People should stay where they were, they should be alert for anything suspicious, they should not give the Germans any assistance, and they should always think of their country before themselves. In January 1941, however, Churchill's chief of staff 'Pug' Ismay expressed his concern, in a letter to Walter Monckton, Director-General of the Ministry of Information, that the public remained insufficiently 'invasion minded'. In March the Ministry was being urged to 'get the public keyed up to a proper state of preparedness' and a new leaflet – 'Beating the Invader' – was issued in June 1941.

Somewhat belying the government's attitude to invasion, however, was the Prime Minister's inability, in February 1941, to answer a straightforward question in the House of Commons from veteran MP for Newcastle-under-Lyme, Colonel Josiah Wedgwood. Colonel Wedgwood asked Churchill 'what exactly was to be the alarm signal for invasion'. Churchill replied, 'I hardly think that these matters are conveniently dealt with at the present moment by question and answer.' It was clear that he did not know the answer, and MPs began to laugh. Once out of the chamber, Churchill wanted to *damn well know the answer quickly*. But his ignorance suggests that, in February 1941, invasion was not a matter of the utmost urgency in the highest circles – whatever the Ministry of Information was telling the country.

It is also worth noting that in November 1940, Colonel Gubbins, the inspirational founder of the Auxiliary Units, and his chief of staff Peter Wilkinson, both left their posts to join the Special Operations Executive. Had invasion still been a priority, would Gubbins and Wilkinson not have remained where they were – as Britain's guerillas-in-chief – rather than being released to create a foreign resistance network? Indeed, as early as 10 October a Joint Intelligence Committee report was warning that the Germans were far more likely to employ their invading forces through the Balkans than attempt a 'hazardous' invasion of Britain.

Yet as the authorities ceased to fear an invasion, the public's fear was growing – as a glance at Mass-Observation's poll data shows. This data gives the percentage of the British population accepting 'the likelihood of invasion' at different periods. In the spring and summer of 1940, the public expectation of invasion was high (possibly as a result of the first invasion leaflet). It fell during the early autumn – which was, paradoxically, the period of the greatest actual threat. (This fall may be attributable to an outbreak of Churchill-inspired denial as well as to the fact that bombing had moved the war's focus beyond invasion.) Then, in the early months of 1941, as the government's efforts to 'get the public keyed up' started to take hold, the percentage of the population expecting invasion rose to an all-time high of fifty-three per cent.

Given this background it is interesting to learn of an Enigma message that was decoded at Bletchley Park on 17 September 1940 – just two weeks after the invasion spies had landed in Kent. The message revealed that Hitler had ordered the dismantling of air loading bays in Holland. This may have sounded innocent enough, but it suggested to knowledgeable observers that Hitler had called off the invasion – at least for the time being. Frederick Winterbotham, responsible for the distribution of decrypted material, brought the message directly to Winston Churchill in his war rooms. Churchill read the message, before turning to Sir Cyril Newall, Chief of the Air Staff, to ask what it meant. Newall replied that it meant the end of Operation *Sea Lion*. Winterbotham describes the Prime Minister's reaction:

Churchill sat back, smiled, pulled out a big cigar and lit it. He said 'Well gentlemen, let's go and see what is happening upstairs.' There was a terrific blitz going on upstairs. The whole of Carlton House Terrace was in flames, and the bombs were dropping all around. Churchill came up smoking his cigar and put on his tin hat. Everybody tried to prevent him walking out because there was so much metal flying about but he went out and I can see him today with his hands on his stick, smoking his cigar. 'My God,' he said, 'we'll get the buggers for this!'

One must be careful about placing reliance on the memories of Frederick Winterbotham. He has, in the past, been criticised for inaccuracies, chiefly, for asserting that Churchill learned in advance of the bombing of Coventry from an Enigma decrypt, but chose to leave the city to its fate so that the enemy would not discover that the Enigma code had been cracked. This assertion is not true – as John Colville, Churchill's Assistant Private Secretary, and a host of historians have demonstrated. But there are differences between the two stories. In the case of Coventry, Winterbotham claimed to have made a phone call to Downing Street, but he never spoke to the Prime Minister and could only guess at what Churchill was thinking and doing. In the case of the air loading bays, Winterbotham attended the Prime Minister in person, and has given a detailed and consistent version of the incident in his memoirs and in an interview with the Imperial War Museum. Not only this, but other indications suggest that the official fear of invasion had indeed subsided in the autumn and early winter of 1940.

Winston Churchill may have been relieved and pumped full of vengeful spirit by the revelation that invasion was not imminent, but the British people would continue to fear the enemy's arrival – encouraged by his government. And there were good reasons for keeping the bow taut. For one thing, the evidence on 17 September 1940 suggested that the invasion had been *postponed* – not necessarily cancelled. And this was indeed the case: Hitler did not cancel *Sea Lion* until 12 October. For another thing, the government could hardly risk allowing the nation's guard to drop. What if – and it hardly bore thinking about – its belief turned out to be wrong? And thirdly, a morale boost was badly needed with the Blitz raging and no end in sight. Common purpose in the face of a perceived threat provided that boost.

The German invasion was, it seems, a confused game of smoke and mirrors being kept alive by both sides – and the British public reacted in every possible way, from dutiful keenness to terror to lack of concern to denial. Fortunately, though, only four invaders arrived on the south coast. Three of them were hanged at Pentonville Prison, while the fourth may rank as the luckiest man ever to appear at the Old Bailey. But whether the jury's verdict was right or wrong, the trial of Sjoerd Pons should be remembered and evoked by those who value the principles of liberty and democracy.

CHAPTER EIGHT

The Enemy Within

In the previous chapter, we learned of the 1940 criminal trial held in secrecy – despite the objections of Sir Alexander Maxwell of the Home Office, who considered it an affront to democratic principles. Yet, in the same year, Sir Alexander's Home Office ordered the immediate imprisonment of tens of thousands of Jewish and anti-Nazi refugees, and then helped to organise the transportation of many of them to the colonies. An attempt to square these apparently contradictory approaches reveals a surprising story about the British government and the British people. And it opens a window onto a less well-founded fear that grew up alongside the fear of invasion: the fear of a 'fifth column' of concealed enemy supporters who were ready to rise up to assist the invasion.*

At the start of the war, there was little doubt among the British people that some form of internment was necessary. There were known and suspected Nazis in Britain, and while the overwhelming

* The expression was probably coined during the Spanish Civil War by General Mola. As the Nationalists besieged Madrid with four columns of troops, Mola claimed that a 'fifth column' existed within the city, made up of Nationalist supporters waiting to rise when the time came.

majority of refugees from enemy countries were clearly Jewish or anti-Nazi, it was possible that Nazi sympathisers – or even spies – might be concealed among them.

During the First World War, British government policy had eventually been to intern all male enemy aliens, and many – including the intelligence officers of MI5 – were confident that the same policy would be adopted in September 1939. This was not, however, the intention of the Home Office. Sincere in its determination to protect the rights of individuals, the department organised a system of tribunals to consider each case on an individual basis. It would have been far less effort to overlook civil liberties in the apparent interest of national security, but Sir Alexander Maxwell, his assistant Frank Newsam and Home Secretary Sir John Anderson were all determined to follow the more challenging and honourable path.

By the spring of 1940, 120 tribunals across the country had sorted over 70,000 enemy aliens into one of three categories: Category A numbered 569 persons who were placed in internment; 6,800 were put in Category B and were subject to restrictions limiting their movements; the 64,200 who were assessed as Category C were subject to no restrictions – as aliens friendly to the United Kingdom. Tribunal chairmen tended to be local magistrates and lawyers, who were encouraged to exercise discretion in their deliberations. Though the intention was to avoid harsh rulings, plenty of eccentric decisions resulted. In Sutton, Surrey, for example, the tribunal placed aliens who owned a car into Category C, and all others into Category B.

A number of tribunals dealt severely with anybody espousing a political ideology. Perhaps a consequence of the Nazi-Soviet Non-Aggression Pact, this resulted in the Category A status of a Jewish socialist who had fought for the Republicans during the Spanish Civil War, and a former Reichstag deputy who had spent several years in a concentration camp. Most tribunals treated recent arrivals with more suspicion than residents of long standing – meaning divided families. One young German Jew who had arrived in England in 1933 was placed into Category C as a long-term resident of good character. His father had been arrested by the Nazis after Kristallnacht and sent to Buchenwald concentration camp. But he had only recently arrived in Britain, and so was placed into Category B – with the result that he was not allowed to travel further than five miles from his new home in Newcastle.

Yet despite the lack of consistency, the system represented a genuine attempt at fairness. As the weeks passed, however, the mood of the country changed, as fear of invasion grew, and fear of a fifth column grew alongside it. This threat was taken very seriously, and British soldiers were taught to be alert to it. During military exercises, men and women were engaged to play 'spies'. Flirting in pubs or posing as farmers, they would chat to unwary soldiers, gathering information about the names and locations of their units – before unmasking themselves as 'fifth columnists'. One young officer even got himself a job as butler to a senior general. He served him for a while, before placing a chocolate box in the general's bed, with the words 'This is a Bomb' on it. 'The troops are learning,' wrote journalist James Lansdale Hodson, 'but more tightening up is needed.'

As Britain tightened up, strange events started taking place. When a young man with a fake identity card was stopped by a Local Defence Volunteer in Oxfordshire, he told his captors that he was a German spy who had landed by parachute. Claiming his name to be Franz Wilhelm Rutter, he was questioned in German, but appeared to recognise only the words 'Ja' and 'Nein'.

Under close interrogation by William Hinchley-Cooke of MI5, the young man changed his story, and revealed that he was really a member of the British Expeditionary Force captured near the French-Belgian border. In his prisoner-of-war camp, he had agreed to return to Britain, to carry out acts of sabotage. He was dropped by aircraft near Witney, where he was told to report to James Florey, a local farmer, who would provide him with explosives and detailed instructions. Florey, he explained, was a Nazi 'confidential agent'.

As a result, James Florey, an extremely well-connected man, was called out of a meeting with the Minister of Agriculture and placed under arrest.

'Why are you detaining me?' asked Florey, 'I am busy hay-making and want to get on with my work.'

'We have not got time to talk about your hay-making,' said an army officer. 'You have got to come with us.'

Florey, his wife and daughters, and his farm workers were placed in cells at Cowley Barracks in Oxford, while Canadian troops searched the farm for evidence. Later that day, General Edmund Ironside – the man responsible for the defence of Britain – arrived at the barracks, and ordered that the Floreys remain in custody. His order, he said, had the full backing of Winston Churchill.

Ironside changed his mind, however, when told that the parachute spy had changed his story yet again. Now he said that he was Leslie Jones, a deserter from a local anti-aircraft battery, who had once worked on James Florey's farm. This story was actually true, and Florey – having caught sight of Jones in custody – had spent the last few hours trying to convince his guards that the parachute spy was a fraud.

The Florey family was finally released after forty hours in custody – and General Ironside instructed Hinchley-Cooke to hand James Florey a personal letter of apology. When Florey arrived home, he found his farmhouse in a state of chaos. Items – including a wallet, a gold pen, and ration coupons – had been stolen. Food and drink were missing. Furniture was broken, private papers and photographs were shoved in the fireplace, and the locks on his desk had been forced. The house appeared to have been the subject of an 'extremely clumsy and violent burglary'. Florey's pigs, meanwhile, had been released and were happily flattening one of his cornfields.

In a letter to the government's legal department, Florey's solicitor claimed that while his client had 'no desire whatsoever' to take

The aftermath of two 50 kg bombs that fell on Vicarage Terrace in Cambridge on the night of 18/19 June, 1940. This was the night the bombs came to Cambridge – almost three months before the Blitz supposedly began.

The following morning, schoolboy Michael Bowyer cycled past Vicarage Terrace on his way to school. In May 2014, Michael returned to the scene of the disaster.

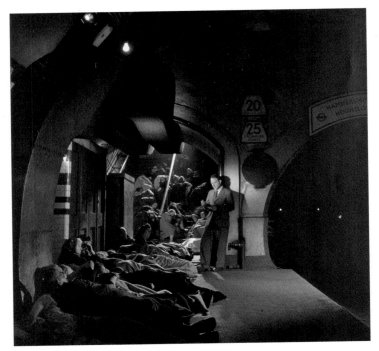

Henry Moore sketches shelterers in Holborn tube station in 1940.

'Women and Children in the Tube' by Henry Moore.

'A Parachute Bomb' by Matvyn Wright. The Thames skyline is silhouetted by fire as a landmine descends. Within moments, it will explode, bringing destruction to an oddly peaceful scene.

'Roof Spotters' by Anthony Gross. Another view of the Thames as two roof spotters scan the sky.

'A Balloon Site, Coventry' by Laura Knight. The presence of barrage balloons forced enemy bombers to fly above 5,000 feet; members of the Women's Auxiliary Air Force were first used to fly them in April 1941.

'Aircraft Production: Girls Working on Wings' by Leslie Cole.

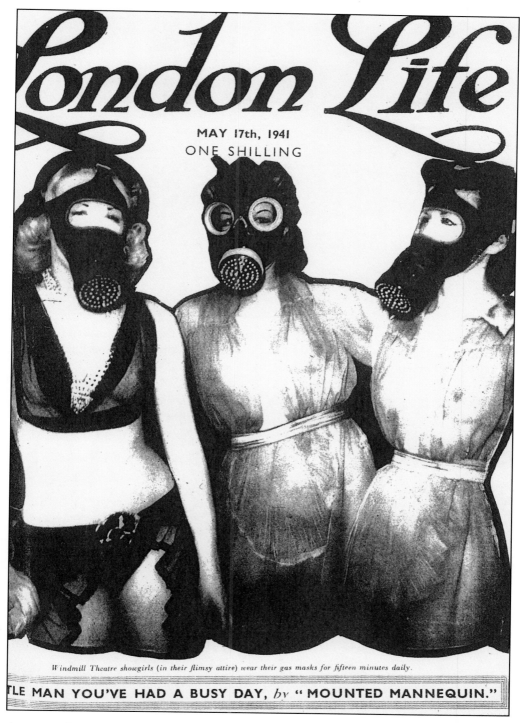

Windmill Theatre showgirls (in their flimsy attire) wear their gas masks for fifteen minutes daily.

TLE MAN YOU'VE HAD A BUSY DAY, by "MOUNTED MANNEQUIN."

A cover of *London Life* magazine from May 1941. 'Blitz Spirit' could be found in surprising locations. And surprising outfits.

'The New Oilfields in the Midlands' by John Ensor. As the people of Britain were making do and mending, so was the land itself. Churchill once described the oilfields of Sherwood Forest as 'the greatest secret of the war'.

WELL Nº 146
DEPTH
7473 Fᵗ

Wartime drillers stand proudly in front of Well 146 at Eakring.

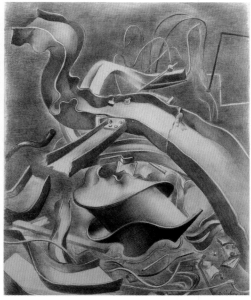

'A House Collapsing on Two Firemen, Shoe Lane, London, EC4' by Leonard Rosoman. This scene was witnessed by Rosoman, an auxiliary fireman, and painted from memory.

'Damaged Steel Girders, Bristol 1941' by Paule Vézeley. Vézeley's drawing blurs the line between abstraction and realism, reflecting the chaos and misrule of the Blitz.

'Road Transport in the Blitz' by Rupert Shephard. Searchlights light up the sky and lorries pull over to the side of the road as a raid begins. A visceral sense of the atmosphere and menace of the Blitz.

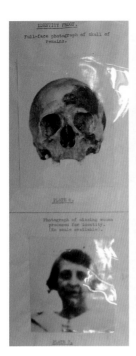

Far left: The remains of a skull found under a stone slab in a bombed-out Baptist chapel in July 1941, and a photograph of Rachel Dobkin, a woman who had been missing for over a year.

Left: When Mary Newman, head of the Photography Department at Guy's Hospital, superimposed one photo onto the other, the correlation was striking. And damning.

'Echo of the Bombardment' by Keith Vaughan. This work in watercolour, ink and crayon might be subtitled 'The Secret History of the Blitz'. The solidity of the buildings represents the outer strength shown by the people of Britain. But the twisted and deformed shapes spewing from doors and windows reflect the stress, the anxiety, the inner turmoil quietly experienced by so many. Ida Rodway – and countless others – might have acknowledged the artist's intention.

advantage of the government, this was a 'dreadful story' in which 'people of British blood' had been turned into suspected fifth columnists. He demanded compensation. In an internal memo, the government's lawyers noted that: 'The difficulty at the moment is that various people unconnected with the case have been putting into Mr Florey's head all sorts of exaggerated ideas about the amount he ought to receive, with the result that he is thinking in thousands while we are thinking in hundreds.'

In the end, a payment of £500 (equivalent to about £20,000 in 2015) was agreed – in spite of the Treasury Solicitor's dry observation that the amount far exceeded the level of damage. That it was paid at all reflected the growing fear of spies and a fifth column.

As the months went by, a new kind of fifth columnist activity began to gain currency – signalling to German aircraft. The *Daily Mirror* reported that Emil Wirth, an elderly Swiss man who had been in the country since 1912, and his English-born wife, had been seen flashing their torches skywards whenever an enemy aeroplane was nearby. The couple were arrested and remanded in custody – but released when it transpired that they had been falsely accused by neighbours with whom they had fallen out.

The litany of false alarms should not, however, mask the reality that spies were being caught, and that a limited number of British individuals were sympathetic to Nazism. George Wall was a twenty-seven-year-old radio engineer charged with recording information calculated to be useful to an enemy. When his house was searched, Wall was found to have copied the details of secret radio apparatus installed at an Air Ministry station on the Isle of Wight. During his Old Bailey trial, Wall alleged that he had collected the information out of interest, but circumstantial evidence counted against him. Witnesses related that Wall had frequently eulogised the Nazis, and given Nazi salutes. He had boasted that he would soon be placed in charge of the station, explaining that 'When the Führer has his grand march up Regent Street on his triumphal drive, those who looked after the Führer will get the best of the jobs.' And a Nazi armlet was found near the documents. Wall was sentenced to six years in prison.

For the vast majority of the war, the Germans' only spies in Britain were those controlled by MI5, but it seems that in 1940 a handful of undetected Nazi spies were at liberty. In April Albert Meems, a fifty-two-year-old Dutch livestock dealer, stayed at the Grafton Hotel in Tottenham Court Road. According to German records captured after the war, Meems was working for the Abwehr. The following month, Wilhelm Mörz was spotted in London. Mörz had been identified as a Nazi spy in Holland before its fall, and he was now posing as a refugee named Nowak. MI5 carried out a search, but he evaded capture and his case file was closed the following year.

Engelbertus Fukken, meanwhile, was an unemployed Dutch radio engineer who parachuted into Buckinghamshire. Posing as a refugee, Fukken made his way to Cambridge and rented a room in St Barnabas Road near the railway station. He failed to register as an alien, but remained undetected. When his landlady began asking awkward questions, Fukken packed up his wireless set and moved to Montague Road, a little over a mile away. The longer he stayed in the country, however, the more precarious his situation became. He had arrived with a limited supply of cash and could not apply for a job for fear of alerting the authorities to his existence. He had, therefore, to hope that the Abwehr would find some way of providing him with money.

In the event, Fukken's money ran out five months after his arrival. He packed his bags, made an excuse to his landlady, and walked into town. He left the bags – including his transmitter – in a locker at the railway station. And then he shot himself dead in a newly built surface shelter in Christ's Pieces, near what has become the Diana, Princess of Wales Memorial Garden.

While he was living in Montague Road, Fukken became friendly with Michael Bowyer's aunt Ruby, who lived a few doors down.

'He wasn't a spy! He was ever so nice!' Nazi agent Engelbertus Fukken lies dead in a newly built air-raid shelter in Christ's Pieces, in March 1941.

Michael remembers his aunt asking why that nice foreigner had killed himself. Michael told her that he was a spy. 'He wasn't a spy!' she said. 'He was ever so nice!' Michael smiles as he says, 'He should have gone to Auntie Ruby for money . . . She'd have helped him!'

It seems, then, that while the fear of spies and fifth columnists far outweighed the reality, it was not entirely fanciful. It was, however, deliberately stoked by elements of the press. The *Sunday Dispatch* was owned by Viscount Rothermere, a pre-war supporter of the British Union of Fascists, and a one-time admirer of Adolf Hitler. Rothermere's newspapers had previously argued for an alliance with Germany, but they now had to demonstrate patriotism – and how better to do this than focus on easy targets? Enemy aliens amounted to sitting ducks. And so, following the Nazi invasion of Norway and Denmark, the *Dispatch* wrote that Hitler had a fifth column in Britain 'made up of Fascists, Communists, peace fanatics and alien refugees in league with Berlin and Moscow'. Other newspapers took up the cry.

Lord Beaverbrook's *Daily Express,* meanwhile, took a firm stand *against* the supposed existence of a fifth column. On 26 April its editorial warned that:

> Witch hunting is a passion of the people. They are easily stirred up to it. Now there is every reason to believe that some interests in Britain are on the verge of stirring up witch hunts in various forms. Against aliens. Against the 'fifth column'. All liberal-minded persons, all who value freedom and liberty in life, should stand against every recrudescence of the witch hunt, no matter what form it may take.

Such a radical stand may seem surprising from a newspaper of the right – but as Peter and Leni Gillman have pointed out, the editorial column was Beaverbrook's personal mouthpiece, and he was, at this time, involved in a love affair with Jewish refugee Lily Ernst.

So despite the best efforts of the Home Office and the *Daily Express* – for rather different reasons – the people of Britain were being led to fear the traitors in their midst. As, it appears, was the Joint Intelligence Committee. This body was responsible for co-ordinating the work of the various intelligence organisations, before presenting its findings to the government and chiefs of staff. On 2 May it met to discuss the invasion of Norway and Denmark – which it had failed to predict. Having absolved itself, by blaming the invasion's success on unforeseeable fifth column activity, the committee then predicted that a British fifth column, though currently dormant, might well be ready to rise up 'at the moment selected by the enemy'. And it went on to employ some rather odd logic. 'The absence of sabotage up to date,' it declared, 'reinforces the view that such activities will only take place as part of a pre-arranged military plan.' In other words, it viewed the lack of evidence of a fifth column as evidence of a fifth column. The committee then prepared a list of twenty security recommendations for the chiefs of staff. At the top of the list was mass internment of enemy aliens.

It is important to note that two Home Office representatives were present at this meeting, and according to the committee's chairman William Cavendish-Bentinck, a 'first-class fight' took place between them and the committee members. Cavendish-Bentinck dismissed the views of the Home Office men as being based on 'political considerations'. For Cavendish-Bentinck and his colleagues, freedom and the rule of law were little more than bureaucratic annoyances.

With the press working on the British public, and the Joint Intelligence Committee working on the chiefs of staff, events began to take their course. Sir John Dill, Vice-Chief of the Imperial General Staff urged – on military grounds – the internment of adult male aliens along the coast in the south-east and east of England, from Hampshire to north-east Scotland. The Home Secretary could not resist. About 2,000 people were rounded up and interned on 12 May.

Andrew Gow, a don at Trinity College, Cambridge, was interrupted at lunch on that day, and told that three of his foreign students had been arrested. He accepted this, writing to a friend that 'it was the sensible thing to do, but it was uncommon hard on some of them'. (One of the students, he claimed, had tried to join the British army.) Yet in October, once they had been freed, Gow's attitude was quite different. 'The incompetence and stupidity with which the matter has been handled are beyond words,' he wrote to his friend. The Home Office had been guilty, in his opinion, of 'five months of shameful bungling'. Whether the fault lay with the Home Office or not, it is revealing to hear an intelligent man, who supported internment in principle, describing the events that followed as 'shameful'.

Those events began two days later, with the return to England of Sir Nevile Bland, the British Minister in the Netherlands. At the Foreign Secretary's request, Bland delivered a short account of Holland's recent experiences. He attributed German success to a fifth column. A German maid, he claimed, had led paratroopers to one of their targets. And he warned that the same would happen in Britain:

> I have not the least doubt that, when the signal is given, as it will scarcely fail to be when Hitler so decides, there will be satellites of the monster all over the country who will at once embark on wide-spread sabotage and attacks on civilians and the military indiscriminately. We cannot afford to take this risk. ALL Germans and Austrians, at least, ought to be interned at once.

On 15 May Bland's hysterical account was discussed in Cabinet. Sir John Anderson was still attempting to avoid mass internment, and he argued that a large-scale round-up would cause a public outcry. But the chiefs of staff were now pressing hard for the internment of all male and female enemy aliens aged between sixteen and seventy in every part of the country, and Churchill was sympathetic. Anderson was simply stalling for time.

In the midst of the fifth column panic, evidence came to light of a genuine threat to British security. Tyler Kent, a code and cypher clerk in the United States embassy, had started making secret copies of private cables between Winston Churchill and President Roosevelt. Kent was an isolationist who believed that the cables disclosed collusion between the two men to draw America into the war. At the time, Kent was sleeping with Anna Wolkoff, a virulently anti-semitic White Russian who was passing information to the Nazis. Through Wolkoff, Kent met Captain Archibald Ramsay, a Conservative MP and founder of the fascist 'Right Club'. Kent decided to pass the cables to Ramsay who could reveal them on the floor of the House of Commons. He therefore gave copies of the cables to Wolkoff to hand on to Ramsay. Wolkoff then made plans to pass them to Germany. Both Kent and Wolkoff were arrested and charged with passing secrets to the enemy. Found guilty, they were imprisoned for seven and ten years respectively.

The Kent/Wolkoff affair had two effects. One was to alert the country to the activities of the far right wing of British politics. As a result, Defence Regulation 18B was amended to allow the detention of those likely to imperil public safety. On this ground, a round-up began of fascists and fascist sympathisers – including Archibald Ramsay and the leader of the British Union of Fascists, Sir Oswald Mosley.

The other effect was to make fears of a fifth column seem justified. As Guy Liddell, director of MI5's counter-espionage branch, noted in his diary on 25 May: 'It seems that the Prime Minister takes a strong view about the internment of all Fifth Columnists at this moment and that he has left the Home Secretary in no doubt about his views.' He added: 'What seems to have moved him more than anything else was the Tyler Kent case.'

As the collapse of France approached, the Home Defence (Security) Executive was created, with specific instructions from Churchill to 'find out whether there is a Fifth Column and if so eliminate it'. The question of internment of enemy aliens was now effectively out of the Home Office's hands. Its efforts to run the show in a civilised fashion were at an end.

On 31 May chief constables were granted the right to intern any German or Austrian men or women where grounds existed for doubting their reliability. Ten days later, chaos erupted as Italy entered the war. With the words 'Collar the lot!' Churchill ordered Anderson to arrange the internment of male Italians aged between sixteen and seventy who had lived in Britain for less than twenty years. Over four thousand waiters, cooks and ice cream sellers were rounded up.

The Home Defence (Security) Executive was, according to Guy Liddell's diary, 'really pandering to the Fifth Column neurosis'. Such a level of paranoia, he believed, was 'one of the greatest dangers we have to contend with at the moment'. And as the country's fear of aliens grew (in parallel, it must be admitted, with well-founded invasion fears), a new strategy was adopted. For the first time in seventy-two years, Britain began transporting prisoners to the colonies.

On 10 June Canada agreed to take 4,000 internees, all of whom, it was understood, would be fervent Nazis – people too dangerous to be allowed to remain in the United Kingdom. And finally, on 21 June, a policy of mass internment was announced by the Home Office. Sir Alexander Maxwell, erstwhile defender of freedom, wrote to chief constables informing them that the government had adopted a policy of interning all male Austrians and Germans in Britain. The round-up began five days later. Over eighty per cent of those interned were Jewish; many were married to British women; even more had tried to join the British army. The arrests brought the total of internees to 27,200. Explaining the policy in the House of Commons months later, Sir John Anderson took full responsibility – but added revealingly that he had been responding to 'the demand' that all enemy aliens should be interned.

In the meantime, the first ship, *Duchess of York*, set sail for Canada, carrying prisoners-of-war and German merchant seamen, as well as about 400 Category B and C aliens. The next ship to sail, on 1 July, was *Arandora Star*, a luxury Blue Star cruise liner with 1,600 people on board – of whom over 700 were Italians, together with many Austrian and German Jews. Just before seven o'clock in the morning of 2 July, having rounded Malin Head, the most northerly point of the island of Ireland, she was struck by a torpedo from a German U-Boat. Over 700 people died – including two-thirds of the Italian contingent.

Two days later, the *Daily Express*, recently a preacher of tolerance, forgot its own sermon. Under the heading 'Germans Torpedo Germans', it described panic among the internees when they realised that the ship was sinking. The report was a recital of national stereotypes: the Germans were great hulking brutes who punched and kicked. The Italians were snivelling cowards who thought only of themselves. And the *Express* was not the only paper to take this line. The *Daily Mirror* quoted a survivor as saying, 'the aliens thought only of their own skins and fought in a mad scramble for the lifeboats.'

Yet on the same day that these reports were published, the Admiralty began speaking to survivors in order to prepare an official report. The most senior crew member, Chief Officer F. S. Brown, said that there was 'absolutely no truth' to the newspapers' stories. He saw no fighting and no aggression. The Admiralty's final report concluded that there was 'little or no panic among the internees'.

One of those who lost his life on *Arandora Star* was Mr Azario, a pet shop owner from Tooting. Eighteen-year-old Colin Perry wrote in his diary that:

> The pet man – as we called him – an Italian subject who had lived peacefully in Tooting for forty-two years, was immediately taken off in a police car for internment. His last words to his wife and daughter were: 'I shall never come back' … Somehow it just seems incredible that an old man who a kept pet stores in Upper Tooting Road has suddenly been snatched away, to forfeit his life in the Atlantic. I can see him now attending his pets …

Other ships sailed to Canada over the following days, taking almost three thousand B and C internees with them. And one ship, *Dunera*, sailed to Australia, although the people on board believed they were going to Canada. This ship contained most of the survivors from *Arandora Star*, and over two thousand Category C internees. In addition there were 320 men who had been on their way to a camp near Liverpool, but, due to administrative confusion, suddenly found themselves on board a ship. One of the Category C internees was the young Jewish man who had been living in Newcastle since 1933. As he was boarding the ship, he felt a sense of menace. The guards, he says, seemed frightened and angry: 'All the first lot of internees going on board had their suitcases taken from them. I saw, looking through one of the holds which was still open, these suitcases being sliced open with bayonets and the contents being thrown overboard.' Everything carried on board by hand was either thrown away or confiscated by soldiers. Identity and emigration papers were torn up. Later in the crossing, an elderly man threw himself overboard when he discovered that his passport – with its Argentinian visa and the promise of a new life – had been destroyed.

'The *Dunera* was not equipped to carry the number that it carried,' says the young man. The result was that people slept anywhere they could below decks, on mess tables or on the floor with portholes and hatches battened shut. There was no daylight and no fresh air – but there was a bucket to serve as a latrine for those being seasick or suffering from diarrhoea. When the men were allowed on deck, they could use toilet seats crusted with a mixture of salt and excrement. The food was often inedible. One man remembers removing maggots from his soup before eating it. 'Everything else tasted too awful,' he says, 'and the greatest delicacy was an occasional raw onion.'

There was an eclectic mix of people on board *Dunera*. The largest group was orthodox Jews, but there were also groups of Sudeten communists, and a band of arrogant young men with Oxford accents. The remainder, according to one man, was 'Jewish, half-Jewish, gentiles, with a sprinkling of Nordic types – whom we vaguely suspected of being U-Boat prisoners'. Among this assortment were lawyers, professors, doctors, writers, artists, photographers, designers, engineers, a grandson of Sigmund Freud, and an acrobat named Zeppi.

'The experience was a great leveller,' says one man of the voyage; 'we were all equal in misfortune.' The guards were members of the Pioneer Corps under Lieutenant Colonel William Scott and Lieutenant John O'Neill (a Great War Victoria Cross winner). When Jewish religious items were seized by the guards – some of which had been saved from wrecked synagogues in Germany – a rabbi who complained was threatened with being thrown overboard by Lieutenant O'Neill. An internee who complained that a guard had stolen his clothing was handcuffed and beaten with fists and a rifle butt. 'Now you will be fucking sorry you spoke,' the guard said. When a bottle was accidentally smashed on the deck, internees were made to run across it in bare feet. But one elderly man stood up to an intimidating guard. 'Try to touch me,' he said, 'and you will go overboard with me.' The guard backed down.

When the internees finally caught sight of Fremantle on 27 August, they were relieved to be disembarking. But their ordeal was not yet over. The ship continued on to Melbourne, where the *Arandora Star* survivors finally went ashore, and then to Sydney, where everybody else disembarked on 6 September. Australian army medical officers, who had boarded at Fremantle, were horrified by the filthy conditions and the sight of emaciated men dressed in rags. Their reaction plainly concerned Lieutenant Colonel Scott, who wrote a report justifying his actions and those of his soldiers. He explained that while his Nazi prisoners were 'of a fine type, honest and straightforward', the Italians were 'filthy in their habits ... and are cowards to a degree', and the Jews were 'subversive liars, demanding and arrogant' who were 'not to be trusted in word or deed'. This document must constitute one of the least effective pleas in mitigation ever delivered. Scott was subsequently court martialled.

In Britain, in the meantime, attitudes to the internment of enemy aliens had changed drastically. On 10 July the House of Commons had finally debated the issue of enemy aliens. Major Victor Cazalet, the Conservative member for Chippenham, opened the debate by acknowledging 'the tremendous public demand for the internment of practically everyone whose family has not lived here for a hundred years'. The authorities, he suggested perceptively, had been stampeded into the policy against their better judgement. And he went further:

We are now starting to pursue the Nazi policy of interning every Jew in this country. I think it is understandable, and up to a point, excusable, but what is not excusable is delay in sorting the cases and in keeping large numbers of people for a long time in internment, when they ought to be released and when there can be no shadow of complaint against them.

Major Cazalet was clear that the country's safety must remain its utmost priority – but he hailed its historical attitude to refugees as 'the brightest page' in Britain's history, and he warned against tarnishing that page.

Eleanor Rathbone, independent member for Combined Universities, cited the case of a sixty-two-year-old chemistry professor. The man had been imprisoned and tortured in a German concentration camp. On his release he had fled to Britain, where, after a year of research work, he had developed a process for utilising sisal waste for use in submarines. This, said Rathbone, was work of national importance. The professor's firm had recently applied to the Home Office for his exemption from internment – but in early July, two police officers arrived at his flat to take him away. He showed them his Home Office application, and asked them to wait until his case had been investigated before arresting him. They refused, and told him that they would return shortly. By the time they returned, two hours later, he had taken his own life. At the subsequent inquest, one of the policemen asked his widow whether he had been Jewish. She said that he was of Jewish origin, but had been baptised a Christian. 'What a pity . . . if we had only known before,' said the officer – who believed that being Christian was a reason for exempting him from internment. With these levels of bureaucracy and stupidity at work, 'it is about as easy to get a man out of an internment camp,' said Rathbone, 'as it is to pull a camel out of the eye of the needle.'

Mavis Tate, Conservative MP for Frome, took issue with Cazalet and Rathbone. 'In the case of certain members in this House, one has only to say the word "Jew" and they lose all sense of reason. I sympathise with the Jews but Germany has learned to make skilful use of them.' Given the nature of this intervention, it is interesting to learn that Mavis Tate would produce a moving and heartfelt interview for Pathé News, recording her experiences as one of the first people into Buchenwald concentration camp after its liberation in 1945. Her experience in the camp affected her very deeply, and may have led to her suicide in 1947.

On 16 July the Secretary of State for War, Anthony Eden, told the House that *Arandora Star* had been carrying only 'Italian Fascists and Category A Germans' when it was sunk. When asked by George Strauss, Labour member for Lambeth North, whether he was aware that *Arandora Star* had actually been carrying refugees who had been imprisoned and tortured by the Nazis, Eden could only reply that he would look into the matter again. And when in Cabinet, Neville Chamberlain, hitherto an enthusiastic proponent of internment, started expressing deep reservations about the injustices caused, it was clear that a tipping point had been reached. At the same meeting it was decided to release those actively hostile to Germany or Italy, as well as others whose internment could not be justified for any other reason. This amounted to the end of mass internment – after the imprisonment or transportation of 27,200 people.

Sir John Anderson broke the news to the House of Commons on 23 July. Major Cazalet thanked him for going a long way towards meeting his grievances, and urged him to begin examining individual cases at once. For while there were still plenty of aliens whom the police had not yet had time to arrest, the process of releasing those who *had* been rounded up would prove long and difficult. A host of committees was created, some tasked with recommending the release of internees in various categories, others with deciding who had been doing work of national importance.

The first releases took place in early August. On 15 August Winston Churchill was pleased to tell the House of Commons: 'I always thought it [the fifth column danger] was exaggerated in this island, and I am satisfied now that it has been reduced to its proper proportion, and is being gripped and looked after with very high efficiency.' Churchill's self-serving memory loss aside, it was clear that fifth column and enemy alien panic was dying down. On 22 August Cazalet pressured the government to increase the pace of the

releases, declaring that he would not feel happy 'either as an
Englishman or as a supporter of this government until this bespattered page of our history has been cleaned up and rewritten.' By the
end of the year, 10,000 internees had been freed – almost half of
whom left their camps to join the Pioneer Corps.

Recently released Italian internees working with a Blitz
demolition squad in London. 1941.

There were many across the country furious about what had happened. Marjorie Redman was a sub-editor at *The Listener* magazine.
In November she visited a German Jewish father and son who had
recently been released. The pair, who had come to Britain in 1932,
told Marjorie that they did not feel like aliens, let alone enemies.
How could anyone possibly suspect that they were Nazi sympathisers? Yet they had been sent to the Isle of Man in an overcrowded
boat and left on deck overnight in the rain before being allowed to
disembark. Other Jewish friends of Marjorie's had been arrested by
the police in the middle of the night, allowed to pack a suitcase
of clothes, and deported without their wives and families. 'Feel

ashamed when I hear all of this,' Marjorie wrote in her diary, 'because we think ourselves better than the Nazis, but these are like their methods we despise.'

There were others who felt differently – including some internees. On 28 September a letter appeared in *The Times*, written by Peter Wiener, a seventy-year-old university teacher. Wiener had been interned on the Isle of Man, and he wrote that he had been treated 'remarkably well' by his guards. He listed a series of improvements that took place while he was in the camp – the accommodation tents became less crowded, hot showers were provided, and a canteen was built. These measures were all 'appreciated very much' by the internees. Wiener concluded by pointing out that 'Britain is greater, stronger, more determined, and more beautiful to-day than she has ever been.'

On 3 October Sir John Anderson was replaced by Herbert Morrison as Home Secretary and Minister for Home Security. As we have seen, Churchill told Morrison that he now wanted a man of the people for the job. But beyond this, Anderson was paying the price for his shelter policy, and for the mess surrounding internment and deportation. Yet the latter policies had not been his responsibility at all. Anderson and his Home Office staff had argued tenaciously for more tolerance and charity towards aliens. They had been defeated by a union of the press, the military authorities and the intelligence community, a motley cabal which briefly convinced the Cabinet that extreme action had to be taken. Anderson and the Home Office should be cleared of ultimate responsibility for a policy that was not theirs – though they were left having to justify it.

And if Cazalet was right to describe this page of history as 'bespattered', the Cabinet nevertheless deserves credit for realising its mistake quickly, and acting while the threat of invasion was still very real. The very fact that Cazalet was able to argue his case publicly at this time was a testament to democracy. As was the fact that the government ultimately turned its back on the ravings of the popular press and the panic of its military advisers and intelligence services. To have done anything else, while fighting the Nazis, would have amounted to hypocrisy. Yet in the circumstances, its actions were courageous.

As British politicians today warn of the existence of a Muslim fifth column, and push for infringements of civil liberties in the name of security, they should be reminded of a time more dangerous than our own. Seventy-five years ago the government began to sacrifice freedoms. But respecting the words of Magna Carta – *To no one will we sell, to no one deny or delay right or justice* – it ultimately chose to do the right thing. Would a modern government do the same?

CHAPTER NINE

Bloody Foreigners

Before the Second World War, London was not a cosmopolitan city. In 1939 less than three per cent of the city's residents had been born abroad – and most of those had come from Ireland. But 1940 brought a sudden influx of foreigners to Britain, and their influence was most notable in the capital. Scandinavians, Belgians, Dutch, French, Poles and Czechs arrived in numbers, fleeing the Nazi advance.

Some came in unusual ways. Writer and humorist Caryl Brahms wrote of a wealthy new resident of Bayswater who had escaped from Nazi-occupied Norway in his luxury yacht. The man had gone down to the harbour, started up the engine, 'heiled everybody in sight', and sailed to England. He had later returned to fetch his girlfriend.

Some had culture shock. In October Maria Chipolina and Juana Lima, refugees from Gibraltar, pleaded guilty at West London Police Court to stealing from Woolworths in Fulham. When arrested, they both hysterically tried to kiss the police inspector's hand. In mitigation, they explained that they had never seen goods on open display in shops, and they had been overwhelmed by the temptation. The magistrate was unsympathetic. It was as wrong to steal in Gibraltar

A soldier and sailor of the Free French Forces attract
the attention of passers-by in Piccadilly Circus.

as it was in England, he said, sentencing the pair to fourteen days in
prison.

Many brought a hatred of the Nazis. Caryl Brahms recorded the
reaction of a Polish fighter pilot, serving with the Royal Air Force, to
the shooting down of a German airman:

> He had just come back from patrol and was terribly excited.
> 'Suddenly,' he said, 'I see a Messerschmitt. Good! Loffley! So I am
> on his tail! So I shoot him up – bupabupabupa – and soon he is in
> flame. Good! Loffley! Ah, but then he jump – bad, I say, that's bad!
> But it's olright! His parachute don't work! Good! Loffley! Okay!'

They brought changes to everyday British life. A young woman from
west London wrote to her friend in America that their arrival had
'the most awful effect on the BBC'. The programmes now seemed to

consist entirely of 'talks in Polish, Welsh, Norwegian and Czechoslovakian, services in French, Dutch and Danish, lessons in playing the mouth organ, and a little chamber music for left-handed players'.

They became scapegoats. Conservative MP Waldron Smithers noted that in the aftermath of air raids in Chiswick, accusations of looting were levelled at the local Belgian refugees. 'Upon investigation by the police,' wrote Smithers, 'the charges were disproved.'

They provoked racial concerns. While noting that Olympia was now full of 'cordiale' Frenchmen, publisher Winifred Musson wondered whether the arrival of refugees and soldiers of so many nationalities combined with the probable deaths of thousands of Englishmen would cause the British race to 'show a few startling changes in a few generations'.

They were influenced by British attitudes. Teacher Phyllis Warner met a Czech refugee who reacted to the Blitz by taking his money out of the bank. But when, after a few days, he realised that Londoners were not doing this, he put it back in. He was, says Warner, impressed by the locals' 'financial phlegm'.

And their novelty sometimes wore off. In September 1941 Caryl Brahms noticed a lot of policemen dotted around Marble Arch like 'perambulating mushrooms'. She asked somebody what was happening, and was told that King George II of Greece was coming this way. As she stood there, an old lady came up to her.

'Are they waiting for the Queen?'

'King George of Greece.'

The old lady thought for a few seconds. 'No thank you,' she said, and walked away.

But it was not just Europeans who came. From the colonies and dominions flocked soldiers, pilots, sailors and war workers. Before the United States entered the war, 125,000 Canadian troops had already arrived in Britain. (The soldiers who ransacked James Florey's farmhouse, for example, were Canadian.) And nearly 45,000 war brides would leave Britain to make new lives in Canada before the end of 1946.

Lance Corporal John Osborne was a Canadian military police officer in London during the winter of 1940. On 19 December he was on night duty at the Provost Corps headquarters in Covent Garden. In the early hours he received a telephone call from James McCallum, a fellow military policeman, asking Osborne to come and meet him at Southampton Row.

Osborne was an experienced soldier who had served in the First World War. He considered himself a friend and adviser to the younger men, and had lent James McCallum money on several occasions. He knew that McCallum was anxious to marry an English girl – but that McCallum's mother was refusing to let the marriage go ahead. When Osborne arrived at Southampton Row, McCallum looked disturbed. 'Hello, Mac, what's the trouble?' asked Osborne. 'Has somebody been knocking you around?'

'No, it's worse than that,' said McCallum. 'I've shot myself.'

'Where?'

'In the arm.'

Osborne took McCallum back to his room, took off his greatcoat – which had a bullet hole at the bottom of the sleeve – and sterilised the wound before dressing it. All the time he was doing this, he avoided asking McCallum what had happened. Eventually, McCallum raised the subject himself. 'I've always shot with the law, Ossy,' he said, 'but this time I've shot against the law.'

'What have you done?'

'I've shot a man high.'

'Is it serious?'

'I don't think so.'

As soon as Osborne had returned to military police headquarters, a plain clothes officer arrived with news that someone had been shot dead in a Covent Garden pub. A man had walked into the Coach and Horses and shouted, 'Hands up! Paper money!' Two revolver shots were heard, forty-two-year-old barman Morris Sholman fell dead, and the gunman – who was wearing an army greatcoat – disappeared.

Osborne was immediately sent out with Detective Inspector Capstick of Bow Street Police Station to make a trawl of local pubs for absentees, missing soldiers and other likely suspects. When his night duty was finally over, Osborne signed out – and thought hard about his conversation with McCallum. He decided to go and see Capstick. Together, they went to the Trafalgar Hotel in Craven Street where they found McCallum lying in bed with his fiancée, Irene Turnbull. 'The man's dead, Jimmy,' said Osborne. As Irene pleaded desperately, McCallum was arrested and taken to Charing Cross Police Station.

During questioning, it became clear that McCallum was under strain. A recent bomb explosion had left him with headaches and nerves. Granted ten days' leave to recover, he had decided to marry Irene, but a telegram from his mother – calling the marriage a 'ridiculous idea' and accusing him of being 'thoughtless' – caused him to cancel the wedding. And he was very short of money. His mother had long been financially dependent on him, and Irene was a new and even greater drain. At the time of the shooting, he did not have the money to pay his bill at the Trafalgar Hotel. This was why he had borrowed from Osborne, and why he had tried to hold up the Coach and Horses.

In his memoirs, Detective Inspector Capstick claims that Irene convinced McCallum to rob the pub and that the gun was discharged during a struggle between McCallum and Sholman. This is speculation – but it may be correct. A police report in the case file states: 'It is probable that McCallum shot himself whilst trying to swing one of the glass screens on the counter in order to find the cash register or to cover the barman. If such were the case the second and fatal shot may have been caused by his reaction to this wound.'

If this is what the police truly believed, then McCallum ought to have been charged with manslaughter. (There was no rule of 'felony murder' in English law, under which an accidental shooting in the course of a robbery could constitute murder.) But he was not charged with manslaughter; he was charged with murder, and his counsel, Charles Du Cann, ran a defence of insanity. On 13 February 1941 the jury returned a guilty verdict – with a strong recommendation for mercy. But the only sentence that Mr Justice Wrottesley was allowed to pass in law was death.

Two weeks later, the death sentence was commuted to one of life imprisonment. And on that same day, McCallum's mother died at her home in Quebec. It is unclear whether a telegram reached her before she died with news that her son's life had been spared.

At his trial, McCallum was given a glowing character reference. He was 'a sober and industrious youth' and 'an excellent soldier' who was 'respected for his determination to achieve efficiency'. His crime, it seems, was out of character. But he was under orders to carry his revolver with him – even while on leave. Here, once again, we see what happens when young men in difficult circumstances are given access to guns.

The Canadians were arriving in Britain in large numbers through-out 1940 and 1941 – and while they had, at this stage, relatively little actually to do, their inactivity does not seem to have led to large-scale trouble. A sense of their behaviour can be gauged from a series of reports compiled by the police authorities in Surrey during 1941. These reports give local updates on levels of crime and civilian morale – and they make frequent mention of Canadian soldiers and their dealings with the public.

In Weybridge, for example, the superintendent reports that 'there have been two incidents of drinking and disorderly conduct but noth-ing serious.' One of these incidents involved the arrest of five Canadian soldiers for disorderly conduct in an Addlestone pub. Particular bad feeling followed the arrests, when a Canadian major told the landlord that he needed lessons in how to handle troops, and that the pub would no longer be receiving his soldiers' business. The landlord, a man of forty-one years' experience, claimed not to be concerned that his pub would be deprived of the major's custom. In fact, he said, he welcomed the news.

In Woking, meanwhile, the Canadians were 'on the whole quiet and well behaved'. The only trouble reported was a soldier convicted of being drunk in charge of a pedal cycle. And in Guildford, 'relations between the Canadian Forces and the general public are very good indeed', the only problems being:

One or two instances recently of immoral conduct between Canadians and the wives of English soldiers, with consequent trouble, and the breaking up of one home, at least, but I do not know that one can attribute the whole of the blame to the Canadian soldiers concerned. The women must be equally guilty.*

In a letter to a friend, a woman from west London describes a Canadian soldier she had met – and perhaps gives a hint of their attraction to British women:

There was a Canadian, too, who'd left a £2 a day job in Toronto, a wife and three kids to join up and fight for the old country. He was a pet – and when I got up, he said, 'Well, I guess I'm sorry you're goin'. I was jus' gettin' to like yer.' It would take an Englishman three years of seeing you every day before he'd say something like that.

And as Canadians came to Britain, so did large numbers of West Indians. In September 1940 the Archbishops of Canterbury and York

* A Canadian soldier named Edward Fryer stationed nearby had a brief affair with local woman Patricia Clapton. The result was a child, Eric, who grew up without a father, believing his mother to be his sister, and his grandmother to be his mother. Eric became one of the most famous rock guitarists in the world. He never met his father.

Canadian soldiers on a day trip down the Thames.

wrote a letter to the *The Times*. Calling attention to British traditions of racial tolerance, they criticised hotels that were forcing black visitors to take their meals in their bedrooms, hospitals that would not admit young black women for training, and the reluctance of British workers to work alongside black workers. The archbishops wanted the people of Britain to understand that an individual's worth was to be measured 'by personal character and ability rather than by the colour of the skin'.

At the same period, a radio programme, *Calling the West Indies*, was being recorded by the BBC in London. Made for broadcast in the Caribbean, it featured West Indian servicemen reading letters to their families. Billy Strachan, a young man living in Kingston, listened to this programme, and to radio appeals aimed at loyal Jamaican subjects. He set his heart on joining the Royal Air Force and learning to fly. His problem was – how to go about it?

He first decided to make contact with a British army unit stationed locally, asking to be sent to Britain. He was politely informed he could find his own way there. His problem was a lack of money, so he went next to local shipping firms – run by white Englishmen – asking for free passage to England. None was interested until he approached the Jamaica Fruit and Shipping Company, the major transporter of bananas. Jamaica Fruit had ships coming from Britain full of people, but no passengers going the other way. Billy was offered passage for £15, a third of the usual price. He sold his bicycle and saxophone to pay the fare, and arrived in Britain in March 1940 with a single change of clothes, and £2 10s in his pocket. He was the only passenger on the ship, heavily outnumbered by bananas.*

At Bristol Temple Meads railway station, Billy was approached by a porter whom he saluted. His first impression of London was of buildings boarded up on every street. He stayed the night at the YMCA in Tottenham Court Road, and on Monday morning began his mission to join the RAF. After some enquiry, he discovered that the Air Ministry was based at Adastral House in Aldwych. He went eagerly along, and told the corporal on the door that he had come to join the Air Force. 'Piss off,' said the corporal.

Billy had not travelled four-and-a-half-thousand miles to be slighted. He stood his ground. A sergeant came to find out what was going on – and Billy tried to explain. 'You don't join the Air Force here!' said the sergeant. 'You're trying to take the mickey out of us!' But to Billy, the Air Ministry seemed the logical place to come. The sergeant asked where Billy lived.

'Kingston.'

'There are recruiting offices in Surrey.'

'I don't come from Surrey. I come from Jamaica.'

---

* It is commonly believed that there were no bananas in Britain during the war. In fact the Ministry of Food banned their import in November 1940, but they were arriving – on ships such as this – before this date.

The sergeant had no idea where Jamaica was.

Into the confusion arrived a passing pilot officer. 'Oh,' he said, 'you're from Jamaica! Welcome! I did geography at university, and I've always been impressed with you West Africans! Come in!'

Thanks to the pilot officer's ignorance, Billy was invited inside, placed in front of a senior officer, and sent for a medical examination. He was passed fully fit, and told to go home to wait to be called up. He explained that his home was thousands of miles away. Another argument ensued, before he was finally put on a train to Blackpool. Billy's Royal Air Force career was underway.

During his basic training, Billy was surprised to hear the reactions of the recruits around him. If they had been born in Jamaica, they told him, they would still be there now. He was called an idiot and a bloody fool. Billy, who had gone to great lengths to serve what he considered the mother country, could not understand these attitudes. And then one morning the corporal in charge looked at Billy and called him 'darkie'.

No one had ever called Billy 'darkie' before. He was angry and humiliated. And then the corporal said, 'Darkie, you are in charge of the squad! I'm making you my deputy!' One emotion piled onto another. Shame gave way to pride. Billy was regarded as a man fit to be promoted. He was to become a wireless operator and air gunner, flying thirty operations in Wellington bombers. He then retrained as a bomber pilot. When asked many years later about his experience of racism during the war, he observed that when one black person arrived anywhere in England, he was welcomed and treated very well. When two black people arrived, they were tolerated. But when three or more came, racism became sharp. It demonstrated, Billy said, 'this inherent fear and threat they see of this different animal'.

Almost six thousand West Indians were to serve with the Royal Air Force during the war, and thousands were also engaged in civilian war work, many at home, but a substantial number in Britain. Just as

John Wade from Montserrat, a lance corporal in the Home Guard.

oil was being drilled locally to lessen the demand on shipping, so Scottish timber production was increased to reduce reliance on exports. And where Americans were brought to Britain to drill for oil, 500 woodsmen were brought from British Honduras to work as loggers in East Lothian, Berwickshire and Dumfriesshire. But that seems to be where the parallels end: the Oklahoma drillers were treated with respect, the Honduran woodsmen were not. Their living conditions were described in the press as 'deplorable', their treatment was harsh, and the majority were forcibly repatriated two years after their arrival. Not all wartime volunteers, it seems, were fully appreciated.

Another group of West Indian volunteers came to work in the munitions factories of north-west England. Almost two hundred workers arrived in 1941, many residing in the newly opened West Indies House in Liverpool. As a port city, Liverpool had an existing black community of about five hundred people. In 1934 J. B. Priestley described the racial mix he found in a local schoolroom:

> There cannot be a queerer class anywhere in the world. The wooly curls of the negro, the smooth brown skin of the Malay, the diagonal eye of the Chinese, they were all there, crazily combined with features that had arrived in Lancashire by way of half a dozen different European countries, from Scandinavia to Italy.

The man responsible for the welfare of the newly arrived West Indians was renowned cricketer Learie Constantine. The first black man to captain the West Indies (if only for a single day of a Test match while the white captain was off the field injured) Constantine was now working for the Ministry of Labour as a welfare officer, based in the Royal Liver Building. Some of Constantine's charges

British Honduran woodsmen arriving in Scotland in 1941.

were young men away from home for the first time. 'We had to do almost everything for them as you would for children,' he later wrote. Others were experienced men with their own businesses, sensitive to any treatment they considered demeaning. But all were faced with an alien and often uncomprehending culture that often proved hostile.

One of these workers was Cebert Lewis from Jamaica. One evening he was standing outside the Majestic Cinema in Liverpool with a young white woman from his factory. He heard footsteps behind him, and a voice suddenly said, 'Your identity card!' He turned round, saw a policeman, and produced his card. The policeman guided Lewis away from the woman, and asked him whether he knew her. 'She is my lady friend,' said Lewis. The policeman then went over to the woman.

'Do you know that nigger?' he asked.

'Yes.'

'Have you known him a long time?'

'Yes, quite a long time.' She explained that they worked together.

'Do your mother and father know?'

'No.'

'What would you do if I went and told them?'

'If there is anybody to tell them,' said the young woman, 'it would be me to tell them.'

The policeman asked to see the woman's identity card, and told Lewis to move on and keep moving – but Lewis protested, saying, 'I am taking her out for the evening!'

'You black nigger!' said the policeman. 'What right have you to be going with a white woman?'

Lewis chose not to pick a fight, and set off back to West Indies House. Once he had gone, the policeman – who had still not seen the woman's identity card – made her empty out her handbag. The card was not there.

'Would you like me to tell your mother?' he said.

'Please, no!' the young woman said. She was frightened – and the policeman came close and put his arm around her. After a while he fetched a senior colleague, and they both asked her questions about 'going out with a nigger'. Eventually a policewoman escorted her to the police station where the questioning continued.

When Lewis arrived back at the hostel, he asked the warden whether the police were allowed to take the young woman away from him. 'It all depends,' said the warden, 'but what you can do is go back and get the officer's number.' So Lewis and a friend went back to the cinema – where they found the policeman now standing with his colleague. But he would not reveal his number; instead, he turned to the senior officer, and said, 'I've had a little bother with this nigger!'

'You are wrong if you call him a nigger!' said Lewis's friend as the policeman began shoving Lewis away.

'Move off when a policeman tells you to move off,' said the senior officer, 'because you niggers make plenty of trouble in this town.'

Eventually, Lewis and his friend went to the Prescot Street Police Station to lodge a complaint. They were told to wait outside as all the officers were too busy. They waited half an hour, before knocking again on the door. Eventually they went home. Lewis then raised the matter with Learie Constantine who, in turn, contacted the Chief Constable of Liverpool. The matter, according to Constantine, was eventually settled when the police made a verbal apology to Lewis, and the Chief Superintendent agreed to take 'steps to prevent any occurrence of a similar nature in future'.

A study of the correspondence in the relevant Home Office file, however, suggests a lack of genuine police contrition. The paper trail leads first from the Colonial Office to the Home Office. The Under-Secretary of State for the Colonies points out that Cebert Lewis had 'volunteered to come over to this country' and is keen to stress that 'colour bar incidents of this sort' can cause serious political repercussions in the West Indies.

The Home Office passes these observations on to the Chief Constable, who comments: 'I do not find fault with the police who dealt with the incident on 17 October.' He gives two reasons. Firstly, the policeman had previously seen the young woman in the company of a black man – and drew the conclusion that she might therefore be a prostitute. Secondly, when the young woman was taken to the police station, she admitted to having twice spent the night with Lewis in a hotel without her parents' knowledge.

Such a robust defence of the policeman – on the grounds of morality – makes a nonsense of the apology received by Cebert Lewis. The warden of West Indies House, Alex Watkinson, subsequently wrote an article in *Time and Tide* magazine which included the following:

> The volunteers were undoubtedly inspired with a real sense of patriotism when they came here. They really believed that Britain was in need of their technical skill, and that they were performing a genuine service by coming here. Their 6000 mile sea journey was no light undertaking, and they were not unaware of its hazards. It is not surprising therefore that they should have expected to meet with a certain sense of obligation in the Mother Country. This they have conspicuously failed to encounter.

It was not just in Liverpool that these problems were occurring. The Under-Secretary of State for the Colonies wrote to his counterpart at the Home Office warning him of many similar complaints about police behaviour in London – specifically in Camden Town and the East End – where 'coloured men from the Colonies' were being 'continually moved on' when 'talking together on the pavements'. The underlying problem, according to the Under-Secretary of State, is that 'the police are inclined to look on them as undesirables owing to their colour'.

Far from receiving the gratitude of the nation, it seems that colonial volunteers were treated as an unwelcome nuisance. This is not what the Blitz consensus would have us believe. Not *everybody* was pulling together. It is, in fact, a surprisingly early manifestation of a problem that would become familiar down the years, from Nottingham and Notting Hill in the 1950s to Brixton and Toxteth in the 1980s. Back in 1941, however, the Under-Secretary of State organised a meeting with Sir Philip Game, the Commissioner of the Metropolitan Police, in order to find a way of raising the status of 'coloured men from the Colonies' to make them 'feel that they are valued members of the community'.

In his letter to the Home Office, the Chief Constable of Liverpool included a copy of the guidance recently issued to the local police in order to prevent any future trouble with colonial workers. It tells us a great deal about contemporary attitudes:

> There are a number of coloured British Subjects resident in Liverpool under the protection of the Colonial Office. They are volunteer technicians working in munition factories and should not be mistaken for the ordinary coloured subject with whom the police now have to deal.

In effect, it is stating that there were now two classes of coloured subject. For political reasons, police constables would have to think carefully before racially abusing colonial subjects. But as far as *ordinary coloured subjects* were concerned, the police could still behave as they wished.

To get a sense of the experiences of 'ordinary coloured subjects', I spoke to Stephen Bourne, an acclaimed historian of black British history.* Stephen told me the stories of two mixed-race women living in London during the Blitz. One was his aunt, Esther Bruce, from Fulham. The other was a lady from Camden Town named Mrs Uroom.

---

* Stephen's books include *Mother Country – Britain's Black Community on the Home Front 1939–45*, and *Black Poppies: Britain's Black Community and the Great War*.

Dudley Levine and Sydney John, both from St Kitts, play cards at
West Indies House in Liverpool.

Stephen's aunt Esther was a working-class woman born in 1912.
She was the daughter of a black father from British Guiana and a
white English mother. Her mother died when she was five, and she
was raised in Fulham by her father, who worked as a labourer and as
an occasional spear-carrying extra in films.*

Esther's overriding memory of the Blitz was of friendliness and
community spirit: 'You'd be walking along and the air raid siren would
go, and people opened their doors and shouted, "Come in here, love!"
and they would give you shelter.' In 1941 Esther left her job as a seam-
stress to begin work as a ward cleaner at Fulham Hospital, and as a
fire watcher at the hospital. In the same year, Esther's father died as
a result of being knocked down in the street during the blackout. (The
blackout was a significant cause of death: Esther's father was one of
9,169 people killed in traffic accidents in 1941 – the highest figure ever

* One of his films, *Sanders of the River*, was criticised by its co-star, Paul Robeson, for
'showing the negro as fascist states desire him – savage and childish'.

recorded for a single year.) Esther was left on her own, until she was asked by a local woman, sixty-three-year-old Hannah Johnson, to come and share her house in Dieppe Street. Esther came to look on Hannah as a mother. Hannah's granddaughter, Kathy, says: 'As far as I can remember Esther was the only black person living in our area. She was part of our community. People knew her. She made friends with everyone. She was always chatting with someone in the street.' When Esther's cousin, Claude, arrived in Britain from British Guiana to take up work in a munitions factory, his first stop was Fulham – and a party was thrown in his honour. According to Esther, everybody 'wanted to welcome him because he was my cousin'.

Stephen Bourne is Hannah's great grandson. He was raised to view Esther as his aunt, and remained devoted to her until her death. Esther was, he says, born into her community, and entirely accepted within it. She never considered herself to be the victim of discrimination of any kind. The same could not be said, however, of Mrs Uroom in Camden Town. The daughter of a black West Indian father and a white English woman, she was married to a West African employed on demolition work. In 1941 Mrs Uroom sent a letter to Winston Churchill explaining the difficulties faced by black people. There were, she wrote, no decent places for black people to live. Landlords would not rent them rooms – while other 'nationalities' had no such problems. 'Can't something be done about coloured peoples?' she pleaded. 'After all, we are British subjects.' She signed off with the hope that Churchill would not cast her letter aside.

Mrs Uroom was invited to meet Colonial Office welfare officer John Keith, who drafted a report of their meeting. Mrs Uroom was 'an intelligent and sensible woman' who told him about 'the difficulties which working-class coloured people have in finding decent and reasonably priced accommodation in London'. She also explained the difficulties faced by black people in Camden Town who were often ejected from air raid shelters by wardens and policemen 'as if they were Jews in Germany'.

Keith was sympathetic to Mrs Uroom, promising that he would raise these complaints with the police and the chief warden in Camden Town. And he told her to encourage others with similar experiences to come and see him. As we have seen, the Colonial Office had recently received unrelated – but very similar – complaints of police racism in Camden Town. A picture emerges of a small community countering immense prejudice.

Beyond these two stories, Stephen Bourne points out that a number of black people were involved with ARP during the Blitz. Eli Box, for example, was a West Indian Royal Engineer who defused a delayed-action bomb in a Welsh garden. Described in the *Daily Mirror* as having 'nerves of steel', Box descended six feet into a narrow hole, lifted the bomb clear, and removed the fuse. 'He was as cool as if he was merely digging out a drain,' a policeman told the *Mirror*. E. I. Ekpenyon, meanwhile, was a law student from Nigeria who became an air raid warden in Marylebone. In 1943 he described his work and its problems:

> Some of the shelterers told others to go back to their own countries, and some tried to practise segregation. So I told the people that though I am an air raid warden in London I am still an African. I said I would like to see a spirit of friendliness and comradeship prevail at this very trying time in the history of the Empire. I further warned my audience that if what I said was not going to be practised, I would advise those who did not agree to seek shelter somewhere else.

H. F. Grey was a police sergeant stationed at Millwall whose racial views seem to have been altered by an experience during the Blitz. One night, in the middle of a heavy raid, he went to the front door of the station. There he saw 'the upturned black and brown faces and white eyes of several negroes'. One of them asked whether they were on the right road for Tilbury.

Sergeant Grey ushered the men inside (there were seventeen of them) and offered them tea and buns. They were Jamaican seamen who had arrived at a west coast port – but were crossing the country to board a freighter docked at Tilbury. It had taken them three days to reach Millwall, and the Blitz had taken them by surprise. They had not been aware that Britain was under attack.

They were shown into the cells where most of them went to sleep on the floor and the benches. As they slept, their skipper spoke to Sergeant Grey, telling him about life in Jamaica. 'He proudly stated,' says Grey, 'that public education had been known in that country for 300 years. I didn't dispute it.' When the sailors left next morning, the skipper handed Grey a coin commemorating Roosevelt's recent election – a souvenir of his travels. Grey was moved by the gesture, and says, many years later: 'I have often thought of that skipper and his crew. They were such a good crowd. It coloured and helped my race relations so much.'

Grey's final observation contains an implied admission that his race relations needed help. But this was unsurprising given that most white British people had never met a black person. Brenda Winterbotham was a young woman in London whose mother came to visit from Wales – and was surprised by the numbers of black people she saw. 'Of course it was easier for me because I was younger,' says Brenda, but this was not necessarily the case. 'Because we'd never seen many before, black people were a bit feared, like black beetles, black soot-covered buildings, you know, dark,' says a Bethnal Green factory worker. In the end, all of these reactions must be viewed within the framework of contemporary attitudes – and these were based on old ideas of British imperial dominance.

In order to justify its existence, after all, the Empire had to be seen to be serving a higher purpose than mere exploitation. This purpose was considered to be the bringing of civilisation to primitive lands and the teaching of child-like colonials to become *more like us*. The corollary was that people from the colonies were considered mentally and morally inferior to white people. 'It is in this cultural atmosphere,' wrote sociologist Kenneth Little in 1947, 'that most children in English society grow up. It is not surprising, therefore, that many of them absorb prejudicial ideas and notions concerning coloured people.'

Such a background of racial indoctrination was why *The Times* was able to publish an article, in June 1930, stating that mixed-race children in Liverpool were of below-average intelligence, that their moral standards were extraordinarily low, and that some of their mothers 'regretted the fact that they had brought these children into the world handicapped by their colour'. It is why, a year later, evolutionary biologist Julian Huxley wrote that there was 'a certain amount of evidence that the negro is an earlier product of human evolution than the Mongolian or the European'. It is why the *Manchester Guardian*, in 1933, could publish a letter stressing the importance 'of maintaining the actual and visible predominance and aloofness of the white man'. And it is the context in which we must understand all of our characters. The Liverpool policemen grew up believing in the inferiority and immorality of black people. Sergeant Grey was surprised and impressed by the humanity of the Jamaican sailors. Billy Strachan's RAF corporal was, in the circumstances, a progressive man. And Esther Bruce's neighbours learned to see beyond a stereotype.

When discussing the issue of race during the war, Stephen Bourne stresses that there was more than one truth. 'It's not all negative,' he says, 'and it's not all positive.' The contrasting experiences of Aunt Esther and Mrs Uroom, of Eli Box and Cebert Lewis show this to be true. Nevertheless, much of the story falls well beyond the consensus. A tale of racially abused wartime volunteers in Liverpool was never likely to be featured in a Pathé newsreel. And the subject of black people in wartime has, according to Stephen, even scared off modern publishers. One reputable company told him that the subject 'didn't fit the image of the Home Front that we want to publish books about'. Wartime discrimination, it seems, did not end with the war.

In a 2013 *Guardian* article about British fascism, author and journalist Will Self writes that 'there remains a sector of our society that still believes ... that black and brown people are inferior (while Jews are worrisomely and magically superior).'

That sector was very much bigger seventy-five years ago, and evidence of this can be found in the confidential reports produced across the country by Home Intelligence. This department of the Ministry of Information kept a close wartime watch on public morale and attitudes. A government-run version of Mass-Observation, its reports were collected from each of the country's ten civil defence regions. One series of reports gathered national attitudes towards Jews – and an examination reveals a startling picture.

In London Jews 'seem to have all the money nowadays'. The restaurants are 'swarming with Jews and hardly a uniform to be seen'. This is because 'Jews can always get out of anything'. In Brighton there is an 'intense dislike for the Jews' that comes from 'their low business morals' and the fact that 'they are not above administering a surreptitious and well-placed kick, if there is any difficulty in boarding a bus'.

In the south their behaviour is arrogant, tricky and greedy. 'After the war, England will be owned by the Jews.' In the east the black market 'is run by Jews', who draw attention to themselves, their girls 'looking like fashion plates ... with the rest of the community in slacks and overalls'. 'No wonder Hitler threw them out!' say people in the Midlands, while in the north Midlands, 'many have the sneaking feeling that Hitler, and those of like thought throughout the ages, were right. This is sometimes linked up with the Jewish rejection of Christ.'

In Wales the subject of Jews is a 'common conversational topic'. This is because they are 'heartily disliked and held in contempt'. The native Jews have 'hides of leather' and a 'knack of scenting good financial propositions', while the refugees 'expect better treatment than our own people'. It is not uncommon for a 'Jewess to elbow her way to the counter to be served'. Anything concerned with 'the black market has something to do with the Jews'. And 'why is it, when other nations have had to build up from scratch, are they allowed to come to established civilisations, start with all the amenities provided for them and drain the pockets of the natives in order to maintain an exclusive free-masonry of Jews?' In fact, getting rid of the Jews was 'the one right thing that Hitler did'. For 'the Jews brought retribution of themselves' and the time is coming when we 'will have to tackle the Jewish problem here as the people of Germany had to do'.

British antisemitism, conventional wisdom often states, is a quieter, more low-key affair than the noisier, aggressive continental model – a study in disapproval rather than hatred. That may be so, but many of the sentiments in these reports are shouted at high volume, not whispered behind anybody's back. And while it is by no means the case that the entire British population was speaking and thinking in this fashion, antisemitism was undoubtedly a growing problem – despite the fact that Britain was at war with the Jews' dread enemy. Indeed, there are very few positive comments in the reports. In the Midlands a lot of the problems were said to arise from 'envy in the general population' and 'abuse from those in competition' after the arrival of Jewish firms bombed out of other areas. In Ebbw Vale there were some 'very fine Jews' who 'take more interest in public welfare than other people'. And in stubbornly unchanging Northern Ireland there was said to be 'no Jewish problem', for here, 'so long as Protestants and Roman Catholics are so deeply concerned with their own quarrels and antipathies, antisemitism is unlikely to thrive.'

In the press many sought to push against the rising tide. J. J. McCall, in the *Glasgow Daily Herald*, criticised the hoary clichés that Jews ran the black market, controlled the banks, overcharged people, and were 'pushy and too damned clever'. Eleanor Rathbone, the independent MP for Combined Universities who argued against internment, published a pamphlet denying that Jews were less courageous, or that they avoided army service. She also pointed out that there were no Jews on the board of the Bank of England, and very few on the boards of the other principal banks.

Yet while it was important that journalists and members of Parliament argued against antisemitism, it is likely that they made little active difference to public attitudes. Prejudice against Jews was as deeply ingrained in the British psyche as prejudice against black people. The Jew (as most of the Home Intelligence respondents could probably confirm) was the dark exploiter seeking to take cunning, almost magical, advantage of innocent gentiles. Stories of his villainy were everywhere – and they could pass for children's fables. In September 1940, for example, a group was queuing outside a west London tube station when somebody told a story. A pub had recently been bombed, and while the rescuers were digging out the wreckage, they came upon an old chest containing 'hundreds of pounds worth of gold and silver'. It took twenty of the rescuers to dig it out, but when they returned it to its owner, he rewarded them with an insulting 'three shillings between the lot of them'. The owner, of course, was 'an old Jew-man'. 'Terrible, isn't it?' said someone.

And some stories might have been written by Dickens to show up the prejudice of the age. In October Lavy Bakstansky, the general secretary of the Zionist Federation of Great Britain, reported being robbed by a soldier who said to him, 'You are a Jew and you and your like will be turned out of Oxford!' before issuing threats and demanding money. Bakstansky gave a detailed version of the incident, before picking the soldier out in an identification parade. The soldier denied the charge, saying that he had never seen Bakstansky before. It was a case ideally suited to a jury, allowing it to observe the demeanour of two witnesses, only one of whom could be telling the truth. But the case never reached a jury. Despite there being no suggestion that Bakstansky had any ulterior motive in accusing the soldier, the magistrates threw it out at the committal stage, on the grounds that no jury would possibly convict. The golden thread of justice could not allow a Jew to be seen exploiting a brave young soldier.

Antisemitism was irrational, of course, just as irrational as the prejudice against black people. In his 1945 essay 'Antisemitism in Britain', George Orwell gives examples from among people of his acquaintance. An intelligent woman, offered a book dealing with Nazi atrocities, says, 'Don't show it me, *please* don't show it to me. It'll only make me hate the Jews more than ever!' A male accountant tells Orwell, 'These bloody Yids are all pro-German. They'd change sides tomorrow if the Nazis got here. I see a lot of them in my business. They admire Hitler at the bottom of their hearts. They'll always suck up to anyone who kicks them.'

And if these examples highlight the naked irrationality of anti-semitism, Orwell makes the point that the usual accusations made of Jews, of their low morals, their greed, their exploitation – the contents of the Home Intelligence reports – were merely attempts to rationalise this deep-rooted prejudice. When the crush in Bethnal Green tube station killed 173 people, for example, the story flew around London that the Jews were to blame. As we saw in an earlier chapter, the incident was caused by a series of chance events: nobody could possibly be blamed. But many intelligent people were willing to accept that it was somehow the result of a mysterious Jewish intervention. Just as the Liverpool policeman was looking for an opportunity to oppress Cebert Lewis, so anti-semitism was waiting for its chance to emerge. It was a neurosis looking for a trigger.

It found its trigger in 1940 and 1941. The sheer intensity of the period – the 'nervous strain' as Orwell describes it – heightened reactions and lowered inhibitions. We have already seen consequences of this, and we will shortly see others – but one was the re-emergence of antisemitism. And this re-emergence was one reason why the country – people and politicians alike – was willing to allow the mass internment of enemy aliens. Even those who protested loudly *against* internment were capable of expressing very different sentiments in private. Orwell writes:

A very eminent figure in the Labour Party said to me quite violently: 'We never asked these people to come to this country. If they
choose to come here, let them take the consequences.' Yet this man
would as a matter of course have associated himself with any kind
of petition or manifesto against the internment of aliens.

Prejudice against black people and Jews is one of the uglier
and less frequently discussed consequence of this time of extremes.
But these were not the only minority groups in Britain. In 1940
Connie Ho was a young mixed-race Chinese woman living in
Limehouse, London's original Chinatown. Thanks to *Limehouse
Nights*, a collection of stories by Thomas Burke, as well as works by
Dickens, Conan Doyle and Wilde, a romantic picture had been
painted of this mysterious corner of east London where opium
could buy oblivion. For Connie, however, it was never a place of
romance. 'I never liked Limehouse,' she says, 'it was very confined
and dirty.' She describes it as being full of shops, cafés, laundries,
tongs (Chinese clubs), puk-a-poo houses*, and a Chinese barber
known as Tipperary Tim who had learned English in Ireland and
spoke with a Dublin lilt.

Despite its literary notoriety, Limehouse was always a small community with never more than about five hundred people. Its families
consisted of Chinese men married to English women, and Connie
was one of many mixed-race children. When she was eight, her
English mother died, and her father went back to Hong Kong –
leaving her to be raised by a friend of her mother's. On the night of
7 September 1940, when Connie was seventeen, a bomb dropped on
the house opposite in which her boyfriend Leslie was living. Leslie's

---

* Puk-a-poo was a popular betting game among the Chinese. A player would mark off
ten Chinese characters on a piece of paper, and would win money if at least four of the
characters tallied with the winning characters. The more characters that tallied, the
greater the winnings.

house was destroyed that night, and Connie's was badly damaged. They were both safe in shelters at the time.

Soon afterwards, the Limehouse school was evacuated to a village north of Oxford called Wolvercote. Many other local residents – including Connie and Leslie – made the trip as well. She remembers knocking on almost every door in the village, until she found someone who would take her in. 'It was a typical English village,' she says, 'but it soon had all these Chinese children running about.' Connie stayed in the village until the raids on London had died down – and she has only good memories of this Chinese corner of Oxfordshire. She says: 'It was really remarkable how well the village took to having a lot of Chinese children. They all had funny names, but the people were very, very good. I never heard of anyone saying anything derogatory. They took us in and we integrated. There was no difference.' Leslie – who later became Connie's husband – agrees that there was no racism in those days. 'The racism against the Chinese came later on,' he says. 'We weren't obnoxious. We were rather passive. By and large we fitted in almost unnoticed. And there was no name calling.'

Connie and Leslie's story is a positive counterpoint to the rather murkier stories of black and Jewish race relations. And the Chinese community even had its own hero – Mr Wu. The subject of six songs written and performed by George Formby,* Mr Wu began life as a Chinese laundryman in Limehouse, before becoming a window cleaner. But once the Blitz was underway, he chucked his laundry and his window-cleaning. Looking 'cute in his new siren suit', he became an air raid warden, ensuring streets were dark. Mr Wu was a patriot, helping to make racism a thing of the past. 'If you've got a chink in your window,' sang Formby, 'you'll have another one at your door.'

Ah . . .

* At this time, George Formby was probably the country's most popular film star and entertainer.

CHAPTER TEN

The First Sexual Revolution

In later life, Quentin Crisp would become 'one of the stately homos of England', and 'an Englishman in New York'. But in 1940, having recently been rejected by the army as 'suffering from sexual perversion', he was an outsider. With his flamboyant dress, effeminate mannerisms and long fingernails, he was an oddity on the streets of London, often attacked verbally, and sometimes physically. At Holborn Underground Station, he was chased from a train, up an escalator, and beaten unconscious. But when the Blitz arrived, he noticed a change. 'Everyone talked to everyone – even to me,' he writes. But the Blitz offered Crisp more than conversation. It brought fear: an emotion he could trust as genuine. For the first time, the outsider started to feel engaged with life. As the ground shook, he took pleasure in walking the streets. And as he walked, he observed a city undergoing a remarkable change:

> As soon as bombs started to fall, the city became like a paved double bed. Voices whispered suggestively to you as you walked along; hands reached out if you stood still and in dimly lit trains people carried on as they had once behaved only in taxis . . . I was

surprised at the frequency with which I found myself sitting opposite some man who between stations decided to try to win fame,
like Mr Mercator, for his projection. The insult implied in these
offers of instant sex no longer troubled me.

And the change was not restricted to tumescent cartographers in railway carriages. As tube dwellers were descending to a world of primal
motivations, all manner of people were discovering one another. The
Blitz, quite simply, intensified sexual desire.

The author Peter Quennell and his lover, Astrid, watched a huge
woodyard set alight on London's Embankment. They stood entranced
as roaring flames separated into streamers, and dissolved into fiery
drops. When they returned to Astrid's house, a wave of bombers
came over, but the couple had no interest in taking shelter:

That night fear and pleasure combined to provoke a mood of wild
exhilaration. The impact of a bomb a few hundred yards away
merely sharpened pleasure's edge; and next day we wandered,
agreeably bemused, around the shattered streets of Mayfair,
crunching underfoot green glaciers of broken glass strewn ankle
deep upon the pavements.

A more chaste version of this story is told by Air Ministry worker
Mary Warschauer. She and her pilot officer fiancé spent a night sitting
on a bench in Hyde Park, a single tin hat between them, watching
anti-aircraft guns firing at enemy bombers. When a large piece of hot
shrapnel fell between Mary's feet, they decided to move on. There was
not a soul about, and they danced the polka up the middle of Oxford
Street. 'Who else in the world has done that?' says Mary.

But passionate responses to the Blitz were not restricted to
momentary visceral reactions. 'People had love affairs they wouldn't
have had before the war,' says Alison Wilson. In 1940 Alison was a
schoolgirl in London – and her mother was one of those people she

describes. Her lover was 'a Scotsman attached to the Ministry of Shipping who was sent to London. He was a married man with two children, and after the war he went back to his family.' Alison's father also took lovers – but these liaisons, she believes, would have taken place regardless of the war. Alison laughs as she acknowledges that her mother was a much nicer person for her affair. When asked why she thinks it started, Alison pauses for a moment. There was a *live for the moment* attitude, she says, because you never knew when you were going to be killed by a bomb.

'As the opposite of death is life, I think I shall get seduced by Rupert,' wrote nineteen-year-old Joan Wyndham, in her diary on 7 September 1940 – the day that Goering began his bombing offensive of London. As good as her word, Joan went to bed with her boyfriend, Rupert, the following night. For a few moments, Joan reports, it was 'bloody painful', but they were soon panting and sobbing in unison. When Joan opened her eyes, Rupert's face was covered in sweat, and he was making exhausted and happy noises. 'If that's really all there is to it I'd rather have a good smoke or go to the pictures,' she thought to herself.

The belief that death might be imminent was at the root of a great deal of unaccustomed behaviour during the Blitz. The number of illegitimate births in England and Wales jumped from 24,540 in 1939 to 35,164 in 1942. Incidents of venereal disease rose by seventy per cent over the same period. Author Ronald Blythe, a young man in 1940, remembers the Blitz, above all, as a time when inhibitions disappeared. 'I don't think things were better then,' he says, 'but there was a huge amount of adventure, excitement, and romance, because there was a breaking down of conventions.' For Ronald, the blossoming of passion and sexuality coincided with the breaking down of class strictures and the arrival of greater tolerance. 'London,' he says, 'was full of foreigners, and women behaved amazingly! It was a permissive period that was more secretive than the 1960s, and never quite admitted.'

It was not just the risk of death that made this first sexual revolution possible. Society was rearranging itself to reveal fresh opportunities. The blackout offered anonymity and excitement. 'Nature tapped out with the heels on the pavement an illicit semaphore,' wrote Elizabeth Bowen in her novel *The Heat of the Day*. The arrival of foreigners, coinciding with the departure of husbands, offered temptation – just as the evacuation of children relieved mothers of parental responsibilities. And even in the absence of direct danger, the routine of violence was raising the nation's temperature, releasing neuroses and bringing all kinds of extreme behaviour within reach.

In 1940 Lillian Rogers, from Tyseley in Birmingham, was the thirty-nine-year-old wife of a garage mechanic, and the mother of a seven-year-old daughter. She also kept a diary for the Mass-Observation organisation, which reveals that she had long been unhappy with her life. Lillian had been forced to leave school at fourteen to help her mother bring up her younger brothers and sisters. Her lack of education had given her a deep inferiority complex, which could manifest itself in feelings of superiority. She considered her neighbours common, writing that they were 'dirty skinned'. The sight of 'Hindus and most blacks' gave her a feeling of physical disgust, while she hoped that the Jewish area of Birmingham would be destroyed by German bombs.

Yet while Lillian was an angry, dissatisfied individual, she had long kept her neuroses concealed. She was a caring mother and an affectionate and thoughtful wife. Her husband was, according to her diary, an 'artist at lovemaking'. Her life would most probably have remained on an even keel, her darker urges buried, had it not been for the Blitz.

Following a series of heavy raids on Birmingham in November 1940, Lillian's daughter was evacuated away. Lillian soon became bored. She attempted to join the Women's Voluntary Service, but was intimidated by its middle-class members, and joined the ARP instead. Suppressed feelings began to emerge. She felt, she wrote, 'wasted and unwanted'. She asked her husband to take her out dancing. He was not keen, so she threw herself into the social life of the ARP post, where she became friendly with a married engineering worker named Clev.

Clev started coming to Lillian's house for 'tea and a chat'. Suspicious, Lillian's husband asked what was going on. Nothing, she told him, except that she and Clev were mutually attracted to each other. Lillian's diary reveals that she was very happy to meet Clev in the blackout – but she would not go further. 'I tease him, I tantalise him, he gets worked up to fever pitch,' she wrote, 'and then I tell him it's time he went.'

Lillian also started going dancing – without telling her husband – and this was how she became involved with a Polish soldier. One day she arranged to meet him at a dance hall – on a day when her husband would be at home. She solved this problem by begging her husband to take her to the dance hall, and while there managing surreptitiously to dance with the Pole without her husband guessing that they had met before. When she subsequently met a Canadian soldier, she told him to come to her house at any time. He did so when her husband was there – leading to a fierce argument.

As the war continued, so did Lillian's adventures. She was keen to complicate her life, and to tantalise as many men as possible without physically betraying her husband. 'I've a nasty mind,' she wrote in her diary. Lillian's problems were deep-seated – but the fact that her daughter was sent away, the arrival of outsiders, the mixing with the WVS and ARP people, the bombing itself, all of these served to release her neuroses. And the story has another element. At a time when the country was supposedly united in a common struggle, when everybody was working as one, Lillian wanted the freedom to do whatever she wanted. Her chief interest – as her diary made plain – was 'fun'. She seems out of step with her times. But in fact, she was anything but.

It is arguable that the national increase in sexual activity was a simple extension of the national sense of unity. Joan Varley was a young woman living in London. One night she boarded a bus, climbed to the top deck and sat at the back. There was only one other person up there, a man sitting at the front. As the bus drove through Westminster, Joan heard a bomb falling. Evidently the bus driver heard it too: he made a sharp right turn. As he weaved through the unscheduled streets, the bomb exploded elsewhere. But as it was coming down, the man had walked down the bus, sat next to Joan, and taken her hand. 'Neither of us spoke a word,' she says, 'and once we were through the bomb area, he moved back to the front seat without a word being said.' The man's action was entirely spontaneous, and would be welcomed by the consensus as a touching example of Blitz Spirit. Yet the intuitive companionship sought and shared in this moment barely differs from Peter Quennell's description of lying beside his girlfriend Astrid, after a night of lovemaking: they were feeling secure in each other, imagining themselves safe, their intimacy allowing them to forget the war. It was a coming together in more than one sense. And if the increase in sexual liaisons really was a manifestation of 'Blitz Spirit', then our modern sexual expectations are traceable back to this period.

A strikingly modern picture is painted in Marghanita Laski's 1946 novel *To Bed with Grand Music*. Published under a pseudonym, it offers an extraordinary insight into changing attitudes towards sexuality and the roles of women in the early part of the war. Its contents are, needless to say, far beyond the scope of the consensus.

The book begins with Deborah and her husband Graham lying in bed together. Graham is being sent to a military desk job in Cairo, and Deborah is upset when Graham tells her that he cannot promise to be physically faithful while he is away. He may be gone, after all, for years. But he is adamant that he will never fall in love with anyone else. 'I'll never sleep with anyone who could possibly fill your place in any part of my life,' he tells Deborah. She, on the other hand, promises that she will be entirely faithful. 'I love you,' she says, 'and even if I wanted another man, my love for you would prevent me from doing anything about it.'

In this way the scene is set for a tale that might have been illustrated by Hogarth. Bored and restless in her Hampshire village, with only her young son and her housekeeper for company, Deborah decides to take a war job in London. While there, under the influence of drink, she sleeps with a young naval officer. She is ashamed of her behaviour. 'I suppose it's you not loving me that makes the whole thing seem just filthy,' she says. The officer, however, is unmoved. He introduces her to a new morality:

It's time you learned something about the facts of life. I don't go to bed with people because I'm in love with them; I go to bed with people because I want them . . . Don't be a little fool. You wanted it last night as much as I did.

Following this encounter, Deborah takes a bath in disinfectant. But then she takes another bath, this time scented with perfume. She lies in it *'deciding what was best to think'*. This throwaway phrase represents a tipping point – for Deborah and for so many real-life British women. Exposed to danger, to opportunity, to loneliness, to temptation, to physical need – what should they think? And what should they do?

Deborah's response is to embark on an relationship with Joe, an American lieutenant, newly arrived in London. The pair behave as though married, and they start to socialise with other 'wartime couples' doing the same. To all intents and purposes this *is* a marriage, formal and permanent within the limits of the war, but with an understood time limit. But once Joe is sent abroad, Deborah slips into another relationship with an American named Sheldon. She never has feelings for Sheldon – she is merely trying to recreate her time with Joe. Her next lover is a sophisticated middle-aged Frenchman, Pierre, from whom she learns to become a good mistress. Pierre tells her:

I think it is a question of wanting always to give pleasure – of being always pleased and never asking for anything a man does not already want to give you, from a diamond bracelet to an embrace.

Before Pierre leaves London, he introduces Deborah to Luis, a Brazilian diplomat, on the understanding that she will become his mistress. While Deborah is seemingly living an independent life, in reality it is beginning to enslave her. From this point on, men come and go, expensive presents and meals are bought and consumed, while Deborah's emotions steadily deaden. 'There is no going back,'Deborah tells herself, 'nothing but going forward to gaiety and loss and loss.'

By the end of the war, the majority of 'wartime marriages' are coming to an end, and the men Deborah meets are no longer gay and witty temporary soldiers and civil servants but jaded middle-aged businessmen. She has outlived her time – but is now so corrupted that she conspires with a man from the War Office to keep her husband Graham in Egypt. The scheme fails, and as she awaits his return, a letter arrives in which Graham suggests that they spend a few days together at 'some big hotel like the Cumberland'. Deborah laughs bitterly, mocks her husband's bourgeois predictability, and tosses the letter aside.

To Bed With Grand Music is a morality tale – but it is not unsympathetic. It undoubtedly serves as a warning to impressionable young women (Deborah is only twenty-four years old) of the dangers concealed in the period's shifting morality. But it also paints Deborah as a very real character, raised to accept the confines of a middle-class woman's life, who is blinded by the sudden opportunities presented in terms of work, sex and love.

Sympathetic, too, are the descriptions of 'wartime marriages', those liaisons intended to last for the duration before being dropped (the sexual equivalent, perhaps, of powdered egg). Had Deborah restricted herself to this kind of relationship, the novel suggests, she might have remained morally and emotionally unharmed. Ronald Blyth remembers:

> One charming couple, they were engaged before the war, she was in London, and he was in the army in the Middle East. They decided when they got married, just after the war, they wouldn't ask each other anything about anything that had happened during the war. That was all in the past.

Thinking back to Alison Wilson's mother, there was similarly no expectation that her affair would outlive the war, or that either partner would leave their spouse. However permissive this period might have been, for the majority of those involved it seems to have involved a *suspension* of the normal rules, rather than an outright rejection.

This was the subject addressed by Noël Coward in his screenplay for the 1945 film *Brief Encounter*, an adaptation of his pre-war play *Still Life*. Laura Jesson, a married woman, embarks on an emotional but unconsummated affair with doctor Alec Harvey. The couple ultimately part, heartbroken, vowing never to meet again. Throughout the film, the viewer believes that Laura's dour but loyal husband Fred has remained oblivious to her passion. But the final scene contains an exchange that might have been written for any number of British couples in 1945:

> FRED: You've been away a long time.
> LAURA: Yes.
> FRED: Thank you for coming back to me.

The film was an acknowledgment of the infidelities that had taken place, and can be viewed as a timely warning – to Alison's mother, Ronald's friends, and Deborah Robertson types – that a line should now be drawn under this strange period of misrule.

Brief Encounter may have served another purpose, however. Its writer Noël Coward was hardly outspoken about his homosexuality. (He once said that he was reticent about revealing it 'because there are still three old ladies in Brighton who don't know'.) The film may reflect, in a coded fashion, the fear that life was about to become a great deal more difficult for gay men, for many of whom the war – starting with the Blitz – had proved a 'golden age'.

Quentin Crisp described heaven for homosexuals as being 'poorly lit and full of people they can feel pretty confident they will never have to meet again'. With its blackout, and the mass arrival of foreigners, the Blitz was a 'feast of love' laid on by 'St Adolf'. Emerging, one evening, from Leicester Square tube station, Crisp found himself disoriented in the darkness. Asking a passer-by what street he was on, he received a kiss on the lips – followed by the answer. Travelling on a bus, a while later, he feared violence when an Australian soldier boarded and sat very deliberately behind him. But instead of causing trouble, the soldier removed a comb from his pocket, and proceeded lovingly to comb Crisps's carefully styled hair.

Perhaps the most unexpected wartime development, in Crisp's eyes, was an enlightened attitude encountered at Bow Street Police Court. Crisp had been arrested by two policemen in Coventry Street, and charged with soliciting. When the court clerk began playing for laughs, Crisp feared the worst. 'You are a male person, I presume?' asked the clerk, turning away from Crisp to the public gallery, arms spread wide. And when Crisp's character witnesses gave evidence, the clerk asked them, in turn, whether they knew that Crisp was homosexual.

'Yes,' they all said.

'And yet you describe him as respectable?'

'Yes,' they said again.

Yet to the surprise of most of those present, the magistrate found Crisp not guilty, an effective acknowledgment that a man could be both gay and respectable. 'This was a distinction,' Crisp noted, 'that ten years earlier, would have been very difficult to make.'

Gerald Dougherty was a wartime ambulance and Light Rescue worker, who shared his memories of 7 September 1940 with author Alkarim Jivani. Having spent the afternoon listening to a Promenade concert at the Queen's Hall, Gerald emerged to a fiery scarlet sky, and the sound of aeroplanes and anti-aircraft guns. Coming to the same conclusion that Joan Wyndham reached that night, he headed for the Fitzroy Tavern on Charlotte Street, a pub known as a gay meeting place. 'I thought I may die tonight, I'm going to see what it's like,' he says.

Gerald was entranced by the atmosphere of the pub. He left with another man, and, together, they ran through Soho trying to dodge the shrapnel as it sparked on the pavements. When they reached Charing Cross, they found there were no trains running, and they climbed into the first class compartment of a stationary train. Gerald says: 'It was most exciting with the bombs dropping and the glass shattering and I thought this is the way to spend the first night of the Blitz – in the arms of a barrow boy in a railway carriage.

Author and publisher John Lehmann spent the *last* night of the Blitz in the Fitzroy Tavern. In his autobiographical novel *In the Purely Pagan Sense*, Lehmann's narrator leaves the pub after closing time on 10 May 1941: 'I found myself going home with a strange, tall, young man in uniform, not really my type in any way, but who had attached himself to me and seemed very eager to be picked up.' As the two men lay in bed together, bombs fell around them. Flames filled the sky, and firemen were busy in the street below. All the while, 'The young man remained on the bed, chuckling macabrely to himself and making Mephistophelian remarks from time to time. I began to feel I had taken home with me a demon sorcerer responsible for the whole phantasmagoric scene.'

There is a confidence to these descriptions suggesting a sense of (relative) freedom. Despite Quentin Crisp's problem on Coventry

Street, the arrest of gay men was no longer a police priority. Along with the general increase in sexual activity, the fact that public attention was focused elsewhere, and the arrival of foreign servicemen, this allowed homosexuality to become as visible as it had ever been – or would be for many more years. As Rodney Garland pointed out in his 1953 thriller *The Heart in Exile*, the underground came closer to the surface of wartime London than it had ever come before.

And in the armed forces, homosexuality seems to have been unofficially tolerated for the duration. According to one Mass-Observation correspondent in the Royal Army Medical Corps, it was well known that sexual activity was taking place in barrack room beds – because the participants were admitting it freely. Accounting for this, the correspondent wrote that recruits now came from all walks of life. Some were already 'well versed in these arts', while the majority had no other outlet for sexual frustration. The correspondent added that a number of men 'are definitely treated as females by the others'. These men sometimes wore make up, were known by female names, and spoke often about the officers and NCOs who liked to 'utilise their services'.

As sexual activity increased, so did awareness of sex. Ronald Gray was a young Royal Artillery gunner who found himself exposed to seemingly endless dirty talk from the men around him. 'I used to hear hair-raising stories of sexual activities,' he says, 'and I was still a virgin. I didn't know how to measure up.' To teach himself, Ronald ordered a 'sexual encyclopaedia' on approval. He studied it for a month before sending it back. It quickly proved its worth:

A sergeant was instructing us on the gun, one day, and the word 'erection' suddenly appeared. And, of course, there were giggles all round. The sergeant said, 'What's that all about then? Who can tell me what an erection is?' Absolute silence. I said, 'The male organ becomes engorged with blood, Sergeant!' 'Oh, very good, Gray!'

Increased sexual awareness had many manifestations. Working in a factory making military uniforms, one married woman slipped her address into the pockets of the uniforms with the message, 'Write to me if you're in the mood and I'll be in the nude.' Vera Reid, a young woman living in London, was approached in the blackout by a man she knew. Excited and emboldened by the darkness, he pretended to assist her, when in fact, he was 'trying his luck'. By the time Vera arrived home, he had unsuccessfully propositioned her several times – and fallen over a paving stone.

The increased freedom was discernible in mainstream entertainment. At the start of 1940, Chrystabel Leighton Porter – once the winner of a competition to find 'Britain's Perfect Girl' – spent her days nude modelling for art students, as well as naturist magazine *Health and Efficiency*. But when she was spotted by the cartoonist Norman Pett, she became the model for the *Daily Mirror*'s massively popular comic heroine, Jane. (She was a logical choice to play a character whose clothes consistently fell off, in front of groups of men, for no apparent reason.) In early 1941, as Jane's full potential became clear, Chrystabel began playing her on stage.

Her stage debut came at a time when the boundaries of theatrical decency were being pushed. In the House of Commons the eccentric radio pioneer and Conservative member for Chatham, Leonard Plugge, asked the Home Secretary whether he was aware of 'the spread of nudity on the London stage'. The relevant authorities were aware of the growing number of complaints, said Sir John Anderson – and Chrystabel's performances would soon add to these complaints.

Her first appearance as Jane came in *Hi-Diddle-Diddle*, an eccentric revue featuring 'an air combat in ballet with a darting Spitfire mowing down Messerschmitts'. Chrystabel, meanwhile, sang a version of 'In the Blue of the Evening' with other members of the cast. Before long, however, she found her theatrical calling – the *tableau vivant*. This involved standing on a small platform in the middle of the stage, and striking a series of dramatic poses – naked except for a few

Artist, model and cartoon. Norman Pett, Chrystabel Leighton Porter and Jane.

wisps of silk strategically placed. Each pose represented a different frame of a Jane cartoon. Laurie Pink was working as a stagehand when Chrystabel came to the Empire Theatre, Bristol. Disappointed to learn that he would not be allowed to stand in the wings as she performed, he cheered up when told that he would be assisting her: 'So there was a God!' he says. 'I had to lie on my back behind the platform and watch Jane pose. Each time the curtain closed, I'd take the silk piece from her and hand her another piece. Laying there on those hard boards I remember thinking, "What a job! What a view!"'

At the end of one show, Chrystabel appeared in a robe, which she would discard, leaving herself momentarily naked as the lights came down. Playing in Hull, the crew of an air-sea rescue boat brought one of their large ship's telescopes into the theatre, and trained it on her as she dropped the robe. The audience roared its approval. When her mother came to the show, Chrystabel told her that she would be wearing a flesh-coloured body stocking that would make her look nude. 'Lovely, my dear,' said her mother afterwards, 'but that body stocking was looking a bit grubby. Shall I take it home and wash it for you?' Sheila Davison, meanwhile, was a ten-year-old audience member. She remembers being 'amazed to see the nude figure of Jane'. Yet for much of the performance, she could actually see very little. Her view was blocked by rows of soldiers on their feet, shouting and whistling.

Chrystabel's performance was a startling development for its time. 'It was the war that made Jane,' says Chrystabel. 'Wartime audiences were wonderful. They were working hard and life was thin.' Stage nudity can certainly be viewed as a reward for wartime sacrifices – though probably aimed more towards soldiers and male factory workers than small children like Sheila Davison. Even in our modern sexualised world, the thought of a ten-year-old girl being taken to a theatre to watch a live strip show is startling.

An even more vivid example of the new freedom was the popularity of weekly publication *London Life*. As we discovered in a previous chapter, this was a 'lifestyle magazine' with an arresting emphasis on sexual fetishism. The cover of a May 1941 edition featured three Windmill Theatre showgirls dressed in their underwear – all wearing gas masks. A more powerful symbol of the sexualisation of the Blitz would be hard to find.

London Life was the trailblazer for magazines of its kind. By 1940 it had already been in existence for twenty years, but according to writer Matt Wingett, it loosened up during the Blitz, pushing the boundaries as far as it could. This, Matt believes, was down to two factors. Firstly, it became subject to weaker censorship. 'The censor's office was busy taking photographs out of the *Daily Mail* and the *Daily Express*,' he says, 'and it was not really bothered with salacious tales about people spanking each other in east London.' And secondly, 'People didn't know if they were going to be alive tomorrow, so they took their fun where they could.'

The fun offered by *London Life* consisted primarily of readers' letters, and home-taken photographs. A selection of stories from Blitz issues offers a flavour of the magazine. 'Yvonne', for example, writes in to share her recent experience of wrestling in the mud with her good friend Marie. Having shed their evening wraps, it seems that the pair began to grapple:

> Suddenly, Marie gave a twist and I was on my back. Although hampered at first by the slimy mud and stained underwear, she nevertheless managed to get her right leg between mine. Each time I squirmed she gave a tighter jerk, whilst I clutched frantically at her green satin undies. For a full five minutes she lay on top of me, tightening and loosening her grip alternately until I could feel the cool, wet ooze saturating through my black satin wear.

In among stories such as these, readers could learn about the folk customs of medieval England, the best ways to survive the dangers of the blackout, and other items of general interest familiar to readers of *Tit-Bits* or *Reader's Digest*. But the focus soon returned to more esoteric matters – such as Long Hair Lover's account of being woken . . .

> . . . to find myself enjoying the most delightful sensations. Thrilled beyond words I became aware that one of my Aunts was waving her unbound hair over my face. I next became conscious of a most exquisite sensation about my feet. My other Aunt had uncovered my tootsies, and was busily engaged in waving her head of hair over my bare feet. They had awakened me with the tickle of their hair: a thrilling experience.

Many of the letters involve recognisable Blitz rituals. Like Winston Churchill, 'Joan Rubber' liked to wear a siren suit. But unlike Churchill (one presumes) hers was made of latex:

> I wear lisle stockings in bed, and have a mackintosh siren suit or a long mackintosh skirt handy, according to whether I am wearing pyjamas or nightie. Then high-heeled rubber boots with a zip front, and a white mack with high storm-collar, complete my emergency attire. All very quick to put on.

'Mountain Mannequin' described her friend Joy's recent attempt to attach blackout curtains while sitting on her brother's shoulders. It seems that when the brother grew tired with the effort, and threw Joy down onto a settee, 'Mountain Mannequin' refused to stand by:

> I felt I wanted to be in this too, so before he had time to recover himself, I sprang right on his back, with a grip that made him gasp. Joy held him by sitting astride his neck. I worked my way forward as Joy slid off the loudly protesting youth, and I settled astride his neck.

The magazine contained advertisements for 'rare books' such as *Bride of the First Night*, *Sexual Life in Ancient Greece*, and *The Book of Nature (Illustrated)*. And there were photographs of cast members of the latest West End plays and revues, including a picture of future *Carry On* star Charles Hawtrey, surrounded by chorus girls, and another of actress Lynn Arlen framed by a pair of bare legs, anticipating the poster for the 1981 James Bond film *For Your Eyes Only*. Its caption reads, 'Apparently the photographer had fallen down as he took the shot through the legs of one of her pals.'

Some of the fetish stories were celebrity-based. Queen Elizabeth (the future Queen Mother) is complimented for her beautifully arched insteps. Some seem surprisingly modern. 'Admirer of Curves' wrote in praise of the fuller female figure, complaining that he was 'sick and tired of these skinny wraiths who have dieted themselves into bad temper and nerves in an attempt to get thin'. 'Ino' told of a twelve-year-old boy who had been dressed as a girl by his mother. At school, he wore gold earrings and a 'corset-waistcoat'. In later life he became 'a very prosperous business man connected with dress design and manufacture'.

It is very easy, in our post-modern world, to assume that *London Life*'s knowing style was intended to be funny. In fact, it was meant as a code allowing those who understood its meaning to fill in the gaps. To many British people in 1940 and 1941, the stories would have made little sense. 'Why on earth,' someone might have asked, 'are his aunts tickling him with their hair?' 'Those who knew, knew,' says Matt Wingett, 'and those who didn't, didn't, and that's why it was able to go on as it did.'

Matt believes that the magazine had originally been intended for an upper-middle-class clique – but that its audience widened as sexual activity increased and sexual awareness spread. For Matt, the growing numbers of readers' photographs printed alongside the letters in 1940 and 1941, and the fact that contributors were starting to refer to each other in their stories, confirms the magazine's role in helping people to connect during a difficult period. 'During the bombing,' he says, 'people were more keen to find something to alleviate the drudgery, pain and horror with a little bit of pleasure.' Perhaps, in the end, the success of this strange fetish magazine can be viewed, like the increase in sexual activity, as one of the less likely manifestations of Blitz Spirit.

There was, however, a dark side to the spirit of freedom. As sexual activity increased, so did incidents of sexual assault. Mary Warschauer, the young woman we last met dancing up the middle of Oxford Street, was approached in the dark in Victoria Street one evening by a man who pushed her backwards and forced her into a doorway. 'I was pretty strong in those days,' says Mary, 'and I gave him the hardest slap in the face.' The man reacted unexpectedly. First he spat at her like a cat, before gripping her shoulders and shaking her until her pinned-up hair fell down her back. He finally ran off.

A twenty-two-year-old WAAF, stationed in Yorkshire, was enjoying the opportunities offered by her new life. 'I learned to drink beer at the pub,' she says. 'It was a coming out for me. I was getting amongst the men. I was enjoying myself.' There was a particular man, however, a French Canadian medical officer, about whom the WAAF had a bad feeling. 'Everybody else used to wander away and leave me with this man. I didn't like it very much.' The feeling turned out to be justified: 'I won't say what happened, but to this day, I resent having to pay for my torn uniform,' she says. 'It wasn't done – but nearly. There was no point reporting it, it would have been his word against mine, and who was I? I think that happened to quite a number of women.'

Freedoms did not spread unchecked, however. Some individuals and organisations – including sections of the press – fought to maintain moral standards. Lord Rothermere's *Sunday Dispatch*, for example, was quick to warn the country of a small naturist organisation – the National Sun and Air Association – which was planning a Christmas nudist party in Cricklewood, in north London. The

Dispatch stated that 'Sailors, soldiers and airmen on leave will join girls in the WAAF' at the party, where they will dance naked 'to the latest "hot" swing numbers and also Boomps-a-Daisy'. For those who prefer not to dance, wrote the *Dispatch*, 'there will be the usual Christmas games, such as Hunt-the-Slipper'.

This strange report provoked a flurry of letters to the authorities. Cecilia Oldmeadow, an author of fairy tales, wrote to the police warning them that the nudist movement, 'so alien to our British ideas of dignity, modesty and reserve', might be infiltrated by Nazi agents. An anonymous letter arrived at Scotland Yard, claiming that the daughters of the association's secretary practised free love, and that the secretary herself would have sex with almost anyone who asked. The Archbishop of Westminster, meanwhile, received a group letter from the Catholic women of Malmesbury, asking him to do something about such an insult to God Almighty. When the party was held, the naturist servicemen present were actually outnumbered by nude pressmen, desperate for a story.

Investigating the nudists, Chief Inspector Leonard Burt, the future commander of Special Branch, was satisfied that nothing immoral was taking place at their meetings and parties. Indeed, he considered the *Sunday Dispatch* article to be more objectionable than their activities, containing, as it did, lies and exaggerations. As a result, he arranged to meet the *Dispatch*'s editor, Charles Eade. The meeting was cordial – but led to an editorial critical of the police. 'A newspaper is a historian of its day,' wrote Eade, 'and if it fails to report what is going on around us, it is not a newspaper.' In an internal memo Chief Inspector Leonard Burt anticipated the findings of the Leveson Inquiry by decades: 'If it be accepted that the newspaper is the historian of its day one would have thought that the editor would pay some regard to the accuracy of the matter that is printed.'

The press was not the only guardian of public morals. The Public Morality Council, founded in 1899 in order to combat vice and indecency, remained supremely vigilant throughout the war. Made up of individuals from the church and the medical, educational and legal professions, it dispatched observers to sniff out immorality wherever it could be found. In June 1940, for example, an observer kept careful watch over the public lavatories at Victoria Station, discovering them to be 'infested' by large numbers of 'male perverts'. The observer also noted that his previous reports of night clubs frequented by 'homo-sexuals' and 'black men' had recently led to a number of closures.

The council's main obsession, however, was prostitution. The same observer listed twelve Soho addresses currently in use as 'disorderly houses'. Another observer reported that as many as forty 'undesirable women' were regularly loitering around the surface shelters in the Bayswater Road. Desperate to catch one in the sexual act, he moni-tored a man and woman speaking outside one of the shelters. As they moved inside, he tried to follow them, but another woman stepped in front of the entrance. The observer hurried to the other side of the shelter, hoping to enter unobserved – but his plan was scuppered when the woman acting as guard called out a warning. By the time he was inside the shelter, the couple had separated – although the man appeared to be 'adjusting his clothing'.

A Public Morality Council patrol of Mayfair, in November 1941, established that Shepherd Market was 'over-run by both English and foreign prostitutes' who were established 'in nearly all the flats of the district'. This, in the council's opinion, presented two problems. Firstly, a substantial security risk was posed by drunken military officers speaking freely to the women. And secondly, the police seemed almost powerless to deal with the problem. They could not bring a prosecution where a single woman worked out of a flat. More than one, however, turned the flat into a brothel in the eyes of the law.

In the case of Yetta Lewis, the police were able to bring a prose-cution. Lewis was working out of a disused shop in Drummond Street, near Euston Station, which she rented for fifteen shillings a week. As several other women also worked there, it was deemed a brothel. The police report of a raid on the premises gives a bleak insight into the life of wartime prostitutes. The shop was described by the police as being in a filthy condition with soiled clothing everywhere. The rooms were lit by candles as the electricity had been disconnected, and 'sanitary arrangements appeared inadequate'. There was not even a bed, just a pile of bedding on a chair. Yetta Lewis had one previous conviction for soliciting – dating back to 1917. She might be considered one of the more unusual veterans of two world wars.

Some prostitutes worked in even worse conditions than these. James Morten was a Metropolitan Police officer who had joined the force before the war. He patrolled the area around Tilbury Shelter in 1940, and he remembers many prostitutes plying their trade there. 'Bearing in mind there was still a lot of horse drawn carriages about,' he says, 'the prostitutes used to be under the carts, on the carts, what have you, going full blast.'

Conditions could vary widely for London's wartime prostitutes. When Marthe Watts came to Britain from France before the war, her style of life was very different from that of Yetta Lewis or the drabs entertaining punters under carts at Tilbury Shelter. Marthe catered to wealthier men, and she charged higher prices. When the bombing started, she and two other French prostitutes (together with their maids) took furnished rooms at Ilfracombe in Devon. The local people, it seems, were unused to the sight of high-class foreign courtesans on the seafront. 'Everyone stared at us,' she writes, 'as we tripped along in our high heels and fancy shoes.'* Two months later, bored and running out of money, Marthe returned to London. She began spending nights at the Palm Beach Club in Wardour Street, where she met the Messina brothers.

Sicilian Giuseppe Messina had built up a chain of brothels in the

---

* In May 2012 actor William Shatner was discussing Ilfracombe on the satirical television quiz programme, *Have I Got News For You*. 'The place is laced with prostitution,' said Shatner to ironic laughter from the studio audience. Yet it seems that for a few months in 1940, *it really was*.

Middle East and north Africa during the First World War. His five sons now lived in London where they each lived off the earnings of a series of women. And with the arrival of so many troops and war workers in the capital, they were cementing their position as the most powerful pimps in London. 'Time was short, money was loose, and morals were out,' writes Marthe, 'and this, of course, is where I came in.'

Marthe had been told that the Messinas were charming people. And when she met Eugenio Messina, the domineering (and best looking) brother, she was, indeed, charmed. For a fortnight, Eugenio took her to the Ritz Hotel, to the Hungaria Restaurant, to the most fashionable spots in town, before taking her for a walk in Hyde Park, and asking asked her to 'join the family'. This would involve becoming Eugenio's lover, as well as his working girl. She agreed.

At first, Marthe's life was good. Eugenio rented her a room at the Ritz, and bought her jewellery and shoes. He redeemed a gold watch and fur coat that she had pawned. But the charm soon waned – and it disappeared on the night that Eugenio told her to sit naked in a chair. Earlier that day, he had seen her chatting happily to a young army sergeant she had met in Ilfracombe. Eugenio was a jealous man – and he punished Marthe by whipping her furiously with a length of lighting cable.

In her professional life, Marthe was presented with a draconian set of rules. She was not allowed to spend more than ten minutes with a client; breaking this rule, even by a minute, brought a punch or a slap from Eugenio. But as ten minutes left many punters unsatisfied, the police were often called to remove angry clients. Another rule forbade Marthe from removing her clothes with clients. On one occasion, this caused an angry soldier to pull a gun on her. She defused the tension by giving him his money back, which, in turn, made Eugenio angry. Other restrictions prohibited Marthe from smoking, from going out alone, from wearing low necklines, even from looking at magazines containing pictures of men. One evening, she met a Royal Marine officer on Piccadilly who was limping with a leg injury. To help him along,

Marthe walked with his arm in hers. When Eugenio was told, he hit her for 'walking with the client in an affectionate fashion'.

While Marthe and Eugenio's two other prostitutes were working from an address in Duke Street, the house was raided. No mention was made to the police of Eugenio. Instead, one of the women pleaded guilty to keeping a brothel. They were then moved to different premises in St James's Place, where care was taken that only one woman was ever inside the house at any given time. They slept together at a different address, however, which was damaged by a flying bomb later in the war. Marthe writes: 'We were fortunate that our rooms were at the back of the house, otherwise we would have been seriously injured. As it was, we were badly dazed, and when the rescue squads arrived, they were not a little surprised to find three almost nude women running around in a bewildered state.'

Stan Poole, meanwhile, was a wartime member of the Auxiliary Fire Service in London. In 2001 he gave an interview to Peter Hart of the Imperial War Museum in which he recalls entering a damaged house in the West End: 'Up the stairs and in the back, there were three women. They didn't have any clothes on! Whether they'd been blown off them or they'd got up in a panic, I don't know. "Come on out!" I said. My language was a bit stronger than that.' It is tempting to think that Marthe Watts and Stan Poole are recalling the same incident – with a deep lack of mutual understanding.

From straight encounters to gay relationships, from the theatre to magazines, from prostitutes to frustrated soldiers, it seems that Britain's moral and sexual life was profoundly affected by the Blitz and wartime conditions. The spirit that drove people to speak to each other on the bus was the same spirit that drove them to hold each other at night. Fear, opportunity, and reward played their part. 'War is a prolonged passionate act,' wrote the author Elizabeth Bowen, 'and we were involved in it.' In fact, huge numbers of people were involved in it, a few of whom we have met. It also provided readers for *London Life*, clients for Marthe Watts, and dangers for all sorts of women.

But as the war was coming to an end, the authorities were very keen to slam the door on the new freedoms, and to revert to pre-war standards of morality. In July 1945 the Archbishop of Canterbury, Geoffrey Fisher, gave a sermon urging Britons to turn away from wartime immorality and sexual indulgence, and to re-embrace Christian lives. A few days later, David R. Mace, the secretary of the Marriage Guidance Council, set out the authorities' case in the *Spectator*. 'Never in human history,' he wrote, 'has family life suffered disintegration upon a scale commensurate with that which the past six years has witnessed.' War had encouraged hedonism; it had promoted romantic love and suppressed solid family life. The result was that one in eight babies was now being born out of wedlock (and one in four *first* babies). And he went further: women were now on the horns of a cruel dilemma. Should they prioritise marriage or career? This predicament, he believed, together with the free availability of birth control, and the decline of religious faith, had served to lower standards of sexual behaviour. Mace wanted a return to chastity and fidelity – and he stressed how this could be achieved: 'We must inculcate through every educational agency at our disposal, sound values and high ideals.' In other words, the nation must be reconditioned to pre-war values.

And this, more or less, was what happened. The marriage rate leapt by fifty per cent in 1946 as the family ideal flourished. Women were encouraged to leave their newly found workplaces, to return to their old lives, and to engage with maternal responsibilities. The media focused on traditional female roles, feminine fashions returned, and government childcare support was reduced.

And the fact was that many ordinary people were as keen as the authorities to return to old values. In 1951 anthropologist Geoffrey Gorer conducted a large-scale social survey, using over 10,000 readers of the *People* newspaper as his sample; their answers demonstrated an overall belief in the importance of marriage and family life over love and sexual satisfaction. The survey also found that fifty-two per cent of people were opposed to any pre-marital sexual experience for men, and sixty-three per cent for women.

Perhaps it is not surprising, therefore, that the post-war period saw reactions against many freedoms. An attack was mounted, for example, on saucy seaside postcards. In 1953 an astonishing 32,603 cards were ordered destroyed by magistrates.* Far more sinister, however, was the attack on homosexuality. With greater manpower now available, the police stepped up surveillance operations, and huge numbers of prosecutions resulted. In 1952, the year in which Alan Turing pleaded guilty to gross indecency, 3,757 people were convicted of homosexual offences – compared with 956 in 1938. This police activity was encouraged by the lawmakers. Referring with satisfaction to the numbers convicted, Home Secretary Sir David Maxwell Fyfe told the House of Commons in December 1953 that: 'Homosexuals in general are exhibitionists and proselytisers and are a danger to others, especially the young, and so long as I hold the office of Home Secretary I shall give no countenance to the view that they should not be prevented from being such a danger.' Not until the publication of the Wolfenden Report in 1957 would official attitudes begin to soften.

The moral change started by the Blitz had been induced by transitory conditions and short-lived opportunities. It had a limited shelf life, and the authorities (and many citizens) were keen to reverse it. But this reversal was itself temporary. Freedoms had been too widely tasted to be forgotten. The family values of the fifties duly gave way to the permissiveness of the sixties – at which point the youngsters who had experienced so much during the war had grown into middle-aged authority figures, with their own fond memories. The Woodstock generation may have thought they were inventing sex – but, in truth, they were following a wartime path.

---

* According to a Blackpool police officer, a plain clothes officer would buy a card and ask the shopkeeper whether he would send this particular card to his daughter. If the answer was 'no', then 'a prosecution may follow'.

CHAPTER ELEVEN

We're All Criminals Now

Coventry, as we have seen, received an attack of unprecedented ferocity on 14 November 1940. Initially the city reeled in shock – but salved by a combination of courage and necessity, its wounds were soon healing. It was not a smooth recuperation. Many problems arose after the raid. One was the lack of available housing. Another – a problem in the eyes of the authorities, at least – was the nightly migration out of the city. But among the most serious was the outbreak of crime.

We last met Jack Miller, an eighteen-year-old in the King's Own Royal Regiment, on the night of the raid. His company had been sent into Coventry to assist with rescue operations. At about midnight, he was shocked to find dead firemen with 'sand-encrusted' faces in the cathedral. But as his platoon went about its grim business, Jack's fellow soldiers went beyond their official duties:

> Sergeants, corporals, men, they went into a jewellery shop, they
> went into every shop. There was no police around – or perhaps they
> were elsewhere. This was very adjacent to the Cathedral. I don't
> think the others noticed us, it was so frenetic. It was only small

stuff, wrist watches and things. What they wanted was money because boozing and women were the *raison d'êtres* for soldiers.

Of the platoon, only Jack and one other did not loot. The men were stationed at Perry Barr in Birmingham, and when that area was bombed in 1941, Jack watched a soldier frantically 'trying to open a cash till that had fused shut'. And these were not exceptional acts. This was common behaviour. In Coventry, after the raid, all manner of thieves with all kinds of motives helped themselves. A thirty-seven-year-old watchman was sentenced to twenty-eight days' hard labour for attempting to break into a butcher's shop because he 'was very hungry'. A twenty-five-year-old Irish labourer of no fixed abode was given the same sentence for taking five bottles of beer from a factory on Windsor Street. A homeless electrician's mate was fined £3 for taking an overcoat from a pensioner's house because he was cold. Edward Crich, a twenty-eight-year-old engineer, was sentenced to three months' hard labour for stealing a Georgian church register from the ruins of the cathedral. 'It is not manly for people to come here to collect souvenirs,' the magistrate told him.

These are interesting cases. In a previous chapter, we learned of the hardships faced by Coventrians; one can certainly sympathise with a homeless person taking food or a coat. It is less easy to excuse soldiers raiding a jewellery shop, or a man travelling nearly forty miles to help himself to memorabilia from the ruined cathedral. But taken together, they offer a hint of the staggering range of Blitz crimes, committed for no end of reasons. Some, indeed, were committed for no reason at all – by men and women who did not know that they were breaking the law.

At the root of the inadvertent crime wave was the Emergency Powers (Defence) Act, passed in August 1939. Overriding the system of Parliamentary sovereignty, it allowed the government to introduce any laws considered necessary 'for the public safety, the defence of the realm, the maintenance of public order, and the effective prosecution of the war'. The resulting laws were known as Defence Regulations. So many regulations were introduced, covering so many areas, that large numbers of God-fearing, law-abiding British citizens were turned into criminals.

Writing in *The Modern Law Review*, Professor Arthur Berriedale Keith criticised the introduction of regulations that were 'natural under a totalitarian regime, but almost inexcusable in a country which respects freedom, and which claims to have taken up arms to vindicate liberty'. Protests by politicians of all parties led to the rewriting of a number of regulations. Nevertheless, the vague wording of some, the zeal with which they were often enforced, and the fact that they were offences of strict liability (meaning that someone could be guilty without knowing that they were breaking the law – or even that a law existed) led to some very aggrieved defendants.

Brenda Winterbotham was a young woman living near Swansea whose father ran the Llandarcy oil refinery. In 1941, when an air raid set fire to five of its storage tanks, he oversaw the operation which saved it. But thanks to the Defence Regulations, Brenda's mother became a criminal. Her crime was to buy a chicken from a fishmonger who had failed to weight it before selling it. Unfortunately, an inspector happened to be present. Brenda explains:

> My father was very ill at this time, and he wasn't eating much, so my mother was desperate to have the chicken so that she could boil down the bones. Even if she ended up in jail, she said that she was jolly well going to have that chicken! So she wouldn't let the inspector take it away! There was a bit of the scrap in the shop . . .

The case went to court, and Brenda's mother was fined five shillings. 'She was a tough Scot,' laughs Brenda, 'and she didn't mind about becoming a criminal.'

The regulations came, and changed, suddenly, and often seemed arbitrary. On 3 June 1940, for example, the police were authorised to remove all car radios 'for reasons of national security'. Shortly after-wards, motorists were required by law to blacken light-coloured vehicles. At a stroke, the driver of a pale-blue car chuckling to *Hi-Gang!* became a serial offender. But if the regulations were tough for people, they were murderous for peregrine falcons. In July these beautiful (and previously protected) creatures were subject to a destruction order. The reason was that the Air Ministry had plans to carry pigeons on board aircraft. The pigeon could be released with a message if an aircraft ditched in the sea, and its radio was not work-ing. But pigeons were a favourite food of peregrine falcons; in order to guarantee their free passage, adult falcons were shot, nestlings were killed and eggs smashed.

Even more zealously enforced were national lighting restrictions. In the belief that a Heinkel bomb aimer at 20,000 feet was alert to a cigarette being lit in a telephone box, offenders were dealt with harshly. John Greaves was fined ten shillings by Jarrow magistrates in 1941 for failing to obscure a light in his bedroom – despite being married the previous day and having only just stepped into his new house. John and his bride appeared in court to argue that they had not yet had time to put up curtains. They were told that 'the first thing they should have done was make sure about the lights.'

A doctor by the name of Musgrave Twentyman, meanwhile, was summoned to Marlborough Street Police Court in November on a lighting charge. He was represented by counsel who introduced him as though he was appearing before a select committee; he was asked whether he had been in medical practice for thirty-eight years, whether he had been a scholar of Christ's College Cambridge, whether he had gained first-class honours, and whether he had studied for one or two other degrees. Eventually the magistrate inter-rupted, asking, 'Did he turn the light on?' 'No sir, I did not,' said Twentyman. 'The case is dismissed,' said the magistrate.

Stories such as this are sometimes cited to suggest that profes-sionals and the middle classes were treated with greater leniency than working-class defendants. But the experience of Metropolitan Police constable Eric Oddy suggests otherwise. Oddy was finishing his patrol one evening when he noticed a light showing from a fanlight above a front door. He rang the bell, and a gentleman of military bearing opened the door.

'Excuse me, sir, but your blackout doesn't comply with rules.'

'Damn it all, man! Been like it ever since the war started! I don't know why you're worried about it!'

'In that case, sir, I'll have your name and address.'

The man turned out to be retired colonel, and Oddy wrote him out a summons. When the case was heard at Clerkenwell Police Court, Oddy explained to the magistrate that the light was the result of the kitchen door being left ajar; there had been no lights on in the hallway. The colonel was nevertheless fined ten shillings.

A year later, Oddy was drinking with a friend in a pub, when two pints of beer were placed in front of them. 'They're from that gentleman over there,' said the landlady. 'Do you know who he is?' Oddy said that he had never seen the man before, but gestured and thanked him.

The man walked over. 'Don't you remember me?' he said.

'No.'

'Colonel Miller!'

'Oh yes . . .'

'You damned well should remember me! Ten bob at Clerkenwell! I thought you were damned fair! Would you two like to come to dinner with me at the Savoy?'

Thanks to the lighting regulations, Eric Oddy's evening took a desirable turn. And the fact was that many 'respectable' people were caught by the numerous regulations. Noël Coward, for example, was fined a total of £2,200 in the autumn of 1941 for two contraventions of currency regulations. One fine related to money spent on a government propaganda trip to the United States, while the other was for failing to disclose American investments to the Treasury. In the former case, Coward had not been aware of the relevant regulations; in the latter, he had instructed his business manager, Jack Wilson, to disclose the securities. Wilson had not done as he was asked.

Coward was clearly affected by his public shaming. 'I would so loathe for anyone to think for a moment that I was not doing my share in every way,' he wrote to Wilson, insisting that, in future, he would take more interest in his own affairs 'however much time it takes and however much it bores me'. But Coward was also aggrieved. He believed that the government was making an example of him – despite the work he had done on its behalf. Indeed, his upcoming film project, *In Which We Serve*, had recently been described by the outgoing Minister of Information, Duff Cooper, as promising to be 'of the very highest propaganda value'.

Coward was not the only notable individual to fall foul of regulations. Weeks earlier, the actor George Arliss had been fined £3,000 for – like Coward – failing to disclose American investments, while in 1944, legendary composer Ivor Novello was sentenced to eight weeks' imprisonment (reduced on appeal to four) at Bow Street Police Court. Novello's company had been issued a permit allowing use of a car for 'work of national importance'; instead he used the car at weekends for his own purposes.

Even Solicitor-General Sir William Jowitt, a man who makes several notable appearances in this book, was brought before the courts. He was summoned to appear at the Police Court, Canterbury, charged with contravening regulations relating to the purchase of animal feed for his Kent farm. And it is hard – initially, at least – not to feel sympathy for Robert Colvin-Graham, the rector of Old Bolingbroke in Lincolnshire, who served twelve days in prison for ringing his church bell on 16 July 1940. A policeman told magistrates at Spilsby Police Court that the rector was seen 'sitting in the belfry, pulling the bell rope'. Colvin Graham claimed that he had no knowledge of the recent regulation which banned the ringing of bells except as a warning of airborne invasion.

The magistrates sentenced the rector to a month in prison – but he was freed on appeal, twelve days later, by the Lincoln Quarter Sessions. The chairman of the appeals committee said that Colvin-Graham 'should never have been prosecuted or convicted' as 'even in times of danger the elementary principles of justice must be observed'. Interestingly, however, the rector's wife, Bertha Colvin-Graham, was a notoriously active fascist who was interned under Regulation 18B just days before the police court dealt with her husband. It seems possible that the magistrates, with their local knowledge, were carrying out a form of ad hoc justice on Robert Colvin-Graham – which the appeal court in Lincoln was quick to reverse.

In addition to the huge number of regulations concerning specific acts, there were other more amorphous regulations intended to combat attacks on national morale. One of these was Regulation 39B (a) which created an offence of making a statement likely to cause alarm or despondency. Described by a prosecutor at Bicester Police Court as a regulation aimed at 'chatterbugs' and 'pessimists', it may be that Arthur Berriedale Keith was justified in calling it a 'drastic interference with expression of opinion'. On 12 July 1940 Mrs Bates of Divinity Road, Oxford, gave evidence before the city magistrates that while reading her electricity meter, Cecil Hughes had told her, 'We should be as well off under the Nazis as we are now' and that 'Ribbentrop deserved Hitler's position if anything happened to Hitler.' It was, Mrs Bates said, 'a queer way for a British subject to talk'. Charged with making a statement likely to alarm, Hughes told the magistrates that the conversation was meant to be 'jocular', that he had light-heartedly said that if Hitler invaded Britain, 'he would make Ribbentrop king', and that the only thing he said against the British government was that things, in general, 'were not up to scratch'. The bench could not decide on a verdict and the hearing was adjourned for a week.

This case seems to be the wartime equivalent of the 'Twitter Joke

Trial', the 2010 trial of twenty-eight-year-old accountant Paul Chambers. Flying to Belfast for a blind date, Chambers had arrived at Nottingham Airport to find it closed by snow. He posted a message on Twitter: 'Crap! Robin Hood Airport is closed. You've got a week and a bit to get your shit together otherwise I am blowing the airport sky high!' It was clear that Chambers' tweet was a joke. The staff at the airport designated it a non-credible threat, which might almost be the technical definition of a joke. It was a bad joke, to be sure, but not very different from countless other weak stabs at humour posted on social media. Similarly, while Cecil Hughes's conversational style did not appeal to Mrs Bates, it cannot have differed greatly from millions of half-joking grumbles delivered across the country in June 1940. Yet one man was faced with prison for sending a menacing message under Section 127(1) of the Communications Act 2003, the other for causing alarm or despondency under Reg. 39B (a) of the Defence (General) Regulations 1939. In Britain, a country famed for its sense of humour, a joke can be no laughing matter.

Two-and-a-half years after his tweet was posted, Paul Chambers' conviction was quashed by the High Court. In the aftermath of the case, a commentator in the *Guardian* newspaper suggested that the public nowadays sees 'hurt and danger around every corner' and that 'we should develop a thicker skin, keep calm, and carry on'. By employing the language of the Home Front, the implication was that nothing like this would have been allowed to happen during the war when people were more robust. But the fact that a week after his first hearing, Cecil Hughes was convicted by a majority of the Oxford magistrates, and fined £5, shows us otherwise. As we have seen, time and again over the course of this book, there is danger in oversimplifying a complex period of history.

Thinking back to the first chapter, we saw how Miss Roach – the central character in Patrick Hamilton's *The Slaves of Solitude* – changed her behaviour during the war, taking unimagined risks, and experiencing new levels of intensity. But these broadening experiences did not mean that she enjoyed the impositions that shrank life in other ways:

> She was not to waste bread, she was not to use unnecessary fuel, she was not to leave litter about, she was not to telephone other- wise than briefly, she was not to take the journey she was taking unless it was really necessary . . . she was not even to talk carelessly, lest she endangered the lives of others.

Miss Roach was certainly not alone in resenting the prohibitions, and the Ministry of Information's patronising manner. The regula- tions were particularly unpopular when their application seemed contrary to fairness and common sense. In 1940, for example, a Leicestershire woman named Mrs Toone refused to accept two evac- uees who were suffering from diphtheria. She made her decision on the apparently reasonable ground that her husband was a school bus driver, and by taking them, she risked infecting an entire school. Yet she was forced to take the children by the High Court, the justices applying the principle that the good of the population outweighed the good of the individual.

Similarly, people objected to the use of entrapment to catch shop- keepers and café owners who broke the rules concerning food. For one thing, entrapment did not seem a very fair (perhaps even 'British') way of ensuring compliance. For another, a surprising number of 'honest' people used the black market, and wanted to keep it going. And thirdly, the 'decoys' or 'stooges' employed by the Ministry of Food and local authorities often used morally dubious tactics. They would recite hard-luck stories or plead at length with a shopkeeper until an item was handed over without the transfer of the necessary coupons. In effect, they were inciting shopkeepers to break the law.

Decoys even tried to confuse shopkeepers into committing offences. In Hendon, shops were targeted by female stooges who came in asking for two ounces of tea. Having removed the relevant coupons from the woman's ration book, the shopkeeper would begin measuring out the tea. The woman would wait until the tea was almost served – and ask for two more ounces. The distracted shopkeeper would often forget to remove further coupons. Fifty-nine well-meaning shop owners ended up in court as a result of this subterfuge. It explains how a grievance arose among small business owners that they were under siege, the authorities looking for the least excuse to prosecute. And the public began to resent the decoys, professional spies whose war work consisted of harassing shop owners, or – even worse – enjoying daily meals in cafés and restaurants in the hope of receiving one rasher of bacon too many.

Yet while it is easy to sympathise with the small business owners, with the patronised public, and with the criminalised vicars, behind all the silly regulations lay the need to create a social and economic framework capable of withstanding the pressures of war. The government was not randomly penalising its citizens. It certainly turned many into criminals – but it did so with intentions as pure as those of the confused Hendon shopkeepers.

These intentions are visible in the government's move to criminalise profiteering by imposing price controls. This measure – introduced by the Prices of Goods Act – attracted criticism as an unhealthy attempt to stifle competition. In fact, like Henry Willink's reorganisation of London's social services in reaction to bombing, it was a pragmatic response to the new circumstances. Together with the system of rationing, it was aimed at ensuring that shortages of essential items did not result in deprivation. And as Neville Chamberlain – the Conservative Prime Minister – explained in early 1940, the prevention of profiteering would avert 'the vicious spiral of the alternate rising of prices and wages'. A price-wage spiral in wartime, after all, might have compromised the war effort and dented national unity. The Prices of Goods Act changed the country's economic landscape exceptionally quickly; shopkeepers who did not modify their business practices faced three months in prison.

The public was encouraged to report instances of profiteering, with the majority of initial complaints related to the price of torch batteries – essential in the blackout. On 6 September 1940 the Central Price Regulation Committee chairman was reporting relatively low levels of profiteering – but by May 1941 the Midlands committee chairman was complaining that problems had arisen. Indeed, far from being controlled, prices were rising wildly, while a Thames Police Court magistrate alleged that large numbers of shopkeepers were 'making enormous profits out of the necessities of the people'.

The chief problem was a legal loophole that merchants had begun to exploit. Maximum prices were not set by the government; instead they were based on a markup over costs. By selling goods back and forth, therefore, profits could be repeatedly increased. The Midlands Committee chairman said: 'Speculation is rampant; goods are changing ownership many times like stocks and shares without even leaving the warehouse . . . prices to the public have, in consequence, risen out of all reasonable proportion, and contributed significantly to an increase in the cost of living.' The problem was overcome in July 1941 when the government started to set maximum prices, and to limit the number of middlemen who could be involved. From then on, price controls became more effective, and profiteering less widespread.

Other forms of profiteering were commonly practised, however. On 2 October 1940, for example, *The Times* reported a sudden increase in rents being charged in Oxford. This followed the influx of Londoners as a result of bombing in the capital. In one 'shocking' case, according to the Chief Constable, £6 a week was being asked for the use of two rooms. This equates to about £240 in modern money, which could sadly no longer be classed as profiteering. But as the number of regulations grew, so, clearly did the opportunities for those keen to exploit the burgeoning system.

Mary Brown was working in the Food Office for the area of Finsbury in London, issuing ration books to individuals, and permits to food retailers. She also helped to staff a centre offering emergency assistance to those who had lost their homes in the previous night's raids. Victims would receive replacement identity cards, clothing coupons, money and anything else they needed. But before dealing with the applicants, Mary and her fellow welfare workers were told exactly where the bombs had fallen. Nevertheless, she says, certain exchanges were common:

> Somebody would say, 'I was bombed out last night.'
> I'd say, 'Where did you live, dear?'
> She'd say wherever it was.
> I'd say, 'Well, that was at least five streets away from where it
>   happened, wasn't it?'
> 'Oh well, I got me windows blown in!'
> 'That's not quite the same . . .'

But these fraudsters were beginners compared with Walter Handy, a man who took the fullest possible advantage of the government compensation scheme. Under this scheme, those who had lost their homes were entitled to a lump sum of £500. Over a period of five months in late 1940 and early 1941, the incorrigible Mr Handy made nineteen separate applications. In today's money, his claims amounted to almost £400,000. For his trouble, he was sentenced to three years' imprisonment with hard labour.

In the next chapter, we will meet many others who exploited the conditions and the circumstances. And we will ask how the Blitz came, in the eyes of many criminals, to be remembered as a golden age.

CHAPTER TWELVE

Golden Age of Crime

The Blitz witnessed a sudden rise in serious crime. The Metropolitan Police war diary notes that crime had actually fallen slightly in London at the beginning of the war as 'criminals took time to adjust themselves to war conditions'. But when intensive bombing started, the figures increased sharply. While in 1939 the Metropolitan Police made 20,134 arrests and recorded 94,852 indictable offences, in 1941 the figures jumped to 25,414 arrests and 99,533 indictable offences. And the official figures are fully backed up by the anecdotal evidence.

Wally Thompson was a persistent criminal from north London whom the senior judge at the Old Bailey, Sir Gerald Dodson, considered beyond reform. For Thompson, the Blitz was a golden period for criminals: 'Air raids, when they didn't drop something right on top of you were the best ally London's crooks ever had.' Billy Hill, a rather more successful villain who became known as the 'Boss of Britain's Underworld' agrees. 'They were roaring days. Money was easy, the villains were well loaded with dough and we were all busy. Either earning it or spending it.' Saying much the same as Thompson and Hill, but viewing the subject from another vantage point, the Bishop of Liverpool commented in 1942 that the country was 'confronted by an outbreak of self-seeking, carried far beyond the limits of ordinary honesty'.

The Blitz's boost to the underworld coincided with the sudden influx of foreigners and colonials. The result was that London's West End became a square mile of bustling prosperity and activity. We have seen how prostitution flourished – but so did crime. Low-life thieves became men of shady substance, while newcomers flooded into the criminal world. And the chief reason was opportunity – which arrived in many forms.

The wartime criminal's greatest friend was the blackout. It is easy, nowadays, to overlook the extent to which the blackout changed lives. Not only did it kill almost eight hundred British drivers, cyclists, and pedestrians every month during 1941, it made every-day existence challenging. Theresa Bothwell, a girl in Birmingham, remembers being sent with her sister to a nearby chemist. Hours later, the girls were found by their father. They were standing together in the dark, crying and hopelessly lost – despite being close to their home. The blackout made the familiar terrifying. And it was a blessing for anybody who wanted to go about their business unobserved.

Wally Thompson, for example. At the height of the Blitz, he planned to break into a warehouse near London Bridge, collect a safe from the warehouse office, and drive it away. And so, one night in the middle of a heavy raid, he parked a lorry in a narrow street. With him were the members of his gang – Batesy, Bob and 'Spider'. Until recently an ARP member, Thompson was wearing his uniform; it allowed him to move about freely and unsuspected.

He had done his preparation. Keeping regular watch over the warehouse, Thompson had discovered that the security guards swapped over at 2 a.m. – making this the best time to break in. He had made a key to open the gates – by blackening a blank with carbon, twisting it in the lock, and noting where the carbon rubbed off. He had stolen a lorry to transport the safe. So now, as anti-aircraft fire raged and bombers droned, he and his men were waiting impatiently.

When the time came, Thompson drove forward. Batesy jumped out, and opened the gates with the key. Spider – an experienced burglar – forced a window, and jemmied the main warehouse door open from the inside. Within moments, they were all inside the office, man-handling the heavy safe out to the lorry. But as they reached the door, a bomb fell. Thompson remembers: 'The ground heaved towards us like an uppercut. I felt myself thrown bodily through the air and flung against the stairs. Swirling, choking dust filled my mouth and nose and blinded me.'

All four gang members were shaken but unhurt. The bomb had landed outside the warehouse, destroying the gates, upturning the lorry, and starting a fire in the building. Thompson was extremely keen to get away – but Spider already had other plans. He had spotted a young girl trapped on an upstairs floor, and was scaling a wall to reach her. Minutes later, a fire engine arrived and sent a ladder up to the ledge where Spider was now hanging with the girl in his arms. He climbed down the ladder – and handed the girl over to a police constable who had arrived. Impressed by Spider's courage, the constable asked him for his details – which Spider declined to give. And with that, the gang slunk away as quickly as they could. Without the safe.

During this period, police forces found themselves stretched very thinly. Regulars were leaving to join the armed forces at a time when crime – and its variety – was increasing. Their replacements were Special Constables and reservists who lacked experience. And new duties had to be fulfilled – such as assisting rescue squads. As a result, fewer police were now available to patrol notorious areas, which had become more dangerous in the blackout. Elephant and Castle in south London, for example, had been notorious before the war for drunken fights and gangs of rowdy youths. In the absence of streetlights and policemen, it had become more lawless still, so that when, one night in early 1942, shouts and screams were heard, nobody paid much attention.

Early that evening, seventeen-year-old James Harvey and his fifteen-year-old brother, Raymond, travelled from their home in Brixton to visit their mother in an Oxford Circus pub. At about 10.15 p.m., they took the Bakerloo Line down to Elephant and Castle to connect with a tram to Brixton. With several minutes to wait, they crossed the road to a coffee stall crowded with young men. They could not get served – the proprietor said that too many cups had been broken that night – and they moved down the street to a second stall.

Meanwhile, a gang of youths led by nineteen-year-old Jimmy Essex was walking towards the brothers. The gang had been tipped off that a young man – James Harvey – was carrying a lot of money in his wallet. As the Harveys moved out of the way to let the gang walk past, they were set upon. Raymond was punched in the face, but the real target was James. The youths surrounded and attacked him, before running off. As they ran, Raymond managed to grab Jimmy Essex, knocking his trilby off, but Essex squirmed out of his grasp and escaped. Looking down, Raymond realised that his brother was lying motionless on the ground, his coat and jacket pulled up over the back of his head. He was snoring as though asleep, and when Raymond bent down, he found a wound at the back of his head. As he called for help, he noticed Essex run back to grab his hat before running off again. Eventually, two people came from the opposite direction – and an ambulance was called. James Harvey died that night at Lambeth Hospital. His wallet was missing when his clothing was searched.

Three members of the gang were arrested – Essex, Charlie Ransford and Johnny Dobbs. Dobbs – who had blood stains on his shirt cuff – initially told the police that he had spent the evening with a female friend, but changed his story, admitting to being with the other members of the gang. He said that after Essex and Ransford had disappeared from the coffee stall, he heard a scuffle, and ran over to find James Harvey lying injured on the ground. Ransford, a deserter from the navy, said that one of the Harvey brothers 'appeared to lash out at Essex' – and this had led to a fight. When he saw that James Harvey was knocked out, Ransford claimed to have done his best to help him. Jimmy Essex, meanwhile, said that he, Ransford and Dobbs had been approached at the coffee stall by somebody telling them that a young man had been spotted with 'a wallet containing £50'. He said: 'To get his wallet, we all crowded him and put our hands in his pockets. He started to shout and it meant we either had to stop him shouting or get away. So we stopped him shouting.' Essex claimed that he had not struck the blow 'that knocked the fellow down'. And he asked, 'Is there any chance of it being manslaughter?'

This was a good question. Essex already had three convictions for assault, and he knew the system. He, Ransford and Dobbs were clearly guilty of manslaughter. They had engaged in an unlawful and dangerous act that was likely to cause injury, during which a person had been killed. But Essex realised that he might face a murder charge – and the consequent death penalty. The principle of joint enterprise allowed Essex, Ransford and Dobbs to be convicted of murder – even if it could not be proved who caused the fatal blow – so long as they had all foreseen that serious harm might occur to James Harvey.

Initially, the three young men were charged with murder. But when the case came to trial, pleas to manslaughter were accepted. Perhaps it was felt that foresight would be difficult to prove, given that street robberies in the area were common but serious harm was rare. Or perhaps there was a reluctance to expose three men to the death penalty, two of whom may not have struck a significant blow. In the event, Essex was sentenced to three years in prison, Ransford to eighteen months, and Dobbs to twelve months.

Local people were unhappy at the court's leniency. These were not sentences calculated to send a warning to young thugs. Jimmy Essex was certainly not deterred. He went on to become a notorious gangster who killed a fellow inmate in Armley Prison while serving a sentence for armed robbery. For this, he received his second manslaughter conviction.

The blackout and the police's difficulties were not the only sources of opportunity in the Blitz. The bombing itself offered huge temptation. Houses, shops and public buildings were wrecked, damaged, and abandoned – creating a pilferer's paradise. William Ryder was a factory worker at Woolwich Arsenal whose parents lived beside the Common. When a bomb dropped on their road, he hurried over to check on their house. On arrival, he was horrified to find the house practically demolished – and looters swarming over it. They were 'sorting out the silver, the knives and forks, and they were even killing the rabbits and chickens that Dad kept'. A woman living in Holford Square in Clerkenwell had a similar experience. Her house had been damaged, and when the police allowed her access, she found that the looters had already taken anything of value. Even the sheets and blankets from her baby's cot were gone.

Looters were becoming a dark emergency service, reaching bomb sites before the medical teams or rescue squads. Actor Ballard Berkeley* was a Special Constable in London, and one of the first to arrive when the Café de Paris nightclub in Coventry Street was bombed in March 1941. An underground space, the Café de Paris was considered safe, but a 50 kg bomb seems to have slid down a ventilator shaft before exploding on the dance floor. At least thirty-four people were killed – including the West Indian bandleader Ken 'Snakehips' Johnson. Berkeley remembers:

---

* Several decades later and after a lengthy film career (including an appearance in wartime classic *In Which We Serve*), Ballard Berkeley would become famous for playing Major Gowen in the BBC comedy series *Fawlty Towers*.

The explosion within this confined space was tremendous. It blew legs off people, heads off people, and it exploded their lungs so that when I went into this place, I saw people sitting at tables quite naturally. Dead. Dressed beautifully without a mark on them. Dead. It was like looking at waxworks.

But some of these waxworks were not complete. Thieves had arrived, and corpses were missing their fingers – cut away to give looters quick access to their rings. 'That, to me,' says Berkeley, 'was the most awful thing.'

One reason why looters could arrive as quickly as the emergency services, was because they sometimes *were* the emergency services. In late September 1940, members of the Auxiliary Fire Service were sent to Carter Lane opposite St Paul's Cathedral. They successfully dealt with the fires – but they also helped themselves to forty-three bottles of whisky and gin from a burned-out pub on the ground floor, and fifty pairs of socks, twenty-four shirts, and all sorts of other items of clothing from a warehouse on the upper floors. They carried the items away in their water buckets, and hid them inside their tender. They were about to drive off, when they were stopped by the police – who had been watching them. All six men were sentenced to five years at the Old Bailey. 'It is a lamentable fact,' said the judge, 'that it has been found necessary to add to the many difficult duties of the police that of watching members of your force.'

This case was unusual in that the looters were caught. A Mass-Observation investigator took a job as a demolition worker in 1941. He found a sharp divide between the 'true navvies' who worked exceptionally hard, and the opportunists who took the job in the hope of picking up loot. On the investigator's first day in the squad, the foreman picked up a woman's purse –and found it empty. 'It's the funniest bloody bomb I ever come across,' he said, 'it's blown every bag open and knocked the money out, it's even knocked the money out of the gas meters!'

According to the investigator, it was normal for the men to take items small enough to be concealed. When a worker found a penny among the debris, half a dozen others began digging in the same spot. After about ten minutes, they had found a little over a shilling. When another worker found candles, soap and matches, the supervisor warned him to put them aside and collect them later – as a policeman was watching from across the road. As for larger items, a certain level of organisation was called for. The supervisor arranged for lead from a damaged roof to be driven away by one of the gang's drivers. And when two sackfuls of coal went missing from a cellar, the investigator was told that they had almost certainly been taken and sold by a particular worker who would 'pinch his own fucking mother'.

Despite the general readiness to loot, the investigator noted a marked 'Robin Hood' attitude: the workers hesitated before looting from poorer neighbourhoods. One worker without such scruples was criticised by another as 'a fucking pig'. 'They're poor people,' explained the ganger, 'else it would be different.' The foreman, meanwhile, disapproved of looting – or else was careful to be heard disapproving. 'I'm no angel meself,' he said, 'but I'm not going to have that going on!'

Some looters were hardened criminals with no scruples at all. The now-demolished Campbell Road in Finsbury Park has been described by historian Jerry White as the worst street in north London before the war. A decaying slum hostile to outsiders and avoided by the police, it was notorious in its day. One of its inhabitants during the Blitz, twenty-six-year-old Jimmy Day, kept a sack with him, eager for the siren. 'I used to pray for a fucking warning,' he says, 'cos a lot of these shopkeepers used to run out and leave their shops, leave everything, their shops empty, all the money and that.' Once a shop was empty, Day could run inside and fill his sack.

Over the period of the most intense bombing between September 1940 and May 1941, a staggering forty-eight per cent of those arrested came from a single group. Not demolition workers, firemen, hardened criminals, or the homeless – but children. Perhaps this is unsurprising. For one thing, children are not very good at resisting temptation. For another, searching through debris must have seemed like an irresistible game. And children had surely never experienced a time of greater upheaval. One can only guess at the excitement and misery caused by disrupted routines, movement around the country, life with strange families, permanently absent fathers and other war-inspired facts of life. Small wonder that many youngsters built collections of other people's possessions.

Looting, it seems, was remarkably widespread. It might even be considered one of those activities that brought people of all ages and classes together – though not in the manner celebrated by the consensus. And it was not as morally clear-cut as it was usually made to seem. There was, after all, a thin line between looting and recycling. According to policeman Walter Marshall, it was ridiculous to charge someone with taking something from a bombed house or shop if they could use it – particularly as, most of the time, it was just going to be thrown away. Teresa Wilkinson was an air raid warden in West Ham. Helping to clean up the ruins of a house, she came across an old copy of *A Mountain Daisy,* a novel by Emily Grace Harding. 'I'd had a copy when I was young,' she says, 'but somehow my copy had got lost. I looked round this house – and all the people who'd lived there were dead – and I thought,"No one will miss that!"'

Perhaps not, but Teresa would have been sent to prison had she been caught. And it should be borne in mind that people were actively encouraged to recycle. 'When you feel tired of your old clothes, remember that by making them do you are contributing some part of an aeroplane, a gun or a tank,' said the President of the Board of Trade, Oliver Lyttelton in June 1941. Yet plenty of people were sent to prison for 'making do'. The head of a Heavy Rescue squad, for example, was punished for picking up a near-empty bottle of gin from the ruins of a pub, and handing it to his exhausted men.

An old age pensioner received six months for taking a bit of rope and an old jug from a ruined house. One thinks back to the homeless man in Coventry who went to prison for taking a coat. As it appeared to the Common Serjeant of London in January 1941, 'Every looter I have tried has been a man of good character. They always are.'

Ranging as it did from the darkly cynical to the frankly innocent, it is difficult to generalise about looting. But this did not stop the press from trying. In November 1940 the *Daily Mirror* demanded that capital punishment be imposed in order to stamp it out. (Looting was punishable by death under Regulation 38A, though the sentence was never imposed.) And our modern politicians seem to have forgotten that looting ever took place. When Prime Minister David Cameron addressed the House of Commons in the wake of the 2011 summer riots, he said: 'The truth is that the police have been facing a new and unique challenge with different people doing the same thing – basically looting – in different places all at the same time.'

Clearly, the challenge was neither new nor unique. Cameron went on to blame a lack of discipline in schools, an absence of morals, and an over-generous benefits system for the incidents of looting. Yet the Blitz looting had taken place before the creation of the welfare state, at a time when caning was common in schools, and the courts were ordering the birching of juveniles and the flogging of adults. The simple fact, shorn of political hot air, was that the majority of the modern looters were reacting to opportunity. In 1940 and 1941 people acted on the spur of the moment in extraordinary circumstances. Exactly the same was true in August 2011.

Economic factors also gave rise to criminal opportunities during the Blitz. As levels of unemployment fell and factory wages rose, the British people had more money to spend. But at the same time, the limited availability of resources and the need to ensure that the poor received a fair share led to rationing. Across the country, people of all classes and backgrounds were keen to circumvent this system; the result was a thriving black market.

This photograph shows shop assistants cleaning up after a raid – but it also explains the prevalence of looting. Opportunity was widespread, and the line between theft and recycling was sometimes fine.

This black market was occasionally used by well-to-do people who considered themselves beyond moral reproach – and so became one element of the 'dark side' of the Blitz that squeezed its way into the consensus. Indeed, the popular image of the 'spiv' (as portrayed by James Beck in *Dad's Army*) was of a lovable rogue who helped to make life a little more bearable. But if the spiv was really 'on our side', then so was the wholesaler who sold him the goods, and the robber who stole them in the first place. (Although one rarely sees cheeky armed robbers in wartime sitcoms.) And if millions of receivers of stolen goods around the country were happy to 'get a little extra', then perhaps Billy Hill, a man who carried out a stream of violent smash-and-grabs and post office robberies, is quite entitled to justify his actions by saying: 'You couldn't blame me, then, if I made the most of a situation which was not of my own making ... I did not merely make use of the black market. I fed it.' Authority figures also fed it. Albert Brown worked alongside his wife Mary in the Food Office in Finsbury. And while Albert never took bribes, he knew others who did. 'We know a gentleman,' he says, 'who made a very good picking when he went from our office to another area.' And there were always individuals and retailers making questionable applications. 'We used to get applications for funeral rations dated two or three months ahead,' Albert laughs. 'And we had applications from prostitutes who said they needed the extra food to keep their strength up on the streets. That's an actual fact! I had to refuse them!'

Even during the worst rationing, according to Billy Hill, the wealthy could get whatever they wanted. 'If there hadn't been any rich people there wouldn't have been any black market at all,' he says. Nancy Jackman was a cook working for a well-to-do family in Norwich. One morning, she was informed by 'her ladyship' that substantial amounts of food would be arriving 'from a relative'. Meat, sugar and butter started to be delivered – in large quantities – by a man whom Nancy had never seen before. 'Then the penny dropped,' she writes. 'It was all black market stuff.' This food was served to the family and their guests, 'but I was told by her ladyship in a note ... that the servants' meals should continue to reflect the current rationing situation.'

Rationing was meant to ensure equality – which, in turn, would encourage the country to work together. Yet much of life remained a case of 'them and us'. In areas untroubled by the Luftwaffe, particularly the south-western coastal resorts such as Bournemouth and Torquay, life could be very good. And the fact was that wealthier people could eat whatever they wanted from restaurants. Albert

Brown remembers being served steaks and lamb chops in a restaurant in Skegness by a proprietor who came to the table after the meal and 'asked us what we wanted to take with us, a leg of lamb, whatever we wanted!' Perhaps grateful for the feast, Albert did not reveal that he worked for the food authorities.

The black market is an interesting subject to discuss with those who can remember the Blitz. Respectable people, who would otherwise not admit to breaking the law, are quite happy to discuss black market dabbles. 'I don't think anybody thought of it as blatantly criminal,' says Ruth Tanner from Walthamstow, 'it was just the way we lived.' Roy Bartlett, the boy from Ealing who injured his leg in his parents' shelter, remembers a friend of his father, who 'did a bit of poaching', supplying his family with a chicken. Glaswegian Elsie Glendinning has memories of her mother buying food from poorer people: 'I don't know what the transaction would be, but my mother got bacon, eggs, cheese and butter, not in great quantities, but these people would sell their rations. You kept it very quiet if you did have any extra. You just took it. "Oh, that's good ... "' In Bethnal Green, meanwhile, one lady remembers local stallholders coming into her factory on Fridays and selling food without coupons 'on the sly'. The workers called it 'Cabbage Friday'. 'Everybody had their crafty ways to survive,' says Tottenham fireman Francis Goddard. 'It was the only way you *could* survive.'

At one end of the supply chain were these ordinary citizens, at the other were men like Billy Hill. And for Hill, these were days of unparalleled opportunity:

Down in the West Country there was a services depot where they stored bedding. I can't remember how many bed-sheets we nicked from that depot. We merely took our lorry down and filled it up ... Thousands of pairs every week. Then there was a warehouse filled with fur coats. I emptied it ... Money? It was coming to us like pieces of dirty paper.

Arthur 'Musher' King, meanwhile, ran a variety of businesses. In winter, he was a licensed coal deliverer, hiring men and horses to deliver coal. In summer, he bought fruit from Covent Garden market and sold it on barrows around London. But all year round, he was in 'the black market game', picking up 'eggs and tomatoes and little sucking pigs' among other things from a village near Hertfordshire, and selling them in London. He began making considerable money, with some of which he bought property (houses were available cheaply during the Blitz) and the rest of which he hid away. One week, he exchanged his eggs for sex with a French prostitute. The following week, he returned with some butter . . .

The black market had its dangers, however. When a taxi drove into the back of Wally Thompson's van in the blackout, the police were quickly on the scene – to find white flour everywhere. Trying to explain why he was driving around a fifty-pound bag of white flour, Thompson made up a story about his brother working at a bakery in Camberwell. A policeman asked for the name of the shop, and, before long, Thompson was serving a six-month prison sentence. Some dangers were less obvious. Fireman Francis Goddard's wife was a waitress in a restaurant with access to steak, salmon, roast beef, pheasant and other luxuries. When Mrs Goddard had the chance, she would bring items home – in her knickers. Francis remembers:

> I'd be in bed and she'd come home and wake me up . . . Out would come a piece of tissue paper, and she'd undo it and there'd be two nice pieces of cold cooked steak and we'd sit there and eat them . . . She might even bring out a great big piece of chocolate. We'd laugh and I'd say, 'I hope you haven't worked too hard! I hope you haven't sweated too much!'

Yet more opportunity for criminals was offered by the increased availability of guns. Some had arrived in the underworld following the evacuation from Dunkirk, but most were carried as a matter of course by servicemen – leading to the disastrous escalation of otherwise mundane quarrels. We have looked at the cases of James McCallum, John Fulljames, and James Burnham. While sentencing Burnham, the Old Bailey judge, Sir Frederick Tucker, expressed his concern at the recent glut of shootings involving servicemen. But firearms were also issued to Home Guards – with sometimes regrettable consequences. Edith Harrison, for example, shot dead her husband, Harold, in Canvey Island. Harold, a forty-eight-year-old council clerk, had been setting off on Home Guard duty when he asked Edith to fetch his rifle. She later told the coroner's inquest: 'I was messing about with a firearm threatening to commit suicide when it went off. I did not intend to harm him. I was so fond of him. What should I do without him?' A verdict of death by misadventure was returned. And as the ages of Home Guards varied widely, it was possible for a young boy to arrive home carrying a Sten submachine gun. This is how Frank Terrel came to leave a Sten gun in his mother's loft for the duration of the war. Returning home in 1947 after five years in the Royal Marines, Frank's mother asked him what he wanted to do with his 'Tommy Gun'.

Yet as freely as guns were distributed, they might have been even more widely available. When the risk of invasion was at its highest, a proposal was introduced that any 'trustworthy member of the community' should be issued with a rifle, or a hand grenade if preferred. Had this proposal been adopted, the levels of gun crime would surely have increased for many years to come.

But it was not just guns that caused problems. The rapid increase in size of the armed forces led to all manner of criminality, from rampaging mobs to desertion to attempts to avoid service. Brian and Patrick Williams were serving members of the armed forces who told the police, in 1941, about a burglary they had committed three years earlier. They hoped that criminal convictions would win their release from the army and navy respectively. Brian was successful; he was convicted, sent to borstal for three months, and discharged from the army. Patrick, however, was bound over, and returned to the Royal Navy.

Unemployed twenty-one-year-old Londoner Jack Brack, meanwhile, became the central figure in a large-scale operation to gain exemptions from military service. At his own examination before a medical board in October 1939, Brack had been rejected as unfit due to heart disease. Several months later, Maurice Kravis, the owner of a Brick Lane snooker hall, offered Brack money to impersonate him at his forthcoming examination. And so, with Kravis's birth certificate and (photo-less) identity card in hand, Brack appeared before the board. He received an exemption for Kravis – and £20 (£800 in 2015) for his trouble.

It may be that the 'brains' behind the scheme was really a man named Louis Cohen who appears to have received a cut from both Brack and Kravis. Certainly, from this point on, Cohen took charge. He interviewed candidates in a Tottenham Court Road office, took their money, and paid Brack a fee. He also ensured that each examination was scheduled for a different venue – to avoid Brack being identified. And as other men were impersonated by Brack, the amounts charged by Cohen increased. James Boulton was charged £100 and Samuel Rivkoff £200 (£4,000 and £8,000) – yet Brack received only £40 (£1,600) each time. He had become a small cog in his own business.

It was not a business with long-term prospects, however. With Cohen spreading the word, and Brack's face becoming known, it was only a matter of time before the police became involved. Ten men – including Brack and all of those he impersonated – were arrested and charged with conspiring to defeat the provisions of the National Service Act. Brack was sentenced to three years, and Louis Cohen, when eventually apprehended, received two years.

At the other end of the spectrum, a young man in north London was breaking the law in an attempt to *join* the army. Twenty-one-year-old

Samuel Martin was convicted of carrying out sabotage in a Willesden factory making parts for torpedoes. Martin's job was assembling 'pistols' – electrical devices which controlled the detonation of torpedoes – and his adventure began on 7 October 1940, when he showed up late for work, saying he wanted to resign from the job. He was told that he could not leave.

The following day, he assembled a pistol with a washer filed the wrong way. This would have caused a jam in the torpedo mechanism. When confronted by his supervisor, Martin said that he was not surprised he had made a mistake, as he was no longer interested in his work. The next day, he assembled a pistol with a crucial part missing – an error that would have kept the torpedo alive for three months had it missed its target. And a third pistol was drilled incorrectly. This, said an Admiralty expert, 'could not have been done accidentally'.

On 18 October Martin was arrested and charged with sabotage. 'I don't know why such a fuss should be made because of a few errors in your work,' he said. 'I did file a collar the wrong way and stripped a thread in a sleeve, but what's in that? I had lost all interest.' During his Old Bailey trial in November 1940 (directly before Pons, Meier and Kieboom were tried, in front of the same judge), the jury returned with a question: 'We all agree that Martin is guilty of deliberately destroying the parts in question solely to get his dismissal but without criminal intent. Please advise us.' Mr Justice Wrottesley advised a guilty verdict. The subsequent sentencing took the form of a conversation between judge and prisoner:

'Men of your age are being killed and being drowned for their country, and are not being paid £5 or £6 per week. You follow that don't you?'

'Yes, my Lord, I have often expressed to my father a desire to get into the Army.'

'What you did was unpardonable. You might have sent your best friends to destruction, and other Englishmen who are running risks you are not running yourself. I am unwilling that a young Englishman at this time should be kicking his heels in prison instead of serving his country. I am giving you an opportunity to show your gratitude.'

'Thank you.'

Samuel Martin had every reason to thank Sir Frederic Wrottesley. He had been found guilty of sabotage, an offence not far short of treason, but the judge merely bound him over. Like Sjoerd Pons the following week, Martin ranks as one of the more fortunate Old Bailey defendants.

But as Martin was hoping to join His Majesty's Forces, plenty of others were running away. Police stations around the country were often contacted with enquiries about local men who had gone missing from their units. Policemen regularly stopped young men wearing civilian clothes, asking to see their identity cards or pay books. And deserters sometimes surrendered at police stations. Eric Oddy, of the Metropolitan Police, recalls a deserter from a north of England regiment handing himself in. The man was placed in the cells, while an escort was sent down to London to take him back up north. Oddy remembers:

> The chappie who came down to escort him was a Londoner, so we handed him over, and the escort said, 'Look, here's a couple of bob, go to the pictures, I'm going to see my mum, meet me here at six o'clock.' And, of course, at six o'clock nobody turned up. The escort thought as he'd handed himself in, he'd show up again . . .

People who were on the run from the military authorities had to live on their wits – which usually meant engaging in criminal activity. Former public schoolboy Harry Tooby, a thirty-six-year-old member of the Pioneer Corps, pleaded guilty before the Banbury Quarter

Sessions in December 1940 to stealing almost 12,000 cigarettes. Tooby had deserted from his unit at the end of August, and taken the cigarettes from Banbury railway station during the blackout. He was asking for two similar thefts to be taken into consideration. 'I have had a most pathetic letter on your behalf from your wife, who is evidently still devoted to you,' the recorder told him. 'Your commanding officer thought highly of your abilities. You were promoted – and you threw away all this.' Tooby was sentenced to six months' hard labour.

Beyond the shirkers and deserters were a surprising number of people impersonating soldiers, sailors and airmen. One such imposter was twenty-nine-year-old D'Arcy Wilson, a barman from Thornton Heath, who dressed as an RAF pilot officer in order to impress women. Wilson already had a wife and children, but when apprehended he was days away from bigamously marrying an eighteen-year-old who believed him to be a test pilot.

The deception was discovered by chance on Oxford Street. As Wilson passed Flight Lieutenant John Forbes Andre Day, he gave a salute. This made Andre Day suspicious. For one thing, a pilot officer would not normally salute a flight lieutenant, and for another, the salute was sloppy. As the two men spoke, Andre Day became convinced that Wilson was an imposter. Placing him under arrest, he marched him towards the Air Ministry. But as they approached Aldwych, Wilson made a dash for freedom. Andre Day chased him, firing two revolver shots into a wall to attract attention. On hearing the shots, George Lacey, a carman on his way to work, dropped dead from shock. Andre Day, meanwhile, hurried round a street corner to find that two passers-by had grabbed his prisoner. The fake pilot officer was eventually sentenced to two months' hard labour in September 1940.

It was not just men impersonating members of the armed forces. Days before D'Arcy Wilson was sentenced, twenty-nine-year-old Pauline Hough pleaded guilty to impersonating a WAAF officer, and was fined £50. But perhaps the oddest – and saddest – example of armed-forces impersonation involved Clive Grunspan, a brilliant young London artist.

Grunspan was a gunner in a Royal Artillery searchlight unit – but this was not how he liked to present himself. In October 1940 he walked into a shop in Marylebone, wearing an army major's uniform – and the ribbons of the Order of the British Empire, Distinguished Service Order, Military Cross, Military Medal, and Croix de Guerre. He told the shopkeeper that he was collecting money for the purchase of mittens for soldiers, but an RAF officer was present, and when he saw Grunspan's home-made pass purporting to have been issued by the War Office, he called the police. When he eventually appeared in court, Grunspan was discharged under the terms of the Probation Act in order to receive psychological treatment. It was clear that he was not well.

Whatever treatment he received seems to have made little difference, however. Five years later, pretending to be blind and wearing the uniform of an RAF Group Captain, Grunspan spent three days at the Berkeley Hotel in Piccadilly. For identification purposes, he gave the hotel his passport in which he had described himself as a general and Victoria Cross holder. Over these three days, he told strange tales of wartime bravery to anybody who would listen, and became friendly with well-known entertainers Pat Kirkwood (who took him dancing at the Savoy), Jack Buchanan (who offered him a box at the theatre), and Fred Emney (who became suspicious when he claimed to recognise a brand of cigar by the smell). Greenspan paid for his stay at the hotel with a dud cheque – and was subsequently arrested. On this occasion, the court was unsympathetic, sentencing him to six months' hard labour. The following year he served another twelve-month sentence for theft. Shortly after his release, Grunspan ended his troubled life by drinking cyanide of potassium in a French hotel room.

With the increase in size of the armed forces at this period, many service marriages came under strain. It was not uncommon for a husband to come home on leave to find that he had been replaced in his wife's affections – and in his bed. Thirty-one-year-old soldier David Walker arrived home unexpectedly in June 1941, hoping to give his wife a surprise. It seems that he succeeded. Walking into his bedroom at five-o'clock in the morning, he found his wife lying next to a strange man – and his youngest child beside them. Walker went downstairs, picked up his rifle and returned. He claimed that a struggle ensued during which the gun was discharged, shooting his wife's lover, forty-year-old reserve policeman Tom Cocker, in the abdomen. Cocker lived long enough to make a statement, saying, 'I know I am dangerously ill and not likely to recover. When Walker came upstairs the gun went off and I fell. I do not want to say anything else.' Cocker duly died, and Walker was charged with murder. But when the case came to trial at Manchester Assizes, the Crown substituted a charge of manslaughter, and Walker gave evidence that he had merely intended to scare Cocker with the rifle, before giving him 'a hammering'. The jury retired for only seven minutes before returning a verdict of not guilty.

It was not just juries who showed leniency to men such as Walker. Judges, too, were loath to make examples of cuckolded soldiers. In November 1940 Robert Capstick, a private in the Pioneer Corps, was found guilty at Derby Assizes of the manslaughter of his wife. But when Capstick came to be sentenced, Mr Justice Oliver seemed extremely keen to absolve him of any blame, stressing that his wife's conduct had caused him to become drunk and fire a rifle shot. 'Far from being a murderer,' said the judge, 'Capstick had, in circumstances in which everybody sympathised, reduced himself to such a condition that he did not know what he was doing.' Capstick was bound over for two years.

Such cases – and such leniency – seem to have been common. For deliberately killing a Canadian soldier who was sleeping with his wife, Lieutenant William Hennant was sentenced to six months' imprisonment. 'I will make the sentence as light as I feel it is possible to make,' said the judge. And William Lovelock, a private in the Oxfordshire and Buckinghamshire Light Infantry, received just twelve months for killing both his wife *and* her lover.

In a case where the husband had previously demonstrated violence, however, pre-war severity still applied. Sapper Clifford Holmes of the Royal Engineers was found guilty at Manchester Assizes of murdering his wife in October 1940. Mrs Holmes had been granted a separation order, on the grounds of cruelty, which her husband opposed. Given leave to try to sort out the problem, Holmes hurried to his wife's rented flat, where he shot and bayoneted her. The jury rejected his defence of insanity, and the Court of Appeal rejected his appeal against conviction. Holmes was hanged in February 1941.

As we travel through the criminal landscape of the Blitz, it becomes clear that a great deal of violence and misbehaviour arose directly out of the new circumstances – as well as interesting reactions to that misbehaviour. At the same time, however, another powerful influence was sweeping the country. Popular American culture ('the false values of the American film', in George Orwell's phrase) inspired many Britons. Viewing life through the prism of Gable and Crawford, their world revolved around dance halls, picture houses, cheap perfume, nylons and jazz music. They might sleep across the landing from their parents, work long hours in a factory, and live in fear of bombs, invasion, and the call-up, but large numbers of young people were more influenced by the dirty glamour of Hollywood than by real life. And one effect of this was to make crime and immorality deeply fashionable.

At its most extreme, the fashion inspired new kinds of crime, as exemplified by the 1944 'Cleft-Chin murder' in which an American army deserter (who falsely claimed to be a big-time mobster) and an eighteen-year-old Welsh waitress (who told him she wanted to be a gun-moll) went on a gangster-style rampage, robbing passers-by and murdering a taxi driver for the £8 in his pocket. Another result was the turning of London's West End, with its gambling, illegality and sexual promise, into the focus of suburban dreams. And the West End's clubland was thriving during the Blitz. The American influence, the need for diversion and the influx of foreigners all kept night spots crowded, and the police on their toes.

A particularly fashionable variety of night club was the 'Bottle Party'. Intended to circumvent strict licensing laws, Bottle Parties were all-night bars posing as invitation-only clubs where the alcohol consumed was theoretically the drinker's own. Hostesses, described in a police report as being 'of the prostitute type', sat with drinkers. Many had dance bands, some offered striptease, and the more popular they grew, the keener the police became to close them down.

One particularly popular Bottle Party was the El Morocco Club, situated in a basement on Albemarle Street. With its black walls and pink curtains, its two celebrity-led orchestras, and its official status as an air raid shelter, El Morocco became one of the hottest spots in clubland. In a feature entitled 'London Harlem', the *Evening Standard* wrote admiringly of the titled men and women who congregated there. The Vice Squad did not share the paper's enthusiasm, however. It was continually sending undercover officers into El Morocco to gather enough evidence to close it down. (One police report, filed after a raid, lists a certain 'Marthe Watts' as being present.) In the end, the police were successful. In August 1940 the Home Secretary told the House of Commons that orders were being made for the closure of six Bottle Parties – one of which was El Morocco. Unfortunately, no recording exists of Sir John Anderson reading the names of the six clubs – 'Boogey Woogey, El Morocco, Hi-de-Hi, Macs, Paradise and Stork' – to his fellow Honourable Members.

Yet despite the growth of crime, and its increased glamour in the eyes of young people, professional criminals remained, in the words of Billy Hill, 'a race apart'. The West End might have been opening up, but the old lags were not going to be pushed aside: 'There were still some clubs where the entrance form was a file in the Criminal Records

Office of Scotland Yard. These were the places I like to keep myself restricted to. I was with my own people and could feel at home.'

Hill remembers teaching a lesson to two young upstarts who were trying to make a name for themselves. One afternoon they attacked a respected old villain in a Soho club. Aware of what was happening, Hill pulled out his knife 'and gave one tearaway my favourite stroke, a V for Victory sign on his cheek' before cutting 'the other monkey to ribbons'. The established criminals, it was clear, were not about to give up their territory.

All the same, the war brought changes to the pecking order. Perhaps the most powerful criminal syndicate at the start of the war – certainly the nearest thing London had to the Mafia – was the Sabini family. Of Sicilian and Irish stock, this notoriously violent clan drew its income from 'protecting' illegal bookmakers, loansharking and other types of extortion. Its power stemmed, in part, from deals struck with the police. If, for example, a Sabini gang member spotted a thief or pickpocket who was *not* in the family's pay, he would whiten his hands with chalk and greet the imposter by slapping him on the back. There was little friendliness in this gesture. Its purpose was to place a white palm-print on the man's back – identifying him to the police as a someone who *could* be arrested.

Life was good for the Sabinis – until the entry of Italy into the war in June 1940. Coinciding, as it did, with a drive by the authorities to crack down on gang crime, the opportunity arose to intern the family members as enemy aliens. Even when other internees were subsequently released, the Sabinis remained in custody. Their absence created a vacuum at the top of the crime world – which rival gangs such as the Yiddishers and the Whites were keen to fill. Desperate not to lose ground, a Sabini associate named Antonio 'Babe' Mancini took charge of the remainder of the gang. In doing so, he set in motion a chain of events that would be instrumental in abolishing the death penalty in Britain twenty-five years later.

In the early morning of 20 April 1941, while Mancini was in the

Palm Beach Club in Wardour Street (where Marthe Watts had met the Messina brothers), a fight broke out between the club's doorman and members of the Yiddisher gang. Once the fight was over, Mancini banned the Yiddishers from returning to the Palm Beach. Ten days later, two members of the Yiddishers, Edward Fleischer and Harry 'Scarface' Distelman, showed up at the West End Bridge and Billiards Club, upstairs from the Palm Beach. As Mancini walked up the stairs to the Billiards Club, he heard Fleischer saying, 'There's Babe! Knife him!' A fight quickly broke out between Mancini, Fleischer and Distelman.

Trying to piece together what happened next is not easy. It seems that Fleischer went to strike Mancini with a chair, while Mancini slashed at Fleischer's wrist with a knife. At some point Mancini stabbed Distelman – who staggered into the street and died on the pavement outside the Palm Beach. Mancini later claimed that Distelman 'was trying to do me', so he had acted purely in self-defence. In truth, the fight was really just another grubby brawl in a tit-for-tat struggle for underworld dominance. It was hard to distinguish one professional criminal from another. Nevertheless, the police charged Mancini with murdering Distelman. He was put on trial at the Old Bailey.

Counsel for the prosecution opened the case by arguing: 'If somebody gets killed in a struggle, that might be called manslaughter ... but if someone enters upon a struggle at an advantage such as possession of a deadly weapon, and in that struggle, he causes death, even if he did not mean to kill, that may amount to murder.'

In fact, a knife had been found next to Distelman's body, suggesting that Mancini may not actually have had an advantage. But this would have been irrelevant to the outcome of the case had Mancini accepted the prosecution's offer to withdraw the murder charge if he pleaded guilty to manslaughter. Had he agreed to the offer, he would have served a few years in prison. But he rejected it, insisting that he had done nothing wrong in defending himself. The jury failed to agree, however, finding him guilty of murder. He was sentenced to death.

Mancini's appeal was rejected by the Court of Appeal. Very unusually for a murder appeal, it came before the House of Lords where it was again rejected – although the Lord Chancellor, Lord Simon, wrote to the Home Secretary, Herbert Morrison, underlining that the killing had been neither deliberate or premeditated, and had resulted from 'a row among a number of excited people' and that 'the attacking was not all on one side'. The Lord Chancellor's tacit – but very clear – suggestion was that while Mancini's act may have amounted to murder in law, the Home Secretary should nevertheless grant a reprieve. Morrison refused to take the hint. Mancini was hanged for murder at Pentonville Prison in late October 1941.

In a letter to his brother, two months before his execution, Mancini writes, 'The verdict will go down in history as there was no premeditation, and it was an accident, so a manslaughter verdict should have been returned.' Mancini fails to reveal that he could have saved his own life. Instead, he writes: 'I can only blame my parents for not giving me the correct environment, when I was a babe: it is hardly fair to blame those that we loved in the past, still it looks to me as such.'

'The hanging of Mancini,' declared the *Daily Mail*, 'warns the gangsters that Scotland Yard intends to clean up Soho.' Mancini's death, from Herbert Morrison's perspective, was a politically motivated sacrifice. And it seems to have worked: an armistice was called between the feuding gangs in the aftermath of the execution. But it would be another fifteen years – April 1956 – before it was publicly revealed that Mancini had been executed following a prosecution offer to reduce the charge.

At this time, an outcry ensued, led by Arthur Bottomley MP, who wondered how Herbert Morrison could have failed to reprieve Mancini in these circumstances, and how the prosecution lawyers, having offered the defendant life, had been able to sit back as he went to his death. Following the outcry, Lord Jowitt (formerly our old friend

Sir William Jowitt) delivered a lecture suggesting that the abolition of
the death penalty must now be in sight.

But of all the wrongdoing that took place during this period, one
act stands apart as the archetypal crime of the Blitz. Where other incidents arose from the Blitz's symptoms – the blackout, men away from
their wives, the shake-up of the underworld, the proliferation of
guns – one was inspired directly by the bombing. And by a simple
question: so many people were dying in air raids, who would question one more victim?

From its first day, the marriage of Harry Dobkin and Rachel
Dubkinski was unhappy. Brought together by a marriage-broker, they
married in a Bethnal Green synagogue in 1920. Within hours, Rachel
had threatened suicide, and two days after the wedding, Harry
walked out. He joined Cunard as a steward, sailing for New York. He
remained in America for eleven months before coming back to
England to find that Rachel had given birth to a son. Summoned for
wife desertion, Harry paid a few weeks' maintenance before going
back to sea. On his return, he received six weeks' imprisonment for
non-payment. He then spent ten years in America, before being
offered money by Rachel's family to come back to her. He took the
money, but left soon after she accused him of stealing a brooch. She
offered him more money to come back a second time. This time, he
stayed for a week. His subsequent years were spent in and out of
prison for failure to pay maintenance.

One morning in April 1941, Harry saw Rachel near his parents'
house. She told him that she wanted to 'make peace'. They met again
that afternoon in a café on Kingsland Road in Hackney. According to
Harry's version of events, Rachel asked him to return to her, and
boarded a bus back home. Shortly afterwards, however, Rachel's sister
Polly reported her missing. Polly told the police that Rachel had gone
to meet Harry – and stated her belief that Harry was involved in 'foul
play'. Polly mentioned Harry's past cruelty. Her sister 'had received
many blows from him'. And when the police checked hospital

records, they found that Rachel had, indeed, received hospital treatment following domestic assaults.

Harry, meanwhile, had recently started work as a firewatcher for a firm of solicitors in Kennington. His job was to patrol the premises throughout the night. Five days after Rachel's disappearance, on 16 April, there was a fire in the blitzed ruins of the Baptist church next door. Harry failed to report the fire – which was spotted by a passing police constable and attended by the fire brigade. When asked by the constable what he had seen, Harry's reply – that he had not caused the fire – seemed to answer another question altogether. A few days later – and equally strangely – Harry wrote to the police volunteering his movements after his wife's disappearance. He was denying guilt before it had even been suggested.

Over a year later, on 17 July 1942, a demolition team began clearing debris from the site of the Baptist church. On lifting a paving stone, a worker found a human body. The head was separate from the body, the lower arms and legs were missing, it was partly burned, and there was no identifying facial tissue. It was taken to Southwark Mortuary, and from there to the forensic department at Guy's Hospital where it was studied by Home Office pathologist Dr Keith Simpson.

It was initially clear to Dr Simpson that this was not a Blitz victim: the body was neatly buried under a stone slab. Two questions needed answering however; how did this person die – and who was it? The answer to the first question arrived when Dr Simpson studied the tiny bones of the voice box and the tissue around them – which had been preserved by lime powder scattered over the body. One of the bones had suffered a fracture that was only observed in victims of strangling. And when Dr Simpson examined the tissue, it showed signs of bruising – which must have occurred while the person was alive. This individual, concluded Dr Simpson, had died by strangulation.

So far as identity was concerned, it was clearly the body of a woman, a little over five feet tall. Study of the fibrous joints of the skull, and of the very few hairs still attached, showed her to be between forty and fifty years old. She had died twelve to eighteen months earlier. When Dr Simpson passed his information to the police, their records indicated a missing woman of similar description – Rachel Dobkin.

On 25 August the police informed Harry that they had found the remains of his wife next door to the site of his old firewatching job. He was taken for questioning at Borough Police Station and charged with Rachel's murder. His trial – in front of Mr Justice Wrottesley at the Old Bailey – grabbed the public's attention, despite coinciding with the stirring news of the Eighth Army's success in North Africa. Newspapers covered the trial excitedly. Even *The Times* provided updates on its home news page. The tide of the war might be turning, and the Blitz might have offered people their own dramas, but the nation had clearly not lost its appetite for a good old-fashioned murder trial.

Except that this trial had a very modern twist. In his opening speech for the Crown, counsel suggested that the corpse had been dismembered 'to make recognition difficult at a time when undoubtedly things were happening in which people were killed and blown to pieces'. It was, in other words, a crime of the Blitz; an attempt to hide a murder amid the destruction and chaos of the bombing.

Harry Dobkin proved to be a poor witness, contradicting his previous statements, confusing his dates, and denying evidence from various witnesses placing him at the scene of the fire. His answers meandered. 'Would you mind directing your mind to the questions that are put?' said the judge. 'Because it takes such a long time if you do not.' It seemed to crime writer Nigel Morland that Dobkin presented 'a sorry picture of panic and fear'. But he undoubtedly gave clear and honest answers to two questions:

'Were you fond of your wife?'
'No, sir.'
'When did you cease to have any affection for her?'
'The day I got married.'

A significant problem facing the prosecution was to identify the victim as Rachel Dobkin. She might have been the right age, height and sex, but this was not sufficient to prove her identity – so two new methods were employed. The first – carried out by Mary Newman, the head of the photography department at Guy's Hospital – involved superimposing a photograph of the skull onto a photograph of Rachel. When this was done, the correlation between the eyes, nose, and forehead was striking. The second method involved obtaining records from Rachel's dentist – who was able to confirm that the four teeth found with the remains of the jaw contained work that he had carried out.

Defending Dobkin was the uncompromising Frederick Lawton, a past member of the British Union of Fascists, who would, in due course, become one of Britain's senior judges (as well as Margaret Thatcher's pupil master). Lawton worked ferociously on Dobkin's behalf. At one point he asked Keith Simpson for the maximum height of the victim. Five feet one and a half inches, said Simpson. 'So if Mrs Dobkin in life was five feet three inches, then this body cannot be that of Mrs Dobkin?' asked Lawton. Simpson said yes.

Lawton then produced a copy of the *News of the World* from May 1941. In the 'Missing from Home' section, a description of Rachel Dobkin supplied by her sister, Polly, stated her to be five feet three inches tall. Moments previously, the prosecution case had been convincing. Suddenly it was in danger of falling apart. Polly was quickly called back into the witness box, where she denied telling the *News of the World* that her sister was five feet three inches tall. She said that she had told the paper that Rachel *was the same height as herself*. Rachel was taken out of the witness box and measured. She was exactly five feet one inch tall.

After only twenty minutes of deliberation, the jury found Harry Dobkin guilty of the murder of his wife. The clerk of the court asked whether he could offer any reason why the court should not sentence him to death. Harry stood straight, and said, very clearly and deliberately: 'I have something to say that this charge against me is very poorly invented, and that is why I do not like giving evidence against the police, but I claim that this charge of murder, as I mentioned, is simply invented by showing photographs.'

Harry Dobkin was hanged at Wandsworth Prison on 27 January 1943. His post-mortem was carried out by Keith Simpson – the man who had fought so hard for his conviction. Yet had the offence been committed a few years earlier – before the introduction of forensic photography and the use of dental records, and had the body not been uncovered by a demolition squad – he would not have been convicted at all. One wonders how many other murder victims were rather more expertly disposed of during the Blitz, and how many grudges and scores were settled as the bombs fell.

When trying to make sense of the crimes of the Blitz, one is struck by the sheer range of offences. From breaches of lighting regulations to cold blooded murders, their scope is staggering. Some were committed by inveterate wrongdoers, others by ordinary people responding to suddenly presented opportunities. The blackout, the bombed-out houses, the proliferation of guns, the regulations begging to be exploited, the absence of police, the desire to avoid the army, the separation of families – all of these things made outlaws of the unlikeliest people.

As did a blurring of moral lines. An ordinary man – with a clearly defined sense of right and wrong – might be fined for the breach of an obscure regulation, he might dabble in the black market, he might find a few extra petrol coupons from somewhere – and before long he was justifying a great deal more to himself. This was how morality became a movable feast.

But beyond the opportunities, beyond the blurred lines, beyond the delinquency of juveniles with no settled routines or father figures, there was a world of uncertainty. Our grandparents and great grandparents genuinely feared that tomorrow would never come. This made them more likely to take risks, and to exist in the moment. The result was good and bad behaviour. In the flash of a bomb, Wally

Thompson's gang member, 'Spider', went from stealing a safe to saving a life. Walter Marshall, a Metropolitan Police officer, recalls a constable at City Road Police Station who received an award for saving two people. Weeks later, he was serving a six-month prison sentence for selling batteries stolen by his son from the Ever Ready factory in Dagenham.

And even when danger was not immediately present, the Blitz's steady brutality sat in the background, raising the nation's temperature, encouraging other moralities and behaviours. Nowhere is this clearer than in the case of George Hobbs, a forty-three-year-old mortuary assistant from Kensington whose job was to prepare bodies for burial. In November 1940, the twenty-three-year-old widow of an air raid victim could not find her husband's ring among his effects. It was subsequently discovered in Hobbs's possession – along with four other rings, two watches, cash and a miniature revolver. Hobbs initially tried to argue that he had bought the goods in a pub – but soon pleaded guilty to four counts of theft and asked for four other offences to be taken into consideration. The Recorder of London sentenced him to three years in prison – but Hobbs's plea in mitigation is revealing. He said that no one could possibly imagine the sight of bodies recovered from bombed premises. This, he said, combined with the dread that he himself might become a victim of an air raid, had an effect on his mind.

It is usual to view pleas in mitigation with scepticism. 'He would say that, wouldn't he?' to quote Mandy Rice Davies two decades later. But, just this once, it is worth paying attention to Hobbs's words. Here was a man who had been doing his job for many years – but it had suddenly become far more extreme, and overlaid with fear. It seems that he had never behaved in this fashion before; possibly he never imagined that he could.

Here is the key to so much of the extreme behaviour of the period. From this place of fear and confusion came Blitz Misbehaviour – as well as Blitz Spirit.

CHAPTER THIRTEEN

It Was the Best of Times, It Was the Worst of Times

The Blitz did not begin suddenly on 7 September 1940. Our period of passion and intensity began in May 1940 with the threat of invasion, turned stranger as bombing began in June, reaching the first of many climaxes in September. The bombing continued beyond the famed 'last night of the Blitz' in May 1941, as did the social, economic and psychological consequences – which are still evident to this day.

And throughout this book, behind the stories and experiences and consequences has sat the idea of Blitz Spirit, sometimes described as though it were a mind-altering drug that swept across Britain in 1940, filling people with love and concern for each other, blotting out stubborn thoughts and obstinate attitudes. Beyond becoming the centrepiece of the Blitz consensus, what actually was this wartime mood enhancer? Was it a tangible concept created by the British people (with assistance from Winston Churchill and Nazi Germany)? Was it a version of established working-class attitudes to deprivation and anxiety, repackaged for a nation at war? In fact – did it exist at all?

Bernard Kregor was a young ARP messenger in Forest Gate, east

London. The bombing made him grow up very quickly. 'I became absolutely a realist,' he says. 'The world was a dark place, and life was a serious business.' Since those days, Kregor has tried to make the best of every day. 'I never ever take anything for granted. That's how I was, and that's how I am to this day.' And if the Blitz turned Bernard Kregor into a serious young man, it did the same for Bernard Kops, growing up in nearby Stepney. He writes, with striking similarity, of the Blitz as a time when he 'stopped being a child and came face to face with the new reality of the world'.

For Kregor, the new darkness gave rise to genuine social unity. Nowadays, people might sit stony-faced on buses and trains, but this, he says, was not the case in 1940 and 1941:

> During the Blitz people spoke to each other, they exchanged their experiences of the raid the night before, what happened, how it affected them. This was different from a year before. And let's face it, it changed back after the war. Didn't take long . . .

Kops disagrees. He felt no sense of belonging. Some people, he says, talk about the Blitz as a time of communal spirit – but that was not his experience. Rather than unity, he remembers only forced humour. It was, he writes, 'an era of utter terror, of fear and horror'.

Here, then, are the dangers of generalising about the effects of the Blitz on British people. Two young men, similar in background, apparently similar in outlook, but sharply divided on the nature and existence of Blitz Spirit.

We have certainly witnessed the capacity of the Blitz to cause all manner of responses – and many have been negative. The agony of Maisie Dance and Gwen Hughes, the misery of Ida Rodway and James Miller, the fear of Viola Bawtree, the discomfort of 'Rosemary Black', the shock of Coventry's citizens, the disappointment of West Indian workers, the despair of the dispossessed, the fear in unpoliced streets, the confusion of honest shopkeepers, the soldiers cuckolded by their wives, the four-year-old evacuee beaten sixty-four times because he wanted a biscuit: the Blitz was inventive in its cruelty. We must never forget the sheer misery it caused.

A modern-day walk down Shawfield Street, Chelsea, reveals Victorian buildings at the north end. Towards the river, these become shiny, red-brick terraces, similar in style to Disney's version of London at its Epcot theme park in Florida. These modern terraces were built in the 1960s to replace those destroyed shortly after 7 p.m. on Friday 1 November 1940. Fifteen minutes after that blast, Irene Haslewood arrived on the scene.

Irene, known as Bobby, was the driver for an ARP stretcher party. Four bearers used to squeeze into her Hillman saloon, with their stretchers strapped onto the roof. Her party was meant to be first to arrive after an 'incident', sorting the living from the dead, giving first aid to the wounded, and placing them onto stretchers. While Irene's squad was doing this, ambulances were arriving to take the wounded to hospital.

The members of a stretcher party hurry to their saloon car in Fulham.

On that Friday night, Irene and her party arrived at Shawfield Street to find half of it missing. Because the raid had come early in the evening, many people had not yet reached their Anderson shelters. The team wandered across the demolished area, calling out for survivors. They searched the houses still standing, but were thwarted by collapsed staircases and heaps of rubble and debris. A young man and woman were found at the top of a building. The woman died almost immediately, but the man, it seemed, could be saved. He had a compressed fracture of the skull, which was carefully dressed, before he was strapped to a stretcher, and brought down several precarious flights of stairs. 'To bring a fully loaded stretcher down,' writes Irene, 'was a work of art.'

Once on the ground, the young man's mother appeared, and threw herself on top of her son. She had to be physically dragged away. Irene writes:

> It may seem incredible but it is none the less the disgraceful truth that no ambulance had yet arrived on the scene. So they had to put the stretcher down in the street to await the arrival of an ambulance. To my dying day I feel that I shall always hear those gurgling snores of the poor devil as his life slowly ebbed away.

The man died later in hospital. He might have been saved had the ambulance arrived promptly. Its late arrival, claims Irene, was due to an argument between two wardens in their Flood Street post. 'I have no comment to make about such behaviour,' she writes.

Just as the consensus has never allowed for the idea that the emergency services were guilty of crime, so examples of their incompetence have rarely been acknowledged. But complaints *were* lodged – and efforts were made, at the height of the Blitz, to learn from mistakes. In early 1941, for example, an inquiry was held by the Civil Defence Regional Officer, after a landmine had killed twenty-five people in Maybury Mansions, a large block of flats on

Marylebone Street. The inquiry was a response to public complaints about the actions of the police and rescue authorities after the explosion. One man stated: 'There is good reason to believe that not only was the search not conducted with the necessary number of men and the energy requisite under the circumstances, but also that it was not undertaken in a skilled manner.' Another man, whose wife was killed by the explosion, added that 'the Rescue Squads did very little', and that had more been done, 'they could in my opinion, have rescued many people'. He said, 'I tremble when I think of the thousands who still have to die under such conditions.' Another witness noted negligent behaviour among the rescuers, including 'one of the men examining gramophone records'.

Maybury Mansions.

The resulting inquiry was forensic in its approach. Witnesses were carefully examined, and a nine-page judgement was handed down. The regional officer concluded that there had been a lack of co-operation between the police and the Rescue Service, that there had been a failure in communication between the rescue site and the Control Centre, resulting in a failure to envisage 'the magnitude of the disaster', and that the Incident Officer had made insufficient efforts to discover the number of people in the building, before 'closing the incident' too soon.

Despite these failings, however, the regional officer believed that none of the deaths could be attributed to 'any lack of energy or skill on the part of the Rescue Service'. On the contrary, he praised the rescue parties, finding that they had recovered casualties 'in the shortest possible time, having regard to the special circumstances'.

The 'special circumstances', as we have continually observed, were demanding. Irene Haslewood's experience as a member of a stretcher squad had begun in earnest on the night of 8 September. As Joan Wyndham and Gerald Dougherty basked in their post-coital glow, as Viola Bawtree struggled with God, as Michael Bowyer prepared to throw beer bottles at the Wehrmacht, Irene was sent to deal with the effects of a bomb that killed fifty-six people in a shelter on Beaufort Street. She writes:

> The scene was of death and devastation. Huge slabs of concrete trapped poor mangled bodies beneath their jagged weight. Poor twisted bodies – blackened and begrimed from the blood and dust. Bits of bodies lay in puddles of water, blood and filth. Dear God! That first glimpse of Hitler's work! I felt my stomach heave for a paralysing second, and I thought I was going to vomit, thereby disgracing myself and my squad for ever. But I managed to gulp heavily and then felt more or less all right again.

Two nights later, a bomb fell opposite the squad's depot. Irene was thrown across the room. The various squads were split up, so that a single bomb could not put them all out of action, and for the next few hours, as Irene and her colleagues waited to be called out, they sat alongside each other on a plank in a pitch-black underground passage. Irene began to feel fear: 'I underwent the monstrous experience of being really frightened. I shivered and shook and hoped to God that my next door neighbours could not feel it.' And when she tried to stand up to go to the toilet, Irene was mortified by what happened:

> I could not stand! . . . Then I remembered that there was a merest drain of whiskey left in my flask . . . Almost at once the miracle happened and I found myself to be in complete control of my nether limbs again. I was able to get up and stand, and then walk – rather unsteadily upstairs.

Fear, we have seen, was the hidden engine driving the country, sending shelterers underground, encouraging apparent fearlessness and genuine courage, and giving 'Rosemary Black' – and many others – the impulse to work and think communally.

For Irene, doing a difficult and dangerous job, fear was a rite of passage, a necessary hurdle to be cleared. But not everybody could contain their feelings. Arthur Dales was a young ARP messenger in Hull whose sixteen-year-old cousin became hysterical in a crowded shelter. Arthur's uncle was the shelter warden: 'My uncle realised that it would be very difficult if all the women and children in the shelter became hysterical so he took his own daughter, picked her up, and knocked her out with a blow under the chin.' One wonders how that punch affected family get-togethers in years to come.

Marjorie Redman, meanwhile, was a sub-editor on *The Listener* magazine, who was lodging with an older London couple. The wife remained fearful throughout the Blitz. On one typical night, she woke in terror, exclaiming that something had fallen nearby. After speculating aloud for some time, she was interrupted by her husband: 'First you say it's an incendiary, then you say it's a time bomb, then you say it's a land mine, and now you say it's a brick. Well, it can't be all of them.'

Yet despite the prevalence of fear, the country never descended into widespread panic or hysteria. Indeed, according to an October 1941 study by Philip E. Vernon, head of Psychology at Glasgow

University, British people were demonstrating far greater mental resilience than psychologists had predicted. There had been fewer psychological disorders, fewer hospital admissions, and quicker acclimatisation to bombing than had been anticipated.

This, in itself, might be considered an indication that Blitz Spirit was a reality – particularly given Vernon's explanations. His primary observation was that people were gaining resilience from the company of others. From tube shelters to family Andersons to volunteerism to the increase in sexual behaviour, the fact was that people were instinctively drawn to each other, and they managed fear better as a result. And secondly, Vernon found that war-work was serving as 'an excellent palliative for potential nervousness'. If we think back to 'Rosemary Black', whose 'agony of experience' drove her to find useful work, it seems that fear could offer its own solutions.

But beyond these factors, there existed a sense of relief that bombing was *survivable*. This had been no foregone conclusion. In 1921 the Italian general Giulio Douhet had argued that armies would, in future, be superfluous as entire cities were turned to rubble by bombers. His arguments were taken up in Britain. In November 1932 Stanley Baldwin told Parliament, 'I think it is well also for the man in the street to realise that there is no power on earth that can protect him from being bombed. Whatever people may tell him, the bomber will always get through.' And Baldwin went much further, predicting that when the next war came, European civilisation would be wiped out. Harold Macmillan, writing in 1956, explained that his generation thought of air warfare 'rather as people think of nuclear war today'. And the fact was that, by 1940, a chilling precedent already existed. Three years earlier, appalled by reports of the bombing of the Spanish town of Guernica by German and Italian aircraft, Pablo Picasso began work on a painting that quickly came to embody the fear and suffering of aerial bombing. On its subsequent tour of major cities, *Guernica* was deemed an accurate – if somewhat figurative –

representation of Europe's likely fate. It was against this background that the people of Britain looked to the skies in 1940. And given their doom-laden expectations, Blitz Spirit might be seen as a huge sigh of communal relief.

Certainly, as our period began, the country was split between those keen to seek terms, and those braced for a bitter fight. Winston Churchill, for example, disagreed with the suggestion of his foreign secretary, Lord Halifax, on 25 May, that Mussolini ought to be sounded out to broker negotiations between Britain and Germany. For Halifax, this did not amount to appeasement; it was plain common sense. For Churchill, simply making an approach would be fatal. Any terms offered, he believed, would place Britain at Hitler's mercy. A month later, Andrew Gow, Fellow of Trinity College Cambridge, wrote in his diary that Britain had a duty to fight, firstly to preserve the liberty of the individual, and, secondly to protect international standards of decency. 'For my own part,' Gow writes, 'provided we win this war I do not care what happens to me; and if we should chance to lose, the thought of surviving is intolerable.'

This was not necessarily the entire country's view, however. The people of Kettering in Northamptonshire returned a young Conservative army officer, John Profumo, as their member of Parliament in March 1940. Profumo would gain considerable notoriety twenty-three years later, but his 1940 election was notable for the fact that his only opponent – a man named William Ross of the Workers and Pensioners' Anti-War Party – received a startling twenty-seven per cent of the vote. Indeed, after success by Independent candidates in a series of 1942 by-elections, a joint message signed by Winston Churchill and Clement Attlee declared that the British electorate had the responsibility 'of indicating to the United Nations, and to neutral countries, that we are united among ourselves'.

But Britain was never fully united. And before the bombing had started, the country could certainly not be said to be pulling in a single direction. George Jackaman was a radio engineer working in

Camden Town in London. When he told his boss that he was planning to become a full-time air raid warden, he was told, 'If you prefer your country to your company, we won't have you back any more.' In Stoke Newington, meanwhile, twenty auxiliary police officers were refusing to carry out guard duties, while in Holloway, thirteen auxiliaries refused to go on duty at all. Complaints about pay and duties were overriding any sense of national obligation.

Once the bombs had begun to fall, Home Intelligence reported that there was 'evidence of growing strain especially among women and children', and that the public should be offered more appreciation, encouragement, congratulations, and explanation. Blitz Spirit needed, in other words, to be boosted. And the public chose to boost its own spirits in questionable fashion – by 'sightseeing' in bombed areas. Morning-after voyeurism became so common that the Home Secretary, Sir John Anderson, had to appeal to the public to keep away from recently bombed areas. In September Anderson told the House of Commons that the public 'had responded' to his appeal, and he would now shelve plans to turn public assembly at recent bomb sites into a criminal offence. Winifred Musson had gone sightseeing to South Wimbledon in August after a raid. She and a friend caught a bus from Hammersmith, and when they finally reached Wimbledon, it was almost dark. 'We imagined picture postcards and 2d to get in,' she writes in her diary, 'but the goggling populace (which we assumed from the paper-strewn streets) had cleared off by then.'

As August turned into September, Home Intelligence reported 'great apprehension' in some London districts, as well as 'despondency' at the prospect of a winter of raids. Once the heavy raids began, mental and physical effects became noticeable. Philip Vernon notes the spread of 'irritability, jumpiness, tension and emotionality', as well as 'muscular incoordination', 'cessation of digestion and sexual appetite', and 'the sinking feeling'. We have witnessed plenty of fearful behaviour in previous chapters – but we have also observed excitement from people whose lives had ceased to be ordinary. In early September Mass-Observation was monitoring the behaviour of seven trainee waitresses, recently hired by Lyons Corner House in Marble Arch. (One of the seven was secretly an investigator.) For the first week of heavy bombing, the waitresses were almost constantly cheerful, their conversations peppered with laughter. Underpinning their enjoyment was fear (their training was continually interrupted by raids during which they held hands as they hurried down to the shelter), novelty (they laughed at funny-looking Belgians in the street, they flirted with male employees, they joked with strangers on buses), and informality (they were permitted to show up late for work in the mornings).

And beyond the newly friendly atmosphere, some people were experiencing exhilaration. A young female Mass-Observation diarist was in Hampstead in London, on 9 September, when the area received its first bombs. After a bomb landed nearby, throwing her to the ground and badly damaging the house in which she was staying, her fear ('a horrid, sick sort of fear') turned quickly to 'pure and flawless happiness'. Decades later, she remembered the event as a 'peak experience' of her life, comparable with having a baby.

As a response to heightened and extreme reactions, came efforts to impose calm. There was a widespread duty, observed Caryl Brahms, to be as 'just the same' as possible in daily life. We have seen that it was considered bad form to allow a siren to interrupt a restaurant conversation. Vera Reid, meanwhile, was amused by a newspaper advertisement urging women to maintain their figures during the current crisis. While the advantage of a slim waist during an incendiary shower might not seem immediately obvious, there was purpose to this kind of banality: the country could not be allowed to disintegrate into panic and turmoil, and the imposition of 'normality' helped to keep chaos at bay. Even if the normality might be as heightened as the fear and exhilaration it was combating.

The 'Britain Can Take It' approach did not appeal to everybody. Its 'chirpy insouciance' was as tiresome to Ronald Blythe as a pub bore describing last night's raid. Such nonchalance was, to Blythe, as affected as 'the awful bonhomie through which we flourished'. Yet as false as the nonchalance and bonhomie may have been, they set a standard to which others aspired. And the result was 'better' behaviour. This was clearly a factor in Philip Vernon's post-Blitz observation that 'many rather timid and neurotically inclined persons seem to have become better adjusted and more confident'.

Examples of insouciance could reach almost comical levels. In October 1940 Marjorie Redman was enjoying a lunchtime concert given by the Stratton Quartet at the National Gallery. In the middle came an unexpected crescendo: a bomb on a delay fuse exploded. Some of the audience leapt up in alarm – but the quartet played on as though nothing had happened. 'People not only subside,' writes Redman in her diary, 'but several by the door say "Sssshhh!" as if someone had talked in the slow movement of Eroica.' There is something absurd and wonderful about a music-lover warning a high-explosive bomb to shut up. Even Canute only attempted to lecture the sea.

As confidence spread, so the national mood grew defiant; this is reflected in the play *Thunder Rock*, more darkly in the behaviour of John Fulljames, and most famously in the ubiquity of Blitz humour, that celebrated denial of fear and uncertainty. At the height of the bombing, the Lyons waitresses yelled with laughter when a bus conductor told them that they should be careful not to talk at night, because 'there may be a Jerry under the bed' (Jerry was slang for a German – and for a chamber pot). The almost hysterical reaction to a ropy old joke seems to reflect the communal need for release. The joke, in fact, was not much better than those delivered by Cecil Hughes in Oxford; the only real difference was that Hughes misread his audience, and ended up with a criminal conviction.

The nation's defiance mirrored that of David Charleston, *Thunder Rock*'s central character. Given the country's history and continuity, it seemed natural that Britain should take the lead in the fight for a better world, and that Andrew Gow preferred to die than to survive in a conquered Britain. Gwyneth Kahn, an American who had recently worked in Britain, received a letter in late 1940 in which an unknown British author writes that Hitler had 'got the British psychology all wrong. The more he hurts the people in the things we love, the more utterly determined and strong and united we become to smash him and finish his reign of evil for ever – never mind what it may cost us.' The notion still persists today that the British people thrive on misfortune.

But before we place too much emphasis on Britain's moral and spiritual superiority, we should remember how the resurgence of Coventry was inspired, in great measure, by sheer necessity. This was a common theme across the country. The nation's defiance was not just a matter of principle, nor simply the result of heightened passions. It was also a practical necessity for people living in a society without social or economic safety nets. In order to survive, ordinary people had to carry on 'normally', and their survival was now threatened as never before. We should not overlook the basic human necessity behind Blitz Spirit.

Nor should we overlook people's ability to turn suffering into a cause for pride and congratulation. In Coventry this pride was bolstered by the interest received from around the globe. In London, as Peter Ackroyd has stated, people 'believed themselves to be especially chosen for calamity'. Pride worked at an individual level, and at a communal level, and the authorities were happy to encourage it, just as they encouraged continued belief in the threat of invasion. 'I don't know anybody who hasn't been bombed, or anybody who hasn't been bombed *badly*, with this gruesome snobbery which is rife,' wrote Winifred Musson in a letter. Pride is, after all, a sin. 'To be able to say that you have not taken your clothes off for a fortnight,' Marjorie Redman told her diary, 'shows that you are a woman of real sensibility – or so you might imagine from the pride with which people give this information.' Just as people were trying to seem as nonchalant and

294 THE SECRET HISTORY OF THE BLITZ

insouciant as possible, so they were trying to impress others with their levels of suffering; and though their motives might have been dubious, the net effect was actually to increase the country's ability to tolerate and endure.

This should not obscure the fact, however, that much of the suffering was real, and that many could neither tolerate nor endure. While Philip Vernon was keen to stress that the Blitz caused less psychological injury than the experts had predicted, his report nevertheless offers a sobering glimpse of the mental damage that *was* caused. Victims ranged from those suffering from 'acute terror' after being caught in the bombing, to those – like Ida Rodway – who were plunged into a state of 'agitated confusion' following the loss of their homes. Vernon describes long-term psychological victims such as a young trainee teacher who underwent a personality change following the death of a friend. The woman 'has fulfilled none of her early promise as a teacher', writes Vernon, her energy and determination used up in internal conflict.

Quentin Crisp spoke of a young friend who suffered a nervous breakdown, spending nights staring at his front door 'in case *they* should come in'. The man's girlfriend eventually committed him to a mental hospital. 'The war did not cause his madness,' writes Crisp, 'it aggravated it by pressing on the soft wall of a hopelessly unrealistic personality.' And as we have seen, it did much the same to Lillian Rogers, unleashing neuroses that would otherwise have remained buried.

It is possible, in fact, that the Blitz caused considerably more psychological damage than has commonly been acknowledged. Psychiatrists' and psychologists' relief that the bombing did not lead to an overwhelming wave of trauma has masked much of the damage that *did* occur. Philip Vernon admits an increase in 'minor' symptoms such as depression, lowering of confidence, increases in drinking and smoking, dissociations of personality and a sharp rise in stress-related illnesses. Eric Oddy, a policeman in London, recalls suffering from a number of such problems during the Blitz, including an outbreak of boils and the loosening of his teeth. 'A lot of people had these things,' he says.

Fellow policeman Les Waters had a four-year-old daughter: 'The Blitz affected her so bad that her hair was falling out. I did feel sorry for her. What a place to live, a quarter of a mile from Woolwich Arsenal.' Once again, as we dig a little deeper, we find a more nuanced story. But the widespread existence of psychological difficulties does not contradict the fact that stoicism increased as the Blitz wore on. Home Intelligence reports confirm that the majority of people began to settle down to the 'new air-raid life cheerfully'.

There were many reasons for this. Some of the most nervous individuals had left the danger areas, while many of those feigning courage had discovered that the bombing was bearable, and so no longer had to feign. At the same time, people were finding tactics and strategies for getting by. One of the most common was the tendency to talk about raids. 'In London, conversation is almost exclusively about air raids,' noted a Home Intelligence report on 21 September, adding that 'it is gossipy, not panicky, and is centred on personal matters'. This desire to share stories was the basis for the social interaction that characterises Blitz Spirit. A temporarily shared interest got people talking to each other; after it went away, they stopped talking. And even before it had disappeared, good old British cynicism was on the scene. At the end of October, Phyllis Warner spotted the appearance of badges reading 'I'm not interested in your bomb!'

Nevertheless, it is clear that Blitz Spirit was real enough. In its purest form, it amounted to the desire to interact, to share whatever was held in common, whether the story of a bomb, the desire to make life better, or the urge to lie together at night. The universality of death made it seem important to make a connection with the living – and to make the most of one's own life. Blitz Spirit was an instinctive realisation that life mattered.

This book has attempted to offer a taste of the reality beyond the consensus. This 'myth', as Angus Calder pointed out in 1991, presents a story stripped of complexity in order to appear historically destined. It is not a story founded on lies. Blitz Spirit was genuine, but its subtlety and complexity were removed by journalists, politicians, civil servants and ordinary people – while the bombs were still falling. This hurried framing of a consensus served a crucial purpose. Just as forced nonchalance and bonhomie inspired the less confident, and overstated endurance encouraged genuine fortitude, so a freshly minted consensus taught the country how to behave. *Britain Can Take It* – and so can you.

Indeed, a search through government documents allows us to pull back the curtain to catch a glimpse of its creation. In January 1941 a Civil Defence Executive committee urged the Ministry of Information to mount a campaign to improve home morale. The committee provided a long list of morale problems, some relating to specific groups (dockers, transport workers, coal merchants) and others to the public generally. The overall problem, according to the committee, was 'under-developed team spirit', and the solution was for the Ministry of Information to mount a positive campaign informing the people of Britain that their action provided 'the finest example of team work the world has ever seen'. Britain was to be encouraged through praise, rather than lectured or rebuked, into living up to the idea that the British are at their best in difficult circumstances. And so, at the height of the Blitz, the real story was scoured and tweaked until it came to resemble a slimmed-down, fresh-faced version of itself.

In truth, of course, there was no single story. People behaved well, they behaved badly – and they sometimes sat in shelters, disengaged from reality, doing nothing at all. Throughout this book, we have seen an extraordinary range of behaviour – and an equally remarkable intensity of behaviour. For which there was plenty of reason. 'The future has quite simply ceased to exist for most of us, and we live quite happily in the present,' wrote a sub-editor at *Woman* magazine to Gwyneth Kahn in the autumn of 1940. 'I live each day now as if it was my last,' wrote Phyllis Warner in her diary in late September.

Living in the present, liberated from traditional constraints, people behaved as they had never done before. In a world that might end tomorrow, in which opportunities suddenly presented themselves, why should a woman not enter a pub alone . . . or lose her virginity? Why not speak to a stranger on the bus, help a neighbour in need, or steal from a bomb site? Here, surely, is the key to the extremes we have witnessed, and to the precious meaning uncovered in many people's lives. After a heavy raid, Phyllis Warner wrote: 'Before this I thought I didn't care a rap whether I lived or died, but these night vigils have taught me that I want to live so badly.' The uncertainty of survival was freeing Phyllis from a multitude of concerns. She was no longer worried about her job, her clothes or her future. Her life felt more satisfying and far more interesting than it ever had before. And once the raids had eased off, her worries started to return. 'Now that I no longer rate my chances of being dead tomorrow at fifty-fifty,' she writes in March 1941, 'I get depressed about the privation, ugliness and suffering that surrounds me, and go dreary about my prospects.' She has even become nostalgic for the heavy raids, observing that with a brief return to the bombing, 'just being alive and whole would supremely content me'.

As the nation's temperature was raised, as its people were lifted to an emotional pitch, the crime, the empathy, the misery, the self-reliance, the fear, the sex, the prejudice, the initiative, the pride, the depression, the defiance, the raised expectations, the anger, the risk-taking, the selfishness, the unity – all were exposed and intensified.

The raised temperature and flight from normality is observable in almost every sphere of existence. Life, for example, was as strange for Britain's pets as it was for its people. In 1939 the ARP published its Handbook No. 12, setting out its plans for dealing with pets in the event of bombing. It is a thorough little document, containing

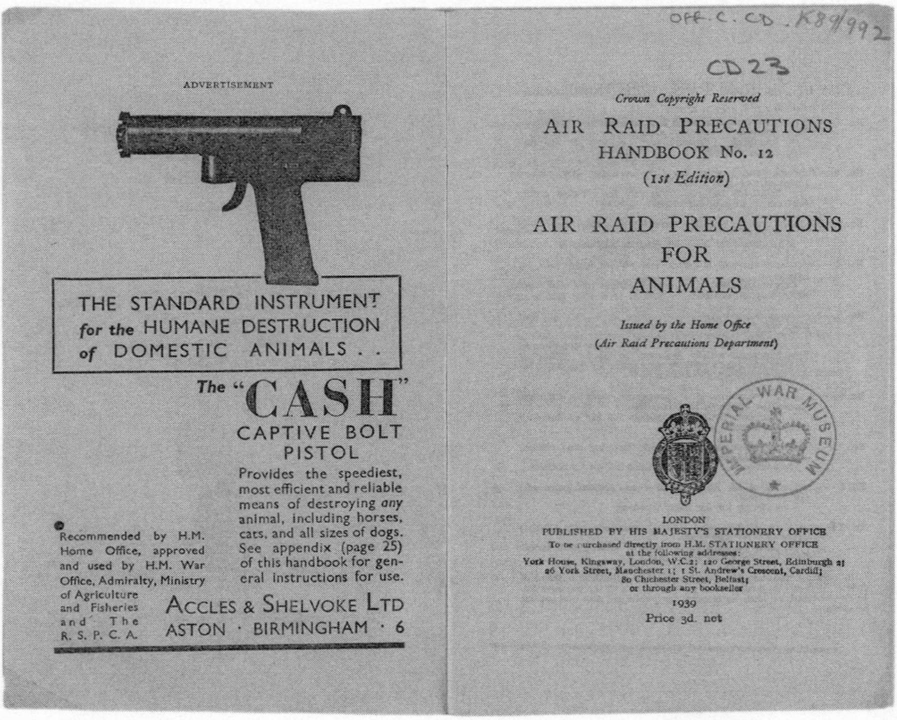
ADVERTISEMENT
THE STANDARD INSTRUMENT for the HUMANE DESTRUCTION of DOMESTIC ANIMALS . .
The "CASH" CAPTIVE BOLT PISTOL
Provides the speediest, most efficient and reliable means of destroying any animal, including horses, cats, and all sizes of dogs. See appendix (page 25) of this handbook for general instructions for use.
Recommended by H.M. Home Office, approved and used by H.M. War Office, Admiralty, Ministry of Agriculture and Fisheries and The R. S. P. C. A.
ACCLES & SHELVOKE LTD
ASTON · BIRMINGHAM · 6
OFF. C. CD. K89/992
CD23
Crown Copyright Reserved
AIR RAID PRECAUTIONS
HANDBOOK No. 12
(1st Edition)
AIR RAID PRECAUTIONS FOR ANIMALS
Issued by the Home Office
(Air Raid Precautions Department)
IMPERIAL WAR MUSEUM
LONDON
PUBLISHED BY HIS MAJESTY'S STATIONERY OFFICE
To be purchased directly from H.M. STATIONERY OFFICE
at the following addresses:
York House, Kingsway, London, W.C.2; 120 George Street, Edinburgh 2;
26 York Street, Manchester 1; 1 St. Andrew's Crescent, Cardiff;
80 Chichester Street, Belfast;
or through any bookseller
1939
Price 3d. net

ARP Precautions Handbook No. 12 and a disturbing advertisement.

information about animals' responses to air raids and toxic gases, first aid tips on treating pets injured by different kinds of bomb, and advice on how to use the 'Captive Bolt Pistol' so that 'the animal is killed and not merely stunned'.

The authorities' basic fear was that cities would be overrun by terrified cats and dogs, all turned out onto the streets by equally terrified owners. The handbook stressed that pets were the personal responsibility of their owners, that they would not be allowed into public shelters, and that anyone evacuated under an official scheme would not be allowed to bring their pets with them. A misjudged radio broadcast, meanwhile, announced that if sending pets to friends outside the city was not practicable, it was 'kindest to have them destroyed'. This advice lodged in the minds of the nation's pet owners, with the result that, over a single hysterical week at the start of the war, three quarters of a million healthy animals were quite unnecessarily put down.

In September 1940, when the intensive bombing of London began, many dogs and cats were abandoned to roam the streets – the outcome feared by the authorities. It fell to the various animal welfare charities, working with the National Air Raid Precautions Animals Committee, to herd the strays to temporary shelters. But these shelters were soon full – and tens of thousands of healthy animals were again put down.

A case recorded in the files of the Citizens Advice Bureaux offers a sense of the complicated relationship between pets and owners during the Blitz. A woman had been forced to abandon her bomb-damaged house, and she was now living in her husband's office. Nevertheless, she returned to the house every day to feed her cat. She was unable to have the cat destroyed, she guiltily told a bureau adviser, because her local animal clinic had been bombed. This sad little vignette neatly illustrates the struggle between emotional attachment and perceived duty in the minds of animal-loving Britons. One can almost sense the woman's relief on discovering that the

A cuddly early warning system: the comfort provided by pets during the
Blitz should not be underestimated.

animal clinic was out of action. Pets were still adored – but the idea
had taken hold that the correct and kind thing to do was to destroy
them. They could not withstand the noise and chaos of bombing, it
was felt, and there was no room for sentiment with the nation's
future in the balance.

So many animals were killed unnecessarily in the early years of the

Individual air raid shelters for dogs in Kensington Gardens.

war that *In Memoriam* classifieds became a common sight in local newspapers, placed by owners quietly ashamed of their behaviour. But there were also organisations, publications and individuals fighting on behalf of the animals. *Dogs Bulletin*, one of many wartime pet publications, wrote in 1944:

Dogs had dug into wrecked homes looking for their owners. Cats have mewed for days outside piles of rubble telling rescuers their owners are buried there. Animals have quietened frightened children. Yet when the history of the war is written, these things will not be recorded.

Or perhaps they will be. Les James was a teenage member of the Cyclist Messenger Service Corps in Hull. Having crashed his cycle in the blackout one night, he was told by a policeman to escort an old man to hospital. The man's shelter had been bombed, he was covered in cement dust and was carrying a birdcage. As bombs fell around them, as emergency traffic sped past, the man stopped in the middle of the road to look inside the cage. Les had to hurry him along. 'Despite his shock and peril,' says Les, 'this man only cared for the welfare of his budgie.' Eventually they arrived at the hospital, where the man resisted all attempts to see to his injuries. He only wanted to uncover the cage and check on his pet. Les remembers what happened next:

> The bird was huddled on the floor of the cage, covered in dust, and apparently dead. However, the welfare volunteer lady, obviously a bird fancier, tenderly picked up the budgie, blew off the dust, and revived it by means of weak brandy and TLC. The effect on the old man was miraculous. He at once became revived and belligerent towards the Luftwaffe. His world had been restored to him. The dangers of the Blitz, the blackout, the shock to his system, his filthy state covered in dust and grime, meant nothing to him compared with the welfare of his only friend.

No story could better illustrate the comfort and sense of optimism that pets brought to their owners during the Blitz.

And sometimes they could do even more. In a previous chapter, we met Roy Bartlett, the little boy who spent so much of his early life in his parents' shelter in west London. Roy had a cat called Stripey. At the start of the war, Roy's parents wanted to have Stripey put to sleep.

A little girl assisting the 'Animals' Home Guard' by bringing food
to cats living in the rubble of their old homes.

'Stripey was *not* going to be put down,' says Roy, 'and eventually
Mum and Dad relented.'Which was just as well – because Stripey had
an important job to do. Whenever he heard the sirens sounding in
outlying districts – long before the humans could hear anything –
Stripey would run into the house, and hide under the sink. He was
a hugely effective – and very cuddly – early warning system.

Nor was it just cats doing unaccustomed work. The raised temperature had profound political and social effects. Foremost was the
fact that women were taking on new roles and responsibilities in
every conceivable sphere. In May 1941 women began flying Spitfires
and Hurricanes as members of the Air Transport Auxiliary, ferrying
them from factories to airfields and operational units. Five foot three
and seven stone, Jackie Moggridge had no problems flying the
Spitfire, that icon of masculinity. 'If you were the type that needs to
use brute force,' she says, 'then you wouldn't be good at the job

because aeroplanes need a delicate touch.' Only once in her flying career did she encounter a flying instrument that she, as a woman, was unable to use. While familiarising herself with the Spitfire, she pulled a tube with a funnel on the end from under the seat. 'What's this?' she asked the engineer. 'That's for gentleman pilots only, miss,' he answered.

The Blitz was, after all, a period of misrule, evoking folk memories of the medieval tradition which saw the normal order of things temporarily turned upside-down, with the status of ordinary people raised, and odd rituals adopted. But by the end of the Blitz, there was a large section of the population keen to see this modern misrule made permanent.

It is this change in attitude that marks the birth of modern sensibilities, modern expectations, and so many of the social, political and economic institutions which we now treasure / take for granted / despise. It begins at the start of our period with the end of Conservative political and ideological supremacy, and the coming to the fore of the Labour Party – peculiarly cloaked as the party of patriotism. For although Winston Churchill was running the war, it was the Labour leaders who were guiding Home Front policy. They introduced what A. J. P. Taylor described as socialism with the difficulties left out. Their innovations were largely unresisted – but they were far-reaching. 'Direction and control,' wrote Taylor, 'turned Great Britain into a country more fully socialist than anything achieved by the conscious planners of Soviet Russia.'

The man who took the guiding hand in the leftward shift was Ernest Bevin. Once a Somerset farm boy, Bevin had risen to become the first General Secretary of the Transport and General Workers Union, and the government's most vociferous opponent. Yet invited by Churchill to become Minister for Labour, he suddenly found himself wielding astonishing power. He was able to direct any worker in the country to take any job, at any wages or hours, and on any conditions that he specified.

But it made good practical sense to bring Bevin into the government. If radical economic measures were necessary to rearm the country, little could be achieved without the full support of the workers and the unions – and Bevin commanded their trust. Crucially, he understood the importance of manpower; financial muscle alone could not build weapons. His most pressing tasks were to restore almost a million unemployed to the workplace, and to persuade workers to accept restrictions for the common good without having to rely on compulsion.

In May 1940, as the beaches of Dunkirk were being evacuated, Bevin spoke to delegates from over a hundred and fifty unions at the largest conference since the General Strike of 1926. He asked the unions to place themselves at the disposal of the state. In practice, this meant accepting that an individual could be directed to any job, and could no longer leave it. It also meant that skilled jobs could be broken down into separate operations, some of which would now be carried out by unskilled workers. But in return, workers would be offered a guaranteed wage, and could no longer be sacked without recourse to a tribunal. In addition, if negotiations between management and union broke down, the matter would automatically be referred to arbitration. These amounted to pioneering safeguards for workers. 'For the first time,' says Jack Jones, the Coventry secretary of the Transport and General Workers Union, 'the trade unions really came into their own.'

During his speech to the unions, Bevin made a prediction: 'This I am convinced of: if our movement and our class now rise with all their energy and save the people of this country from disaster, the country will always turn with confidence to the people who saved them.'

So far as Bevin was concerned, war socialism was not simply an expedient measure, valid for the duration. It amounted to the building blocks of post-war Britain. And it was not just committed socialists who saw the war as the basis for a fairer society. No one had ever accused Foreign Secretary Lord Halifax of being a socialist, yet on 30 July he wrote to Minister of Information Duff Cooper stating that, in the peaceful future, 'human conscience in this country is not going to stand for a system that permits large numbers of unemployed' and that it was now 'necessary to have greater regard to the human values and not allow them to be smothered by considerations of old-fashioned financial purity'. In his reply, Cooper said that 'the minds of a great many people whom you would not expect to agree are moving in the same direction.'

This exchange between two staunch Conservatives came as they discussed a Cabinet memo, drafted by Harold Nicolson at the Ministry of Information, proposing that the government should prepare a statement of British war aims. Hitler, after all, had his own freely expressed war aims, and it was felt that Britain ought to have something positive with which to reply. Nicolson suggested the following:

> We should admit that the old order is changing and must give way to the new . . . Every effort must be made to provide real equality of opportunity for the younger generation, since it is upon their action and intelligence that the New Order will depend. We must cease to think in the old terms of risk and profit and think only of the needs to be met and the resources of labour and material available to meet them.

A War Aims Committee of the War Cabinet was duly formed, with Attlee, Halifax, Chamberlain, Bevin, and Chancellor of the Exchequer Sir Kingsley Wood among its members. To assist the committee, Professor Arnold Toynbee, director of the Royal Institute of International Affairs, was asked to deliver a set of guiding proposals for post-war reconstruction. Toynbee's paper advocated equal access to medical services, a system of family allowances, social services for all, an overhaul of the education system, and an end to a society based on privilege. As Hitler was poised to invade Britain, so the predominantly Conservative War Aims Committee found itself setting out the decidedly un-Tory foundations for the post-war welfare state.

When the concerted bombing of London began, discussion of change began to appear frequently in the media, offering – as it did – hope to an embattled people. An editorial in *The Times* on 4 October indicated that Britain would not be content with a return to the past. The country was fighting not to restore, but to build. 'Out of this horror must come the building of a better housed as well as a better fed British people.'

The fact was that bombing was hastening some of the proposed changes into existence. The government's unpreparedness for mass homelessness in London led to those progressive measures introduced by Conservative MP Henry Willink in October 1940. These measures – including the sweeping away of 'poor law' attitudes – were paving the way for the welfare state. Four months later, architect Donald Gibson's plan for rebuilding Coventry was adopted. A local housewife, Mrs Adams, told the BBC that she was delighted by the prospect of life in a modern Coventry. She wanted a shopping centre where she could buy everything in one place, instead of 'scampering around' until she was fit to drop. Above all, she said that she wanted a modern house that was easy to keep clean, with an electric washing machine, a Frigidaire, and plenty of electric points. 'Why should we put up with brass taps, old fashioned skirting boards, and dark corners that collect the dust?' Mrs Adams asked. 'We want a house that'll save our legs a bit . . .'

As the Blitz raged, the Cabinet War Aims Committee continued to meet, preparing material for a major speech to be delivered by Churchill. Its basis was to be Toynbee's paper, but in November 1940 Halifax added three vague moral principles, which, he accepted, would need stiffening. The Chancellor of the Exchequer proposed that mention be made of any future system offering security to its citizens, while Bevin suggested a further principle: 'The direction of our economy is to achieve social security and the provision of a reasonable standard of living and social welfare.'

Ultimately, a document heaving with progressive rhetoric was delivered to Churchill. His speech would proclaim that the nation's social conscience had been aroused by the war, that abject poverty would no longer be tolerated, and that economic, social and educational practices would have to be overhauled in order to secure a reasonable standard of life for all.

But – to the disappointment of many – Churchill never broadcast this collectivist manifesto. Harold Nicolson's diary entry for 22 January 1941 reads: 'Winston refuses again to give his statement on war aims. The reason given in Cabinet is that precise aims would be compromising, whereas vague principles would disappoint. Thus all those days of work have led to nothing.'

Perhaps Churchill considered the views too socialistic. Perhaps he was simply too focused on a military victory. But the disappointment was shared outside political circles. Marjorie Redman noted that if, 'after all the suffering of the population, we do not know what we are fighting for, it is a poor do'. And as historian Paul Addison has noted, though reconstruction would not come about through Churchill, 'gradually it flowed around and past him, like a tide cutting off an island from the shore'. Yet the former Liberal had not entirely jettisoned his old concerns: in December 1940 Churchill told the pupils of Harrow – his own school – that advantages and privileges ought, in future, to be shared by the many, while, a year later, he told James Chuter Ede that the ruling class should henceforth be chosen 'by the accident of ability'. However sincerely these views were held, they were clearly not meant for public consumption.

But Churchill's job, so far as the public was concerned, was to make them believe that Britain could win the war. He was not needed to sell the peace. As Home Front policy shifted to the left, and as the media promoted the idea of a People's War, common attitudes were changing. It could hardly have been any other way. People had taken on fresh responsibilities. In these pages we have read of volunteers of many kinds, of soldiers, sailors and airmen, of police and rescue and firemen and women, of shelterers (engaged and disengaged), of government workers (bureaucrats and local authority stooges), of factory workers, of oil drillers and of many others whose roles changed with the times.

Many of these newfound roles were hard and dangerous, involving difficulties imposed by a government which needed its people as never before. It needed them to fight, and to work in its factories producing its aeroplanes, tanks and guns. It needed them to bear the bombing patiently, and to accept shortages of food, clothes, and luxuries. It needed them to accept being told endlessly what they could and couldn't do, being suddenly relocated to strange parts of the country, being separated from their children, and spending thousands of hours in grim, damp shelters. And if life was going to be difficult, there would have to be compensations.

And so, for many, wages improved, and became guaranteed. Yet beyond this, people found themselves contributing to society in a manner they never had before. Being made to feel important translated into a sense of self-respect. As the relationship between the government and its citizens altered, London Underground shelters were opened up, sexuality was tolerated, and consumers were allowed the odd dip into the black market. And, crucially, people were offered hope – not just of victory, but of a better, fairer future. And once this had been offered, there was, in truth, no going back. The period of misrule would have to be made permanent. The People's War would become the People's Peace.

We must not forget, of course, that many thousands of people were killed during the Blitz. Ministry of Home Security statistics indicate that 1,698 British civilians died as a result of enemy action between 3 September 1939 and 6 September 1940, 22,069 between 7 September 1940 and 31 December 1940, and 19,918 between 1 January 1941 and 1 January 1942. Over the same period, more than

50,000 people were admitted to hospital with serious injuries. There were, as we have seen, considerable numbers of psychological casualties, including many – like Ida Rodway – whose lives were destroyed. There were numberless others who though neither injured nor traumatised, could not see beyond the misery of the period. Bernard Kops, for example, remembers the Blitz only as a struggle for survival, devoid of any hope or optimism. And this was, it must be remembered, a time when peace on Britain's own terms seemed an unlikely prospect. Britain, its Empire and its Commonwealth were standing alone against Germany, and its people were expecting an invasion; as, for much of the time, was its government.

In the midst of such uncertainty, Earl Winterton, Conservative MP for Horsham and Worthing,* argued that any consideration of long-term aims would 'cause a feeling in the minds of neutrals and the enemy that we are anxious to make peace'. But others, such as Lord Addison, the Labour leader in the House of Lords, wanted no return to 'the disgusting scramble' of a system based upon mass unemployment. Addison believed that, rather than decrying discussion of long-term aims, 'we should as far as possible project into the period of peace as much as we can of the glorious unity that now possesses us'.

This unity was inspiring people like Bloomsbury artist Jimmie Phillips. On 29 December 1940, the night the City of London caught fire, he wrote to a friend:

Strange to say, one does not get a feeling that one must get away from all this, but rather that God is giving us an opportunity to help the less fortunate and thereby build up a fellowship that will aid in the building of a better world. Things are happening fast in this staid old country of ours. Class distinction is fast being rooted out ... Materialism is not so strong today as it was ... It's now 11.30 and the room is lit up as though it were broad daylight. It seems

* As an Irish peer, Winterton was able to sit in the House of Commons.

that the whole of London is ablaze. Am going for a stroll to see if
I can help in any small way ...

And it was not just individuals who found inspiration. Government
institutions were setting aside traditional financial restraints in an
attempt to help citizens; in July 1940 the national milk scheme began
providing a free daily pint of milk to children under five, and to expectant and nursing mothers whose family income was below forty
shillings per week.* In 1941 the vitamin welfare scheme was introduced, eventually entitling young children and mothers to orange juice
and cod liver oil. According to Richard Titmuss, it was no longer
argued – as it had been before the war – that the people were not suf-
ficiently wretched to merit such provision, or that it amounted to an
invasion of parents' rights. Supercilious excuses and penny-pinching
indifference were giving way to a climate of care.

Titmuss describes the period of the Blitz as 'the year when needs
were made manifest and complacencies shaken'. This was the start, he
says, of needs being dealt with in a more humane and compassionate
fashion. Pensions, for example, began to lose their poor-law stigma, and
supplementary payments released a million pensioners from poverty.
'It was fortunate for the nation,' writes Titmuss, 'that this revision of
ideas and rearrangements of values came so early in the war.' The effect
was the protection of the vulnerable, an increased sense of collective
responsibility, and a far higher standard of national health than ever
before.

In a House of Commons debate on 17 October 1940, Minister of
Health Malcolm MacDonald acknowledged that the nation's well-
being was now a priority: it was essential that the men and women
producing the armaments must be maintained in good health. But he

* Over the period of the war, the percentage of families entitled to free milk dropped
from thirty per cent to two per cent – demonstrating how poverty was alleviated by the
economic effects of the war.

went further, – describing the Blitz as the birth pangs of a new nation. 'The lessons taught by the war,' MacDonald said, 'must be remembered in peace.'

And this enthusiasm for a post-war 'New Jerusalem' gathered pace in the summer of 1941, as the newly appointed President of the Board of Education, Rab Butler (a Conservative), began drawing up plans for an overhaul of the education system. He proposed to raise the school leaving age, and to make free secondary education available to all. A skilled politician, Butler overcame the opposition of Churchill and of the Anglican and Catholic churches to publish a workable White Paper, which he prefaced with a quote from Disraeli – 'Upon the education of the people of this country the fate of this country depends.' The bill became law in early 1944, allowing a new generation of children (including this author's father) to receive a free and extensive education, and subsequently to attend university.

The Coalition Cabinet of May 1940. For all their differences and often-rigid attitudes, the members of Churchill's government usually did the right thing in the end.

Just as the Blitz shocked people out of their rhythms, and encouraged extremes of behaviour, so the government was jolted into action by this extraordinary time – and by rising public expectations. Examining its behaviour, we see that – generally – it acted efficiently and with concern for its people. And while events often took it by surprise, it usually did the right thing in the end.

It encouraged, for example, the collective reorganisation of London's welfare services by Henry Willink. It offered deep shelter, and acknowledged the right of the people to trek out of towns and cities – albeit belatedly. It freed large numbers of Jewish and anti-Nazi internees while the threat of invasion still persisted. It caught almost every Nazi spy. It pursued progressive modes of reconstruction, in areas ranging from health to housing. It practised as it preached: drilling for high-grade oil in Sherwood Forest was surely the ultimate example of 'make do and mend'. And all this as it fought an unprecedented kind of war. Of course, the government also introduced a huge number of regulations and restrictions, arbitrarily criminalising swathes of the community overnight, but it might be argued that it was being forced to improvise in unprecedented circumstances . . .

And even when conditions seemed insurmountable, Blitz Spirit came to the fore – spontaneous yet manufactured, real yet simplistic. It inspired Caryl Brahms to write in her diary, in December 1940:

These are the days to be alive in. These days now. They are hard, unhappy, lonely, wasted, infuriating, terrifying, heartbreaking days. But they are history. And in them we are a part of history. We are lucky to be living now.

The Blitz was the best of times because it was the worst of times and the folk memory of the period – and particularly of Blitz Spirit – remains with us. In March 2015 an army bomb disposal team defused a Second World War bomb in Bermondsey in London. Local residents were evacuated to nearby hotels and to a sports centre. One of these 'evacuees' told the press, 'Before, nobody talks to each other, but after what's happened, people just realise life's too short, let's just mingle.' This woman was expressing Blitz Spirit because that is what we have learned to do. After the London bombings of 7 July 2005, Metropolitan Police Commissioner Sir Ian Blair said that, 'If London could survive the Blitz, it can survive four miserable events like this,' while the *Daily Mirror* advised the nation to 'adopt the famous Blitz Spirit'.

When Blitz Spirit is called upon nowadays, it is really the consensus that is being invoked. It encourages good behaviour in difficult circumstances – just as it was created to do in 1940 and 1941. Built upon the solid foundations of genuine Blitz Spirit, it helps us now, as it helped us then. Time has barely altered its function; *Britain Can Take It* – and so can you.

But time *is* altering our relationship with the social benefits that grew out of the period. The Blitz was the dark crucible of the National Health Service, of free education for all, of the collective spirit that guided much of the last century. Today's politicians and policy makers were born long after these benefits evolved, and this, perhaps, is why they are now being allowed to erode. It would be very sad if the true legacies of Blitz Spirit were lost – because we fail to remember how hard they were won.

Acknowledgements

This book has been a pleasure to write. I am lucky to have spent eighteen months immersed in an extraordinary period of British history that lasted half as long. This book will have succeeded if it paints an unexpected picture of a brutal time when lives were lived in the present, and the seeds of modern Britain were scattered among the ruins.

I have been very fortunate in the number – and calibre – of people who have helped me, and the archives to which I have had access. The Imperial War Museum Sound and Document Archives have been mines of superb information. In particular, I would like to thank Richard McDonagh, Richard Hughes and Peter Hart in the Sound Archive, and Jane Rosen in the Research Room. Also at the IWM, I would like to thank Ralph Perrot, Dan Marriott, Marie France, Steve Turner and Rachael Hodson.

At the Museum of London, Digital Curators Hilary Young and William Lowry were endlessly helpful and patient. At the Coventry History Centre, John Hewitson guided me through numerous documents. At the BP Archive at Warwick University, Bethan Thomas and Joanne Burman went to great lengths to locate documents, as did the librarians at the Energy Institute in London. Kevin Topham at the Duke's Wood Oil Museum was cheerful and knowledgeable. In Cambridge, I received a great deal of help from historian Tim Harding (and, of course, from Michael Bowyer who features heavily in the book).

The staff of the Southampton Archives at the Civic Centre were helpful – while Don Robertson expertly guided me around the city's wartime shelters (including the medieval cellar from which Gwen Hughes and

her children were the only survivors on the night of 30 November 1940).
The London Metropolitan Archives in Clerkenwell contained a great deal
of interesting material – including the records of the Public Morality
Council. I would also like to thank the staff of the Surrey History Centre
in Woking, and of the National Archives at Kew. I have had a number of
PRO documents opened under the Freedom of Information Act 2000 –
which has proved to be a remarkably painless operation; the documents
available at Kew are beyond compare, marrying contemporary fact and
colour so effectively that the reader (or this one, anyway) slips his
chronological moorings for days at a time.

So far as libraries are concerned, the London Library in St James's
Square has a superb selection of books, journals and newspapers from
the period. It is also a wonderful place to work – I am typing these words
on the fourth floor. I have hugely enjoyed working at the Inner Temple
library where the staff were generous in dredging up books (mostly relating to wartime regulations) which had not seen daylight since sugar
rationing. (In addition, lunch in Middle Temple Hall became a semi-reg-
ular event, the staff unclear whether I was a spruced-up tramp or a
lesser-known judge.) The British Library, meanwhile, was valuable, firstly,
for the availability of the most obscure books and articles, secondly, for
its oral history archive (and very comfortable listening booths), and
thirdly, for its wonderful collection of national and local newspapers.
These often alerted me to incidents or courts cases which I could follow
up elsewhere.

I have had expert assistance from a number of people. I am hugely
grateful to Andy Saunders for his help with aerial matters (and also with
Chrystabel Leighton Porter). I spent a happy day in Cambridge with
Michael Bowyer, taking photos of each other in front of ordinary houses
and confusing the locals. Writer and editor Paul Hamblin offered great
assistance – particularly in relation to the Coventry chapter. I am also
grateful to Gemma Newby, my superb radio producer. Matt Wingett
opened my eyes to the wonders of *London Life*, Stephen Bourne was very
generous in sharing his knowledge of black wartime history, Judy Sahm
offered inside information on the role of the Citizens Advice Bureau,
while Claire Price was insightful regarding pets. The great Ronald Blythe,
author of *Akenfield: Portrait of an English Village*, was very kind in sharing
his honest and subtly expressed memories.

I would like to thank those who helped me to set up interviews: the

RAF Museum's excellent curator Peter Devitt introduced me to Bernard Kregor, James Clarke led me to Denis Warren (with whom I spent an enjoyable day at the Imperial War Museum), Fiona Laird placed me in touch with Alison Wilson and Brenda Winterbotham, and Sarah Waddell introduced me to her great aunt, Elsie Glendinning. All of these were superb (and often surprisingly frank) interviewees. I would also like to thank Jeroen Kemperman of the Institute for War Holocaust and Genocide Studies in Amsterdam, and Yvonne Prins of Centraal Bureau voor Genealogie at The Hague, for their research into the life of Sjoerd Pons after the war.

I first discovered the existence of Sherwood Forest oil thanks to Sheila Stallard, and learned a great deal more from Kevin Topham. The novelist Kate Thompson was very generous in providing her contacts, and a number of stories that she had come across. (It was also good to talk to somebody else who knows the sound a deadline makes . . .)

A number of people have kindly read over sections of the book. First of all, I am grateful to the senior historian at the Imperial War Museum, Terry Charman, whose knowledge is unparalleled. I would also like to thank Jonathan Cullen and Simon Dinsdale who read through parts.

On the production side, I am enormously grateful to Kerri Sharp, my editor at Simon & Schuster, to Iain MacGregor, to Jo Whitford, to John English, to Sue Stephens, the excellent publicity manager, and Claire Brenard, the Art Curator who showed me around the IWM's impressive collection. My thanks also to Liz Bowers and Madeleine James in the IWM publishing department.

I have had huge support from this team – and from Jim Gill, my agent at United Agents. There are many others whom to thank for their support:

Max Arthur, Osian Barnes, Turtle Bunbury, Will Brooks, Lucy Briers, Alexandra Churchill, Richard Clothier, Victoria Coren Mitchell, Marshall Cope, Ruth Cowan, Bob Cryer, Ian Drysdale, Bill Emlyn Jones, Bridget Fallon, Simon, Robert, Gillian and Lionel Frumkin, Tanya Gold, Edward Grant, Kate and Aidan Greenwood, Meekal Hashmi, John Hayes Fisher, Susan Greenhill, Mishal Husain, Simon Irvine, the Keenes (Edward, Mollie, Olivia, Rosalind and Lillian), Suzy Klein, Lionel Levine, Judy Levine, Kim Levine, Marshall Levine, Andrew Lycett, Mhairi Macnee, Charles Malpass, Emily Man, Santo Massine, Dru Masters, Jon Medcalf, Deborah Moggach, Harry Mount, Robert Newman, Fred Perry, Jess

Redford, Andy Robertshaw, Malcolm Rushton, the Rowes (Chris, Sara, Charlie and Matti), Dorothy Sahm, Tanya Shaw, Michael Sparkes, Chris Spencer, Piers Torday, Duncan Neale, Orlando Wells, the Woods (Mike, Annabel, Henry and Arthur), David Weston and those whom I've shamefully forgotten to mention. My thanks, also, to the UK 1940s Radio Station which kept me 'In The Mood' when there was no end in sight. To Claire Price I give my love as well as my thanks.

Sources

There have, of course, been a large number of books written about the Blitz – and a few are even worth reading. Above all, Juliet Gardiner's *The Blitz: The British Under Attack*, manages to be both forensically researched and entertaining to read. Winston Ramsey's *The Blitz Then and Now, Volume 2* is a wonderful work of reference, and often a good deal more thoughtful than might be imagined. Angus Calder's *The Myth of the Blitz* may take the form of a tightly reasoned argument, but it is also written with great affection for the period and its people. *Living Through the Blitz* by Tom Harrisson is an anthropologist's view of the Blitz, laced with subtlety and surprises. Norman Longmate's *How We Lived Then* is less revelatory, but gives a detailed overall picture of certain sections of society. For a journalistic taste of the period, two authors stand out: Leonard Mosley and James Lansdale Hodson. Mosley's *Backs to the Wall: London Under Fire* is vivid and perceptive, while Hodson's trilogy: *Through the Dark Night*, *Towards the Morning* and *Before Daybreak* amounts to a self-aware (and often very funny) critique of the period. Hodson is not afraid to criticise, and is worth reading simply for the concluding essay in the final book – 'The England That I Want' – in which he touchingly sets out his hopes for the future.

CHAPTER ONE

In considering the nowadays little-performed play *Thunder Rock*, I have quoted from the 1940 Hamish Hamilton edition. There is an interesting discussion of the play in *Britain Can Take It: The British Cinema in the*

Second World War by Anthony Aldgate and Jeffrey Richards. The story of Albert and Maisie Dance can be found at Succession Number 18258 in the IWM Sound Archive. In the same archive, Ethel Clarke is at 5362 and Joan Batt at 21874. My information about the attack on Cambridge comes from several sources: from *Air Raid!* by Michael J. Bowyer, from my interview with Michael, from information gathered by historian Tim Harding, and from Andy Saunders' entry in *The Blitz, Then and Now, Volume 2* (Andy himself corresponded with Joachim von Arnim in the mid 1980s). It should be pointed out, however, that the victims of the Vicarage Terrace bombing were not the first to die as a result of German air action. On 16 March 1940, James Isbister, of Brig o'Waithe, Orkney, died when a Junkers 88 jettisoned its bombs during an attack on Scapa Flow. On 1 May, Frederick and Dorothy Gill were killed when a Heinkel 111 crashed into their house in Clacton-on-Sea, injuring 160 people.

CHAPTER TWO

In the National Archives, there are two files on the extraordinary case of John Fulljames: DPP 2/741 and PCOM 9/876, and two files relating to Ida and Joseph Rodway: MEPO 3/2169 and CRIM 1/1239. Richard Titmuss's excellent official history, published in 1950, is entitled *Problems of Social Policy*, while Gioya Steinke's Rest Centre recollections can be found in the IWM Sound Archive at 18724. Lily Merriman's memories are from the Finsbury Project, a series of interviews carried out in Islington Day Centres, which is held by the Museum of London Digital Archive. Merriman's interview is at 12.19A, while Eileen Brome's interview is in the Museum of London archive at 86/359/1. Doreen Kluczynska's sobering workhouse memories are at 20893 in the IWM Sound Archive, and Maggie Edwards is at 13975. Henry Willink's press conference is covered on page 4 of *The Times* on 1 October 1940. The account of Elizabeth Robson (née Atkin) is in the London History Workshop Collection, held at the Museum of London. Social worker Bernard Nicholls relates his memories of working with (and slapping . . .) the long-term homeless 4631 in the IWM Sound Archive; Isabel Catto is at 9741 in the same archive, while Vera Reid is at 12001 in the IWM Documents Archive.

CHAPTER THREE

With regards to the many ways in which fear could strike, and the forms it took, C. P. Snow's recollections are from Leonard Mosley's *Backs to the Wall: London Under Fire*, while the diary of Viola Bawtree, a fifty-seven-year-old woman living in Carshalton in 1940, can be found at 1807 in the IWM Documents Archive. The Church Army's reassuring little booklet can be found at A/PMC/071 in the London Metropolitan Archives, while Rosemary Black's story is from Leonard Mosley. Richie Calder's quote is from his book *Carry On London!*, published in 1941. Margaret Vear was interviewed for the Finsbury Project, and is at 12:20A in the Museum of London. The words of Herbert Morrison and Arthur Greenwood are from *Hansard*, the situation regarding tube shelters in the First World War is in the National Archives at MEPO 2/1735, and the account of Bernard Rice is in the Royal Air Force Museum at Hendon, at X002 – 5429/001/008.

The discussion of events surrounding shelter in the tubes has been pieced together using a number of National Archive files: HO 45/18540, HO 186/321, HO 186/149, HO 207/404, CAB 21/773 and MH 76/577. The *Daily Worker*'s giddy special correspondent was writing on the paper's front page on 13 September 1940, while Bernard Kops's memories are in the Museum of London's Digital Archive, as well as in his memoirs – *The World is a Wedding*, published by MacGibbon and Kee in 1963. Philip Piratin's account of the communist invasion of the Savoy hotel shelter is in the IWM Sound Archive at 10210. The Peter Ackroyd quote is from *London: The Biography* at page 566. The quote from Colin Perry is taken from *The Boy in the Blitz* at page 192, while James Morten's account of the Bethnal Green disaster is at 15219 in the IWM Sound Archive. So far as shelter (or lack of shelter) accounts are concerned, Betty Brown is at 20804 in the IWM Sound Archive, John Fowles is at 18202, Elsie Glendinning's story was told to the author, while the account of the July 1941 meeting of the British Psychological Society was described by Dr Robert Thouless in the journal *Nature* (Volume 148, No. 3746) published on 16 August 1941. Herbert Morrison's defence of surface shelters (and his memory of Churchill's words when appointed Home Secretary) appear in his autobiography, published in 1960 by Odhams Press – while the conflicting voices are those of policeman Walter Marshall and fireman John Cooper, both in the IWM Sound Archive at 23849 and 16639 respectively. Alda Ravera – who actually slept in one – is in the IWM Sound Archive at 28537. Gwen Hughes's memories of trekking are at LT 004 (Tapes 4 and 5) in Southampton City Council's Blitz Oral History Archive, while the Society of Friends report is quoted by Richard Titmuss, the Official Historian of Social Policy. Tom Harrisson's quote is from page 166 of *Living Through the Blitz*.

CHAPTER FOUR

Roy Bartlett's full and vivid account of shelter life is at 30421 in the IWM's Sound Archive. The *Daily Mirror* report of the unspeakable mother and daughter from Hailsham (and the apparently enlightened magistrate) is on page 3 on 25 April 1940. Gwen Hughes's harrowing memories of the night that she and her children were buried in a medieval cellar in Southampton – and were the only shelterers to emerge alive – is at LT 004 in Southampton City Council's Blitz Oral History Archive. The odd but fascinating claims arising from accidents in and around air raid shelters can be found at the National Archives at HO 207/459. The cases of Simpson, Ptonopoulos and Sumner are from *The Times* on 10 September, 19 September and 8 October 1940 respectively. Percy Clark was the focus of press coverage on 11 September 1940, while the sad case of James and Ann Miller was featured in the Daily Mirror on 14 November 1940. The file of James Burnham (amounting to the indictment papers) is in the National Archives at Crim 1/1236. The judge's pointed comments about what happens when excitable young men are given access to guns are in *The Times* on 18 October 1940.

A full transcript of Caryl Brahms's diaries – a trove of wit and perception – is at 2427 in the Imperial War Museum Documents Archive. The Public Morality Council material was found in the London Metropolitan Archives at A/PMC/071. The startling *London Life* magazine, meanwhile, can be found in the British Library at Cup.701.a.5, and I have had access to Matt Wingett's own collection of copies, and his attitudes to them. The story of George Hall is included in *An Underworld at War* by Donald Thomas. (This book is a detailed and fast-moving overview of the period's crime ranging from pre-war racetrack gangs to post-war treason trials. It is well worth reading.) Vera Reid records watching the development of shelterers at 12001 in the IWM Documents

Archive. The Mass-Observation material comes from a variety of sources. The first account, in which an unknown wartime commentator points out the chaotic and undisciplined nature of much early tube shelter life, can be found on pages 102–7 of *The Saturday Book 3*, a 1943 annual, edited by Lionel Russell, and published by Hutchinson. Although this account was partially reprinted in *Speak For Yourself* (a Mass-Observation Anthology published in 1985), many of the most interesting observations are missing from the reprint. The second account, of a different tube station, is contained in Chapter Five of *Living Through the Blitz* (as is the account of Tilbury Shelter). The *Daily Express*'s revelations concerning 'droppers' appeared on page 4 of the paper on 1 November 1940. Police reports on the behaviour of the public in shelters are in HO 207/503 at the National Archives, while Flight Lieutenant Guy Gibson's revealing memory of public attitudes in the winter of 1940 is on page 133 of his autobiography, *Enemy Coast Ahead*, published posthumously by Michael Joseph in 1946.

CHAPTER FIVE

The material in the Coventry chapter comes mainly from the superb collection of original letters and documents held by the Coventry History Centre. I have drawn heavily on documents from PA 2684 – a diary of events in response to the raid of 14/15 November and from CCA/3/1/9897 – a file relating to a post-war visit of American officials to the city to study the post-Blitz reactions. Joan Thornton's letter about the August 1939 IRA bomb is at PA 1692/4. The *Tribune* article after which the chapter is named was published on 31 May 1940, and the account of the air raid warning system is from the Metropolitan Police War Diary in the National Archive at MEPO 3/3066. The report of Chief Fire Officer Cartwright is in the Coventry History Centre at PA 1480/13, the account of Sergeant Richard Mitchell is in the IWM Sound Archive at 11364, and Guy Burn is at 10631. Jack Miller is at 92.177 in the Museum of London Digital Archive, while John Sargent's memories are held in the Coventry History Centre at JN 940.544. The letter commending the activities of Head Warden Alcock is at PA 2105/2/11.

Ritchie Calder's 'Interim Report on Coventry' appeared in the *New Statesman and Nation* on 23 November 1940, while Reginald King's bitter recollection of his inability to rescue people trapped in a basement shelter can be found on page 261 of *The Blitz Then and Now, Volume 2*. Mr Harrison's memory of his day at the Daimler factory is at PA 1420/1-2, while Dilwyn Evans's surprise at meeting the King is in the IWM Sound Archive at 20792. The extent of damage to factories is at page 265 in *The Defence of the United Kingdom*, Basil Collier's official history. Donald Gibson's difficulties in patching up the broken city are at CCA/3/1/9897, while the material on the WVS and Pearl Hyde is at PA 17532/1-2, and PA 1753/1, and the *Yorkshire Post* article was on the paper's front page on 4 November 1940. Harold Holttum's description of the city a fortnight after the raid is at 10459 in the IWM Sound Archive, while the BBC Home Service programme featuring Donald Gibson was an edition of *From All Over Britain* entitled *The rebuilding of Coventry*, broadcast at 9.45 p.m. on Friday 12 November 1943. Additional material on the rebuilding comes from *Concretopia: A Journey Around the Rebuilding of Postwar Britain* by John Grindrod, published by Old Street in 2013, while George MacDonald Fraser's words are from page 177 of *Quartered Safe Out Here*, his 1992 wartime memoir.

CHAPTER SIX

The material relating to Eakring, its astonishingly high grade oil, and the government's attempts to *Make Do and Mend* on a grand scale comes from a variety of sources. Initially, I was very fortunate to meet Kevin Topham at the Duke's Wood Oil Museum – a lovely building hidden in the depths of the forest. It is well worth a visit: Kevin's enthusiasm and experience are infectious. (Indeed, he and his colleagues have won a 2015 Queen's Award for Voluntary Service.) Bethan Thomas and Joanne Burman at the BP Archive at Warwick University, meanwhile, could not have been more helpful in guiding me around their fascinating collection. I spent two fruitful afternoons in the library at the Energy Institute in New Cavendish Street, while the National Archives held important documents, and the British Library held wonderful interviews in its *Lives in the Oil Industry* oral history collection, a joint project between the British Library and the University of Aberdeen. *The Secret of Sherwood Forest, Oil Production in England During World War II* by Guy H. Woodward and Grace Steele Woodward is an interesting overview of the story relating to the Oklahoma drillers. I found *The History of the British Petroleum Company, Volume 2: The Anglo-Iranian Years 1928–1954* by James Bamberg to be useful in certain regards, while Janet Roberts has published an informative booklet entitled *Oil Under Sherwood Forest*.

Information concerning the nation's oil position in 1940 and 1941 can be found in the National Archives at POWE 33/1175 and POWE 33/1176. Cadman's desire for the creation of a Petroleum Department is demonstrated in his correspondence at T 273/194. The original Eakring mining licence is at POWE 33/538, while Petroleum Department papers relating to Eakring, including the report into Herman Douthit's death are at POWE 33/1378. Philip Southwell's article 'Petroleum in England' can be found in the February 1945 edition of *The Journal of the Institute of Petroleum,* Vol. XXXI, No. 254, at pages 27 to 39. The stories relating to Jack Clarke and Sandy Ross are from *Eakring 1939–1945*, a booklet from Duke's Wood Oil Museum. Among many useful documents in the BP Archive are *Eakring: Oil in the UK* at 69109, the minutes of Petroleum Board Meetings at 37144 and volume XX of *NAFT* (the British Petroleum magazine) from September 1944. That same month saw an article entitled 'Anglo-Iranian's New Commercial Oilfield Somewhere in England' in *Petroleum Times*. The interviews used from the *Live in the Oil Industry* collection, meanwhile, were those of Lewis Dugger (F14727–F14731), Ivan Mitchell (F17372–F17373), and Denis Sheffield (F12249–F12251). A fair amount of the material in this chapter related to events that took place after May 1941 – but the inspiration and drive behind, and framework beneath, all of these events come squarely from our period.

CHAPTER SEVEN

The information concerning the German spies arriving on the south coast in early September 1940 comes from a considerable number of files in the National Archives. KV 2/11, KV 2/12, KV 2/13, KV 2/1452, KV 2/1699 and KV 2/1700 were previously available; readers can now also access KV 2/107, HO 144/21471, HO 144/21472, CRIM 1/1243, PCOM 9/890 and PCOM 9/891. Taken in their entirety, these files paint a full picture of events before, during and after the trial. Lord Swinton's justification for secrecy and Sir Alexander Maxwell's request for openness are at HO 144/21471 – which also contains an interesting (unsuccessful) appeal for clemency for Kieboom (by his counsel, Christmas Humphreys) on the basis that Kieboom was sentenced to death even though Pons was found Not Guilty – when there were no significant distinctions between the cases forwarded by the two men. Hugh Trevor-Roper's post-war memo is at CAB 154/105, while the diaries of Guy Liddell (the chief of MI5's 'B' Division) are at KV 4/185 to KV 4/196. Colonel Robin 'Tin Eye' Stephens's account of Camp 020 is at KV 4/13 to KV 4/15. Christopher Harmer's memories are from his private papers.

The Southern Command officer's memories are from WO 199/2198, a file concerning events which occurred when the invasion was expected during September 1940. Michael Bowyer's memories are from his interview with the author, while Kenneth Johnstone is in the IWM Sound Archive at 9185. Churchill's views on the likelihood of invasion – and his challenge to Sir Dudley Pound – are at CAB 66/9/221 in the National Archive. James Lansdale Hodson's observations on Churchill can be found on page 55 of *Before Daybreak*. Oliver Lyttelton's superb summary of Churchill's role in the national emergency is in the IWM Sound Archive at 2739, while the reactions of Joan Seaman and Oliver Bernard are in the same archive at 14821 and 11481 respectively. Concerning invasion scares and committees, James Oates is at 17984, Hilda Cripps is at 18337, while the interview with Denis Warren is the author's own.

The information concerning 55th (Sutton and Cheam) Battalion Home Guard is from two pieces by C. E. Greenshields published in the *Sutton and Cheam Herald* on 20 and 27 October 1944. Stanley Brand's memories are in the IWM Sound Archive at 27347, Stan Poole's are at 22198, George Pellett's at 16911, Percy Clark's at 13612, Peter Wilkinson's at 13289, and Walter Miller's at 19382. Caryl Brahms's diary is in the IWM Documents Archive at 2427, while Elsie Glendinning, Brenda Winterbotham, Bernard Kregor and Ronald Blythe were all speaking to the author. The exchange between Churchill and Colonel Wedgwood is quoted in *The Times* on 12 February 1941, while the Joint Intelligence Committee report is quoted in Volume 1 of the *Official History of the Joint Intelligence Committee* by Michael S. Goodman. Frederick Winterbotham's account of his visit to Churchill is both in his book *The Ultra Secret*, and in the interview he gave to the Imperial War Museum Sound Archive at 7462 (this is where the section quoted here can be found).

CHAPTER EIGHT

Concerning fears of a fifth column, the military exercises in which soldiers played at being spies are described on page 33 of James Lansdale Hodson's *Before Daybreak*. The extraordinary case of James Florey and family (and the discussion of compensation . . .) is covered in file number TS 46/25 at the National Archives. The *Daily Mirror*'s report of Emil Wirth is on page 2 on 13 September 1940. The case of George Wall and his Nazi sympathies is in the National Archives at CRIM 1/1223, Albert Weems is at KV 2/2428, Wilhelm Mörz is at KV 2/2106, and Engelbertus Fukken (who posed as a refugee under the rather more palatable name of Willem Ter Braak) is at KV 2/114. *Collar the Lot! How Britain Interned and Expelled its Wartime Refugees* by Peter and Leni Gillman is an excellent account of the internment of aliens – although harsh in its damning assessment of the government given the release of aliens while the risk of invasion (as well as the pressure from the press and military) still persisted. A Home Office file concerning the treatment of internees sent to Australia (although believing they were being sent to Canada) on board *Dunera* can be found in The National Archives at HO 213/1959, while files relating to their lost and damaged property are at HO 215/213 and HO 215/214. Lord Snell's enquiry into *Arandora Star* (which was handed to members of the War Cabinet in October 1940 at Churchill's request) is at CAB 66/13/12.

CHAPTER NINE

The sad little story of the two Gibraltarian refugees is from *The Times* of Wednesday 2 October 1940, while Caryl Brahms's memoirs are in the IWM Document Archive at 2427. The observations of eccentric MP, Waldron Smithers, are from a Ministry of Home Security file into the effects of enemy bombing at HO 199/453. The papers of Winifred Musson and Phyllis Warner are at 19540 and 3208 respectively in the IWM Documents Archive. The papers relating to the case of Canadian military policeman, James McCallum are in the National Archives at MEPO 3/1274, while Detective Inspector Capstick's memoirs, published by John Long in 1960, are entitled *Given in Evidence*. (Charles Du Cann, McCallum's defence counsel was something of a polymath. He authored a 1955 self-help book entitled *Teach Yourself to Live*, as well as *Antiques for*

Amateurs and *The Love Lives of Charles Dickens*.) The Surrey police reports are held by the Surrey History Centre in Woking, while the woman's letter explaining the attraction of Canadians is in the IWM Documents Archive at 16391.

The archbishops' letter to *The Times* was published on 12 September 1940, while Billy Strachan's memories were told to Conrad Wood of the Imperial War Museum; they are held in the museum's sound archive at succession number 10042. A Colonial Office file on the health and welfare of members of the British Honduras Forestry Unit is at CO 876/41 in the National Archives, while the depressing story of Cebert Lewis, and its unsatisfactory aftermath, are contained in HO 45/24471, a file marked 'Police Complaints by Coloured Immigrants'. J. B. Priestley's words are from his 1934 travelogue *English Journey*, and Learie Constantine is quoted from his autobiography *Colour Bar*, published by Stanley Paul in 1954. The material relating to Esther Bruce and Mrs Uroom are from the author's interview with Stephen Bourne, from Stephen's book *Mother Country, Britain's Black Community on the Home Front 1939–1945*, and from Stephen's article on Aunt Esther, published in the *Guardian* on 9 July 2011. E. I. Ekpenyon's memories are from page 10 of a 1943 book entitled *Some Experiences of an African Air-Raid Warden*, published by Sheldon Press, while H. F. Grey's racial epiphany is described in his private papers in the Imperial War Museum Documents Archive at 4556. Brenda Winterbotham was speaking to the author, the Bethnal Green factory worker was speaking to Kate Thompson, and Kenneth Little's sociological observations are from his 1947 study, *Negroes in Britain: A Study in Race Relations*. *The Times'* comments about mixed-race children were printed on Page 21 on 16 June 1930, while the *Manchester Guardian* letter was published on page 18 on 29 September 1933.

The startling Home Intelligence reports on antisemitism in Britain can be found in the National Archives at HO 262/9. J. J. McCall was writing in the *Glasgow Daily Herald* on 28 May 1943, while Eleanor Rathbone's pamphlet, *Falsehood and Facts about the Jews*, was published the following year. The story of the miserly 'old Jew-man' is from page 102 of the *Saturday Book 3*, published in 1943, and the material about Lavy Baktansky was found in the *Oxford Times*, 18 October 1940. George Orwell's essay 'Antisemitism in Britain' was published in 1945, while Aaron Goldman's interesting discussion of wartime antisemitism, 'The Resurgence of Anti-Semitism in Britain during World War II', can be found in Volume 46, No. 1 of the journal *Jewish Social Studies*, on page 37. On a rather different front, Connie Ho's memories are held in the Museum of London Digital Archive at 92.116.

CHAPTER TEN

Quentin Crisp's observation that the Blitz turned London into 'a paved double bed' can be found on page 154 of his 1967 autobiography, *The Naked Civil Servant*. Peter Quennell's night with Astrid is described in *The Wanton Chase*, his 1980 memoir. Mary Warschauer talks of dancing up Oxford Street in her interview with the Imperial War Museum Sound Archive at Accession Number 16762. The interviews with Alison Wilson and Ronald Blythe are the author's own, while Joan Wyndham's diary was published by Heinemann in 1985, entitled *Love Lessons, A Wartime Diary*. The telling story of Lillian Rogers can be found in Chapter Six of *Nine Wartime Lives*, published by the Oxford University Press in 2010, while Joan Varley's interview with the IWM Sound Archive is at 28454.

Marghanita Laski's brave and vivid novel *To Bed With Grand Music* was published by The Pilot Press in 1946 – under the nom-de-plume 'Sarah Russell'. This gives a sense of how shocking the book seemed at the time; for while the behaviour it described was surprisingly common, it was certainly never part of the consensus. Gerald Dougherty's decision 'to see what it's like' is related in *It's Not Unusual* by Alkarim Jivani, published in 1997 by Michael O'Mara books, and John Lehmann's description of the last night of the Blitz (not how The Longest Night is usually remembered . . .) is from *In the Purely Pagan Sense*, published by Blond and Briggs in 1976.

The RAMC Mass-Observation correspondent, described in *Civilians into Soldiers: War, The Body, and British Army Recruits 1939–45*, by Emma Newlands, is at TC29, Box 2/E (Assorted Short reports from Observers in the Army). Ronald Gray's self-taught course in sex education is at 30493 in the IWM Sound Archive while Chrystabel Leighton Porter's interview is at 11246. Further information is from Andy Saunders's book on Chrystabel – *A Pin-Up at War* – published by Leo Cooper in 2003. The copies of *London Life* can be viewed on microfilm at the British Library at shelf mark Cup. 701.a.5. The quotes from Matt Wingett are from the author's own interview.

The taped memories of the WAAF stationed in Yorkshire are in the Southampton Civic Archives at CO 125 (B1). The National Sun and Air Association has its own Metropolitan Police file in the National Archives, subtitled, 'Complaints About Their Activities', while the records of the Public Morality Council can be found in the London Metropolitan Archives; the material quoted here is from files A/PMC/040 and A/PMC/071. Material relating to Yetta Lewis, an unusual veteran of two world wars, is from MEPO 3/2133, a Metropolitan Police file held in the National Archives. The memories of James Morten and Stan Poole are in the IWM Sound Archive at 15219 and 22198 respectively, while Marthe Watts published her memoirs under the title *The Men in my Life* in 1960. The information relating to saucy seaside postcards, meanwhile, is from the website of the British Cartoon Archive, based at the University of Kent.

CHAPTER ELEVEN

Jack Miller's memories of soldiers looting are held in the Museum of London Digital Archive at 92.177. The examples of crime given are from the pages of the *Midland Daily Telegraph* on 19 and 22 November 1940, and *The Times* on 22 November. Arthur Berriedale Keith, barrister and professor, was writing in Volume IV, No. 2 of the *Modern Law Review* for 1940. The interview with Brenda Winterbotham is the author's own, while the examples of wartime regulations (from car radios to peregrine falcons) can be found in the National Archives at CAB 75/8. John Greaves's first court appearance as a married man was described on the front page of the *Daily Mirror* on 22 September 1941, while the case of the magnificently named Musgrave Twentyman appeared in *The Times* on 19 November 1940. Eric Oddy's account of his hard-won Savoy meal is at 15220 in the IWM Sound Archive, while the details of Noël Coward's regulation breaches (and his reactions to them) are contained in letters to Jack Wilson written on 29 May and 31 October 1941, and a letter from Duff Cooper to Brendan Bracken written on 1 July 1941. These are set out between pages 439 and 452 of *The Letters of Noel Coward*, published by Methuen in 2007.

As for the apparently unfortunate vicar, Robert Colvin Graham, his case is discussed in *The Times* on 5 October 1940 – but the rather more subtle local machinations behind his conviction and imprisonment only reveal themselves when one discovers the Prime Ministerial papers held by the National Archives – specifically PREM 4/39/1, which demonstrates that his wife, Bertha, was a prominent fascist recently detained under Regulation 18B. The trial and conviction of Cecil Hughes (the 'Twitter Joke Trial' of its day – and evidence that history does, indeed, repeat itself) are to be found in copies of the *Oxford Times* of July 1940. The bench of magistrates was unable to make up its mind at the initial hearing – and following the case on microfiche copies of the newspaper in the British Library reading rooms, my heart sank when they finally reached their majority verdict. The article in the *Guardian* urging us to keep calm and carry on appeared on 27 July 2012; it should serve as a warning that we should not always trust our attitudes to the past.

The quote from Hamilton's *The Slaves of Solitude* is from page 134, while the story of Mrs Toone is raised by Arthur Berriedale Keith on page 85 of his *Modern Law Review* article. The use of female stooges in Hendon can be found in Chapter Five of *A Very Peculiar Story* by David Arscott. The quotes from the chairman of the Food Price Regulation Committee for the North Midland Region, and from the Thames Police Court magistrate, are both from *The Times* – page 2 on 1 May 1941 and page 2 on 3 May 1941 respectively. An interesting discussion of wartime price controls can be found in *The Journal of Economic History*, Vol. 47, No.1 at page 197; the article, written by Geoffrey Mills and Hugh Rockoff, is entitled 'Compliance with Price Controls in the United States and the United Kingdom During World War II'. Mary Brown's memories of tentative attempts at fraud are at 12.21B (20.1048/225) in the Museum of London Digital Archive.

CHAPTER TWELVE

The Blitz crime figures are taken from the Metropolitan Police War Diary, at MEPO 3/3066 in the National Archives – while filling in the details of these crimes has been made far easier and a great deal more entertaining by two books written by wartime criminals. *Boss of Britain's Underworld* by Billy Hill is an account by a ruthless man who was climbing to the top of the criminal ladder. *Time Off My Life* by Wally Thompson, meanwhile, is the memoir of a journeyman criminal, far more willing to reveal his faults and mistakes – including a vivid description of receiving the cat-o'-nine-tails at Pentonville Prison. Together, these books shed unusual light on life during the Blitz, and on attitudes commonly obscured. Hill's memories of 'roaring days' are on page 97 of his book, while Thompson's assertion that air raids were the criminal's best ally can be found on page 140 of his. Theresa Bothwell's memory of the blackout is in the IWM Sound Archive at 18729, while the details of the Jimmy Essex case with its more tragic blackout consequences (and its illustration of the fine legal line between manslaughter and murder, between eighteen months in prison and execution) is in the National Archives at CRIM 1/1411.

So far as the temptation from bombed-out houses is concerned, William Ryder's account is at 19662 in the IWM Sound Archive while the tale of looting in Clerkenwell comes from a Finsbury Project interview with 'Ellen B' at 12.14b in the Museum of London Digital Archive. Ballard Berkeley's memories are at 5340 in the IWM Sound Archive while the deposition papers relating to the Carter Lane thefts by members of the AFS are at CRIM 1/1238 in the National Archives. The fascinating and rare insight into the attitudes and behaviour of demolition workers can be found on page 99 of *Speak for Yourself: A Mass-Observation Anthology*, while Jerry White's interview with Jimmy Day is in the Campbell Road Collection at the Museum of London Digital Archive. The looting/recycling divide is illustrated by Walter Marshall and Theresa Wilkinson (at 23849 and 21596 respectively in the IWM Sound Archive). The head of the Heavy Rescue Squad convicted of looting the gin bottle is described on page 83 of *An Underworld at War*, the story of the pensioner who received six months for taking rope and a jug is in *The Times* on 18 September 1940, while the Common Serjeant's deflated observation is from the same newspaper on 8 January 1941.

Prime Minister David Cameron's misunderstanding of both history and of the causes of looting were set out in the Commons on 11 August 2011. And the Blitz does not stand alone as a clear twentieth-century precedent ignored by the Prime Minister; in *The First World War on the Home Front*, Terry Charman describes the widespread (and blatant) looting that took place in May 1915 during anti-German riots.

The Black Market recollections of Albert Brown are at 12.21B (20.1048/225) in the Museum of London Digital Archive, while Nancy Jackman recorded her memories in *The Cook's Tale: Life Below Stairs as it*

Really Was, published by Coronet in 2012. Ruth Tanner's interview is in the IWM Sound Archive at 15291, Francis Goddard is at 24196 in the same archive, the tale of Bethnal Green was told to Kate Thompson, Arthur 'Musher' King was speaking to Jerry White (contained in the Campbell Road Collection in the Museum of London Digital Archive), while Elsie Glendinning was speaking to the author.

Sir Frederick Tucker's sentencing remarks in the case of Burnham were set out in *The Times* on 18 October 1940, and the accidental shooting of Harold Harrison by his wife is reported on page 3 of the *Daily Mirror* on 10 September 1940. The story of Frank Terrel and his Sten gun can be found on page 45 of *The British Home Front 1939–1945* by Martin J. Brayley, while that of the Williams brothers can be found on page 51 of *An Underworld at War*. The papers in the strange case of Jack Brack and his enlarged heart are in the National Archives at CRIM 1/1201, while those in the equally surprising case of Samuel Martin are at CRIM 1/1241. Eric Oddy's memory of the deserter who deserted his escort is at 15220 in the IWM Sound Archive, the sentencing of Harry Tooby was reported in the *Oxford Times* on 6 December 1940, the apprehension of D'Arcy Wilson by John Forbes Andre Day was reported by *The Times* (and in greater detail by the *Daily Mirror*) on 12 September 1940, the sad case of David Grunspan was widely reported (including in *The Times* on 16 October 1940).

There are many examples of the lenient reactions of judges and juries when confronted by cuckolded soldiers who had exacted rough justice on wives and wives' lovers. The story of David Walker was reported in the *Manchester Guardian* on 1 December 1942, and Robert Capstick in the *Midland Daily Telegraph* on 12 November 1940. Other examples (including William Hennant and William Lovelock) are set out on pages 143 and 144 of *Soldier, Sailor, Beggarman, Thief: Crime and the British Armed Services*, a 2013 book written by Clive Emsley. The case of Clifford Holmes was reported in *The Times* on 28 January 1941, while George Orwell's deprecation of 'the false values of the American film' is from his essay 'The Decline of the English Murder', published in *Tribune* magazine on 15 February 1946.

The El Morocco Bottle Party had its own police file, now in the National Archives at MEPO 2/4501, while there are four files relating to the murder (in law, at any rate) of Harry 'Scarface' Distelman by Antonio 'Babe' Mancini. CRIM 1/1314 contains depositions, DPP 2/933B contains case papers, PCOM 9/807 contains material relating to Mancini's period in custody, while HO 45/25560 contains documents concerning the appeal to the House of Lords. Similarly, there are four files relating to the murder of Rachel Dobkin by her husband Harry – surely the Blitz's archetypal crime. CRIM 1/1457 and DPP 2/933B contain depositions and case papers, while PCOM 9/956 and MEPO 2/2235 contain prison and police material. In addition, there are two contemporary accounts of the case; the first is by the crime writer Nigel Morland who attended the trial and wrote of it in *Pattern of Murder*, published by Elek Books in 1966, while the second (and more interesting) is by Keith Simpson, the Home Office pathologist whose extensive efforts gained Dobkin's conviction. Chapter 5 of Simpson's gripping memoirs (*Forty Years of Murder*, published by Harrap in 1978) is devoted to the Dobkin case, and it complements the National Archive material well. In addition, the description of Dobkin's statement to the court prior to sentence is taken from the report of the *Morning Examiner* on 24 November 1942. Walter Marshall's memories, meanwhile, are in the IWM Sound Archive at 23849, and the reports into the macabre behaviour of mortician George Hobbs are in *The Times*, first on 23 November 1940, and after sentence, on 8 January 1941.

CHAPTER THIRTEEN

Relating to the nature and existence of Blitz Spirit, the Bernard Kops material is from his interview held in the Museum of London Digital Archive, and from *The World is a Wedding*. The interview with Bernard Kregor is the author's own. The extraordinary diary of Irene Haslewood is in the IWM Documents Archive at 12994, while the inquiry into the response to the bombing of Maybury Mansions is in the National Archives at HO 186/641. The pugilistic response of Arthur Dales's uncle to his own daughter's fear is described in Arthur's interview at 14595 in the IWM Sound Archive, while the diary of Marjorie Redman is in the IWM Documents Archive at 16303. Philip Vernon's authoritative paper 'The Psychological Effects of Air-Raids' was published in October 1941 in Volume 36(4) of *The Journal of Abnormal and Social Psychology* on page 457. A. F. S. Gow's belief in Britain's duty to fight is set down on page 42 of *Letters from Cambridge*, while page 168 of *By-Elections in British Politics* by Chris Cook and John Ramsden suggests how the state of the nation might be gauged by wartime by-election results. The memories of George Jackaman are part of the Finsbury Project at 12.18a in the Museum of London Digital Archive, while the complaints by members of the Metropolitan Police war reserves about pay and duties are in file MEPO 3/573 at the National Archives.

Winifred Musson's memories of bomb sightseeing are at 19540 in the IWM Documents Archive, while the behaviour of the Lyons Corner House waitresses and of the diarist who experienced flawless happiness after a narrow escape, are featured in *Living Through the Blitz* at pages 69 and 82 respectively. Caryl Brahms is at 2427 in the IWM Documents Archive, Vera Reid is at 12001, Marjorie Redman is at 16303, Gwyneth Kahn is at 16391, and the interview with Ronald Blyth is the author's own. Peter Ackroyd's quote about Londoners being chosen for calamity is on page 739 of *London: The Biography*, Quentin Crisp's memories of his friend's nervous breakdown are from *The Naked Civil Servant*, the recollections of policemen Eric Oddy and Les Waters are in the IWM Sound Archive at 15220 and 15222 respectively, and the diary of Phyllis Warner is in the IWM Documents Archive at 3208. The Civil Defence Executive's encouragement to the Ministry of Information to improve national morale – that extraordinary snapshot of the consensus in mid-creation – is in the National Archives at INF 1/849.

An original copy of ARP Handbook No. 12 relating to pets in wartime (with its advice on how to use a Captive Bolt Pistol on Tiddles) can be found at MAF/118 in the National Archives, while Les James and Roy Bartlett are both in the IWM Sound Archive, at 15226 and 30421. Jackie Moggridge is in the same archive at 8668.

A. J. P. Taylor's analysis of wartime socialism is on page 507 of *English History 1914–1945*, and Alan Bullock's *Ernest Bevin, A Biography* offers an interesting discussion of Bevin's central role in the nation's political shift. Jack Jones's comment about the trade unions coming into their own is at 11857 in the IWM Sound Archive. So far as the War Aims Committee of the War Cabinet is concerned, I have gathered information primarily from four files held at the National Archives: INF 1/862 and INF 1/863 are Ministry of Information files containing correspondence relating to post-war aims (such as the letter from Halifax to Duff Cooper and Harold Nicolson's suggestions for positive aims); CAB 87/90 contains minutes and papers from meetings of the committee (such as Arnold

Toynbee's progressive suggestions, and the contributions of Halifax and Bevin), and PREM 4/100/4 contains the Prime Minister's papers on war aims. Harold Nicolson's disappointment at Churchill's failure to deliver a broadcast can be found in a diary entry on page 235 of his *Diaries and Letters*, published by Weidenfeld and Nicolson in 2004. His speech to the boys of Harrow is described on page 126 of *The Road to 1945* by Paul Addison, while his discussion with James Chuter Ede is set out on page 119 of *The Life of R. A. Butler*, Anthony Howard's 1987 biography, published by Jonathan Cape. The enthusiasm of Mrs Adams for a drudgery-free future, meanwhile, is from the BBC programme *The Rebuilding of Coventry*, broadcast on the Home Service.

The Conservative MP Earl Winterton's belief that discussion of post-war aims would be dangerous, and the Labour peer Lord Addison's enthusiasm for discussion are both contained in CAB 21/1581 – a file on war aims held in the National Archives. (The file also contains the transcripts of a 1942 House of Lords debate on War Aims in which the pro-German Duke of Bedford calls for peace to be offered to Germany, and the Liberal Duke of Montrose argues for post-war devolution for Scotland.)

The Blitz casualty statistics are taken from Terence O'Brien's *Official History of Civil Defence*, published in 1955 by HMSO, while the measures which led to human needs being dealt with in a more humane and compassionate fashion are discussed in Richard Titmuss's *Official History of Social Policy*. The wartime bomb which caused twenty-first century chaos in Bermondsey was discussed in the *Guardian* on 24 March 2015; it was here that the local resident was quoted as saying that the bomb has caused people to come together and to realise that 'life's too short'. Blitz Spirit, it seems, has barely changed in its purpose or its nature. Driven by fear and extremes, the period caused people to behave in new ways. Across the country, they behaved well, they behaved badly, and they started relating to each other differently. As the world became a less permanent and more mobile place, social, economic and political expectations increased – and we are living with the results today. That, in effect, is the Secret History of the Blitz.

Bibliography

Ackroyd, Peter, *London: The Biography* (London: Chatto and Windus, 2000)

Addison, Paul, *The Road to 1945: British Politics and the Second World War* (London: Pimlico, 1994)

Addison, Paul, *No Turning Back: The Peacetime Revolutions of Post-War Britain* (Oxford: Oxford University Press, 2010)

Addison, Paul and Crang, Jeremy, *Listening to Britain: Home Intelligence Reports on Britain's Finest Hour* (London: Bodley Head, 2010)

Aldgate, Anthony and Richards, Jeffrey, *Britain Can Take It: British Cinema in the Second World War* (Oxford: Basil Blackwell, 1986)

Andrew, Christopher, *The Defence of the Realm: The Authorized History of MI5* (London: Allen Lane, 2009)

Ardrey, Robert, *Thunder Rock, A Play in Three Acts* (London: Hamish Hamilton, 1940)

Arscott, David, *Rations: A Very Peculiar Story* (Luton: Andrews UK, 2012)

Balon, Norman, *You're Barred, You Bastards!* (London: Sidgwick and Jackson, 1991)

Bamberg, James, *The History of the British Petroleum Company; Volume 2. The Anglo-Iranian Years 1928–1954* (Cambridge: Cambridge University Press, 2009)

Beardmore, George, *Civilians at War: Journals 1936–1946* (London: John Murray, 1984)

Bearse, Ray and Read, Anthony, *Conspirator: The Untold Story of Churchill, Roosevelt and Tyler Kent, Spy* (London: Macmillan, 1991)

Bissell, Andrew, *Southampton's Children of the Blitz* (Bournemouth: Centenar, 2010)

Blythe, Ronald, *Writing in a War: Stories, Poems and Essays of 1939–1945* (Harmondsworth: Penguin, 1966)

Blythe, Ronald, *Private Words: Letters and Diaries from the Second World War* (London: Viking, 1991)

Bourne, Stephen, *Elisabeth Welch: Soft Lights and Sweet Music* (Lanham, MD: Scarecrow Press, 2005)

Bourne, Stephen, *Mother Country: Britain's Black Community on the Home Front, 1939–45* (Stroud: The History Press, 2010)

Bowen, Elizabeth, *The Heat of the Day* (London: Jonathan Cape, 1949)

Bowen, Elizabeth, *The Mulberry Tree: The Writings of Elizabeth Bowen* (London: Virago, 1986)

Bowyer, Michael J., *Air Raid! The Enemy Air Offensive against East Anglia 1939–1945* (Wellingborough: Patrick Stephens, 1986)

Brasnett, Margaret, *The Story of the Citizens' Advice Bureaux* (London: National Council of Social Service, 1964)

Brayley, Martin, *The British Home Front 1939–1945* (Oxford: Osprey, 2005)

Brock, Colin (ed.), *The Caribbean in Europe: Aspects of the West Indian Experience in Britain, France and the Netherlands* (London: Frank Cass, 1986)

Bryden, John, *Fighting to Lose: How the German Secret Intelligence Service Helped the Allies Win the Second World War* (Toronto: Dundurn, 2014)

Bullock, Alan, *Ernest Bevin: A Biography* (London: Politico's, 2002)

Cabell, Craig, *Dennis Wheatley: Churchill's Storyteller* (Staplehurst: Spellmount, 2006)

Calder, Angus, *The People's War: Britain 1939–1945* (London: Jonathon Cape, 1969)

Calder, Angus, *The Myth of the Blitz* (London: Jonathan Cape, 1991)

Calder, Angus and Sheridan, Dorothy, *Speak For Yourself: A Mass-Observation Anthology 1937–1949* (London: Cape, 1984)

Calder, Ritchie, *Carry on London!* (London: The English Universities Press, 1941)

Calder, Ritchie, *The Lesson of London* (London: Secker and Warburg, 1941)

Charman, Terry, *The First World War on the Home Front* (London: Andre Deutsch, 2014)

Citizens' Advice Bureaux Handbook (London: National Council of Social Service, 1941)

Clapson, Mark and Larkham, Peter J. (ed.), *The Blitz and its Legacy: War-time Destruction to Post-War Reconstruction* (Farnham: Ashgate, 2013)

Collier, Basil, *The Defence of the United Kingdom* (London: HMSO, 1957)

Colville, John, *The Fringes of Power: 10 Downing Street Diaries 1939–1945* (London: Hodder and Stoughton, 1985)

Constantine, Learie, *Colour Bar* (London: Stanley Paul, 1954)

Cooper, Nick, *London Underground at War* (Stroud: Amberley Publishing, 2014)

Cook, Chris and Ramsden, John, *By-Elections in British Politics* (London: Macmillan, 1973)

Costello, John, *Love, Sex and War: Changing Values 1939–1945* (London: Collins, 1985)

Crisp, Quentin, *The Naked Civil Servant* (London: Jonathan Cape, 1967)

Day, Barry (ed.), *The Letters of Noel Coward* (London: Methuen Drama, 2007)

Dove, Richard (ed.), *Totally Un-English: Britain's Internment of 'Enemy Aliens' in Two World Wars* (Amsterdam: Rodolpi, 2005)

Ekpenyon, E. I., *Some Experiences of an African Air-Raid Warden* (London: Sheldon Press, 1943)

Elmsley, Clive, *Soldier, Sailor, Beggarman, Thief: Crime and the British Armed Services* (Oxford: Oxford University Press, 2013)

Fielding, Stephen, Thompson, Peter and Tiratsoo, Nick, *England Arise! The Labour Party and Popular Politics in 1940s Britain* (Manchester: Manchester University Press, 1995)

Fraser, George MacDonald, *Quartered Safe Out Here* (London: Harvill Press, 1992)

Gardiner, Juliet, *Wartime Britain 1939–1945* (London: Headline 2004)

Gardiner, Juliet, *The Blitz: The British Under Attack* (London: HarperPress, 2010)

Garfield, Simon, *Private Battles: How the War Almost Defeated Us* (London: Ebury, 2006)

Gibson, Guy, *Enemy Coast Ahead* (London: Michael Joseph, 1946)

Gillman, Peter and Gillman, Leni, *Collar the Lot! How Britain Interned and Expelled its Wartime Refugees* (London: Quartet Books, 1980)

Goodman, Michael S., *The Official History of the Joint Intelligence Committee, Volume 1* (London: Routledge, 2014)

Gow, Andrew Sydenham Farrar, *Letters from Cambridge* (London: Jonathan Cape, 1945)

Grafton, Pete, *You, You and You: The People Out of Step With WW2* (London: Pluto Press, 1981)

Grindrod, John, *Concretopia: A Journey around the Rebuilding of Post-War Britain* (Brecon: Old Street, 2013)

Grayzel, Susan, *At Home and Under Fire: Air Raids and Culture in Britain from the Great War to the Blitz* (Cambridge: Cambridge University Press, 2012)

Haapamaki, Michele, *The Coming of the Aerial War: Culture and Fear of Airborne Attack in Inter-War Britain* (London: I. B. Tauris, 2014)

Hamilton, Patrick, *The Slaves of Solitude* (London: Constable, 1946)

Hancock, W. K. and Gowing, M. M., *British War Economy* (London: HMSO, 1949)

Harrisson, Tom, *Living Through the Blitz* (London: Collins, 1976)

Heenan, John C., *Not the Whole Truth* (London: Hodder and Stoughton, 1971)

Hewison, Robert, *Under Siege: Literary Life in London 1939-1945* (London: Weidenfeld and Nicolson, 1977)

Hill, Billy, *Boss of Britain's Underworld* (London: The Naldrett Press, 1955)

Hinton, James, *Women, Social Leadership, and the Second World War* (Oxford: Oxford University Press, 2002)

Hinton, James, *Nine Wartime Lives* (Oxford: Oxford University Press, 2010)

Hodgson, Evelyn and Nash, Evelyn, *Bramley's Home Front: A Surrey Village during World War II* (Bramley: Bramley Historical Society, 2007)

Hodgson, Vere, *A Few Eggs and No Oranges* (London: D. Dobson, 1976)

Hodson, James Lansdale, *Through the Dark Night* (London: Victor Gollancz, 1941)

Hodson, James Lansdale, *Towards the Morning* (London: Victor Gollancz, 1941)

Hodson, James Lansdale, *Before Daybreak* (London: Victor Gollancz, 1941)

Hoggart, Richard, *The Uses of Literacy* (London: Chatto and Windus, 1957)

Holmes, Colin, *John Bull's Island: Immigration and British Society* (Basingstoke: Macmillan Education, 1988)

Houlbrook, Matt, *Queer London* (Chicago: University of Chicago Press, 2005)

Howat, Gerald, *Learie Constantine* (London: Allen and Unwin, 1975)

Howard, Anthony, *RAB: The Life of R. A. Butler* (London: Jonathan Cape, 1987)

Jackman, Nancy and Quinn, Tom, *The Cook's Tale: Life Below Stairs as it Really Was* (London: Coronet, 2012)

Jivani, Alkarim, *It's Not Unusual: A History of Lesbian and Gay Britain in the Twentieth Century* (London: Michael O'Mara Books, 1997)

Kops, Bernard, *The World is a Wedding* (London: MacGibbon and Kee, 1963)

Kynaston, David, *Austerity Britain: 1945–51* (London: Bloomsbury, 2007)

Laski, Marghanita (as 'Sarah Russell'), *To Bed with Grand Music* (London: Pilot Press, 1946)

Lehmann, John, *I am my Brother: Autobiography II* (London: Longmans Green, 1960)

Lehmann, John, *In the Purely Pagan Sense* (London: Blond and Briggs, 1976)

Levine, Joshua, *Forgotten Voices of the Blitz and Battle for Britain* (London: Ebury, 2006)

Lewis, Peter, *A People's War* (London: Methuen, 1986)

Little, Kenneth, *Negroes in Britain: A Study in Race Relations in English Society* (London: Kegan Paul, 1947)

Longmate, Norman, *How We Lived Then* (London: Hutchinson, 1971)

McKibbin, Ross, *Class and Cultures: England 1918–1951* (Oxford: Oxford University Press, 1998)

McKibbin, Ross, *Parties and People: England 1914–1951* (Oxford: Oxford University Press, 2010)

Maclaren-Ross, Julian, *Memoirs of the Forties* (London: Alan Ross, 1965)

Morland, Nigel, *Pattern of Murder* (London: Elek Books, 1966)

Morrison, Lord, *Herbert Morrison: An Autobiography* (London: Odhams Press, 1960)

Mortimer, Gavin, *The Longest Night: 10–11 May 1941* (London: Weidenfeld and Nicolson, 2005)

Mosley, Leonard, *Backs to the Wall: London Under Fire* (London: Weidenfeld and Nicolson, 1971)

Newlands, Emma, *Civilians into Soldiers: War, the Body and British Army Recruits 1939–45* (Manchester: Manchester University Press, 2014)

Nicolson, Nigel (ed.), *Harold Nicolson: Diaries and Letters 1907–1964* (London: Weidenfeld and Nicolson, 2004)

Nixon, Barbara, *Raiders Overhead: A Diary of the London Blitz* (London: Lindsay Drummond, 1943)

O'Brien, Terence, *Civil Defence* (London: HMSO, 1955)

Ogley, Bob, *Surrey at War: 1939–1945* (Westerham: Froglets Publications, 1995)

Overy, Richard, *The Bombing War: Europe 1939–1945* (London: Allen Lane, 2013)

Padley, Richard and Cole, Margaret, *Evacuation Survey: A Report to the Fabian Society* (London: Routledge, 1940)

Pearl, Cyril, *The Dunera Scandal: Deported by Mistake* (London: Angus and Robertson, 1983)

Perry, Colin, *Boy in the Blitz: The 1940 Diary of Colin Perry* (Stroud: Sutton Publishing, 2000)

Ponting, Clive, *1940: Myth and Reality* (London: Hamish Hamilton, 1990)

Quennell, Peter, *The Wanton Chase* (London: Collins, 1980)

Ramsey, Winston (ed.), *The Blitz Then and Now, Volume 1* (London: Battle of Britain Prints International, 1987)

Ramsey, Winston (ed.), *The Blitz Then and Now, Volume 2* (London: Battle of Britain Prints International, 1988)

Ramsey, Winston (ed.), *The East End Then and Now* (London: Battle of Britain Prints International, 1997)

Rathbone, Eleanor, *Falsehood and Facts about the Jews* (London: Victor Gollancz, 1944)

Richards, Jean, *Inform, Advise and Support: The Story of Fifty Years of the Citizens Advice Bureau* (Cambridge: Luttworth, 1989)

Russell, Leonard (ed.), *The Saturday Book 3: A 1943 Annual* (St Albans: Mayflower Press, 1943)

Saunders, Andy, *A Pin-Up at War* (London: Leo Cooper, 2003)

Saunders, Andy, *Finding The Few* (London: Grub Street, 2009)

Roberts, Janet, *Oil Under Sherwood Forest* (Janet Roberts Booklets, 2009)

Simpson, Keith, *Forty Years of Murder* (London: Harrap, 1978)

Smith, Adrian, *The City of Coventry: Twentieth Century Icon* (I. B. Taurus, 2006)

Spender, Stephen, *Citizens in War, and After* (London: G. G. Harrap and Co, 1945)

Taylor, A. J. P., *English History 1918–1945* (Oxford: Clarendon Press, 1965)

Thomas, Donald, *An Underworld at War: Spivs, Deserters, Racketeers and Civilians in the Second World War* (London: John Murray, 2003)

Thompson, Wally, *Time Off My Life* (London: Rich and Cowan, 1956)

Titmuss, Richard M., *Problems of Social Policy* (London: HMSO, 1950)

Todd, Selina, *The People: The Rise and Fall of the Working Class 1910–2010* (London: John Murray, 2014)

Watts, Marthe, *The Men in My Life* (London: Christopher Johnson, 1960)

White, Jerry, *Campbell Bunk: The Worst Street in North London Between the Wars* (London: Pimlico, 2001)

White, Jerry, *London in the Twentieth Century: A City and its People* (London: Viking, 2001)

Winterbotham, Frederick, *The Ultra Secret* (London: HarperCollins, 1974)

Woodward, Grace Steele and Woodward, Guy H, *The Secret of Sherwood Forest: Oil Production in England during World War II* (Norman: University of Oklahoma Press, 1973)

Wyndham, Joan, *Love Lessons: A Wartime Diary* (London: Heinemann, 1985)

Picture Credits

Index